2700

MAKING IT
WHOLE

Every thought involves a whole system of thoughts, and ceases to exist if severed from its various correlatives. As we cannot isolate a single organ of a living body and deal with it as though it had a life independent of the rest; so from the organized structure of our cognitions, we cannot cut one, and proceed as though it had survived the separation.

Herbert Spencer, *First Principles*

MAKING IT WHOLE

A Victorian Circle and the
Shape of Their World

Diana Postlethwaite

OHIO STATE UNIVERSITY PRESS : COLUMBUS

Library of Congress Cataloging in Publication Data

Postlethwaite, Diana, 1950—
Making it whole.

Includes bibliographies and index.
1. English literature—19th century—History and criticism. 2. Philosophy, British—
19th century. 3. Philosophy in literature. 4. Great Britain—Intellectual life—19th
century. 5. Eliot, George, 1819–1880. Middlemarch. I. Title.
PR469.P45P67 1985   820'.9'008   84-20677
Cloth: ISBN 0-8142-0372-8

195656

FOR MY FATHER
R. Deane Postlethwaite (1925–1980)

CONTENTS

ACKNOWLEDGMENTS

Although this book is the product of a long evolutionary process, its origin can be dated with certainty to the day a decade ago that I left a warehouse sale at the Yale University Press, happily burdened with seven blue-covered volumes: Gordon Haight's edition of *The George Eliot Letters*. Free from library due dates, I indulged in the luxury of reading them from cover to cover. It was therein that I met the members of this Victorian circle, and began to sense the rich interrelationships of their world. In the *Letters* and in his biography, Professor Haight first gave us the historical George Eliot; his meticulous scholarship has been a continuing inspiration to me. If Gordon Haight introduced me to the facts, J. Hillis Miller introduced me to the theories. My gratitude to him for stimulating my interest in the Victorians, and for his support and advice in my early researches.

Thanks are also due to Elisabeth Helsinger for her helpful reading of the manuscript, and to Robert Richards for encouragement at a crucial juncture. My greatest academic debt is unquestionably to my students. As I have taught them, they have taught me; time and time again, they have sustained me emotionally as well as challenged me intellectually. Among so many, I must single out Meri-Jane Rochelson Mintz, Jim Harbaugh, Evy Asch, Bill Kuhn, Sharon Walsh, and Dan Whitmore. I wish I could name them all.

The love, strength, and faith of my husband, Paul Thiboutot, have been the gift of grace that made it whole.

In the Victorian age, the humanist and the scientist still spoke a common language. A logician could read contemporary poetry; a novelist could debate the latest development in evolutionary theory. The increasingly alienated discourses of the twentieth century have created an intellectual climate that mediates against an accurate reflection of the Victorians. Today, the literary critic and the historian of ideas often move in different worlds; the investigator of popular culture may be given short shrift by the more traditional historian of the period; science and literature share little common ground. This study attempts to bridge some of these distances, and to achieve a most Victorian ambition: to make it whole.

The pages that follow will depict a Victorian circle whose members are drawn from a diverse range of intellectual vocations: John Stuart Mill and Auguste Comte; George Combe and Robert Chambers; Charles Bray and Harriet Martineau; George Henry Lewes and Herbert Spencer; George Eliot. They number among them respected scholars and inflamed ideologues, novelists and philosophers of science; men of letters, renegade industrialists, and bluestockings. They are not the Bloomsbury group or the Cambridge Platonists; neither a cozy biographical circle of intimate friends nor a united band of sectarian disciples. Yet the biographical interrelationships among them are intricate and important. In some cases they were drawn together by friendship or love; in all cases they were bound by a shared set of beliefs. As their circle takes shape in these pages, it encompasses a vision distinctively Victorian. What ultimately unites these thinkers is a Victorian frame of mind.

George Eliot's heroine Dorothea Brooke finds herself amidst a prototypical Victorian cosmos: "Her world was in a state of convulsive change."[1] Jerome Buckley opened his study of *The Victorian Temper* with the assertion that "the Victorian period achieved little of the stability we have learned to associate with a semi-mythical classical culture. It moved from form to form, and nothing stood. Almost every Victorian thesis produced its own antithesis, as a ceaseless dialectic worked out its designs."[2] Although stability may have eluded the collective sensibility of what John Stuart Mill characterized as an "age of transition," individual Victorians of widely-varied persuasions strove arduously for the third term of that great nineteenth-century dialectic: synthesis. Transition points toward resolution. The "transitional period" of "weak convictions, paralysed intellects, and growing laxity of principle" will terminate in a "renovation . . . in the basis of . . . belief, leading to the evolution of some faith, whether religious or merely human, which they can really believe."[3]

Mill's words are apt: all of these Victorians had faith in evolution, and all of them evolved new faiths—hardly orthodox, yet more than "merely human." Walter Houghton draws attention to the note of Evangelical fervor that can be heard in the new rationalist affirmations of faith: "Though for them the revelation was not religious but scientific, the same note of joy, part relief, part excited hope of discovering a new philosophy of man and the universe, is found among the rationalists."[4] It could be said of the Victorians in this circle that the revelation was both religious *and* scientific. Intellectually, the men and women in my circle are the heirs of British empiricism, sons and daughters of Francis Bacon and John Locke, eighteenth-century rationalism and association psychology. Yet they are fascinated by the unknowable, the intuitive, the transcendent. They did not consider the material and the spiritual irredeemably alienated. Although none were orthodox believers (and all were, in varying degrees, denounced as spiritually subversive by their critics), every member of this circle believed, ardently and unwaveringly, in a *via media*. For them, to explore the mechanisms of the human brain or the progressive development of the natural world was not to deny man's moral and spiritual nature. Although their efforts to conciliate science and faith are not always persuasive, they are unerringly sincere.

This intellectual temperament had its roots in romantic precursors of the preceding generation. In his survey of the transition *From Classic to Romantic*, Walter Jackson Bate argued that "nothing is more characteristic of British thought as a whole than its simultaneous confidence, not only in the empirically concrete, but also in an almost intuitional absorption of the experience of concrete phenomena, and in the exclusive working of that intuition through the empirically known."[5] Bate's work provided a lively formulation of an intriguing paradox: the romantic emphasis on feeling and imagination was a product of the mechanistic eighteenth-century psychology of Locke and Hartley. M. H. Abrams elaborated on these truths in *The Mirror and the Lamp*: "[Although] almost all the important romantic theorists commented on the disparity between imagination and scientific perception. . . . It is important to realize . . . that by far the greater number refused to admit that there is any inherent and inescapable conflict between science and poetry. . . . The most common procedure was to regard these, when properly employed, as parallel and complementary ways of seeing."[6] But typically, critics of the Victorian period have failed to recognize the continuity of this romantic sensibility into subsequent decades. Abrams himself belies the subtlety of his previous analysis in his desire for a tidy ending to both the romantic period and to his book: "It was only in the early Victorian period, when all discourse was explicitly or tacitly thrown into the two exhaustive modes of imaginative and rational, expressive and assertive, that religion fell together with poetry in opposition to science."[7] In an essay on "Moral Problems and Moral Philosophy in the Victorian Period," Jerome B. Schneewind defined these two modes in terms of the Utilitarian and Intuitionist schools of thought, and traced their conflict from Bentham's *Introduction to the Principles of Morals and Legislation* (1781) to Henry Sidgwick's *Methods of Ethics* (1874) and F. H. Bradley's *Ethical Studies* (1876). Schneewind's essay provided a useful corrective: it revealed that there *was* a native British intuitionist school in the Victorian period, previously neglected by most historians of ideas.[8] Just as Bate and Abrams revised the stereotype of the emotive, romantic cloud-poet, so Schneewind refined too-exclusive notions of a Gradgrindian Victorian reasoning-machine. But Schneewind's polarization of these two schools denies the nature of Bate's characteristically British bedfellows. Similarly, a recent study of the period titles the collision of the utilitarian / rationalist / empiricist and the intuitionist / idealist / mystic an "omnipresent debate," and concludes that any attempt at synthesis was doomed: "The premises are irreconcilable."[9]

But even a brief survey of some classic works of the Victorian period reveals persuasive and powerful urges toward the synthesis of opposing tendencies. John Henry Newman might at first seem an unlikely prototype for a Victorian synthesist. Newman's *Apologia Pro Vita Sua* chronicles the cardinal's ill-fated search for a *via media*, in the course of which he was to "receive a shock which was to cast out of [his] imagination all middle courses and compromises forever." His gradual journey across the slippery ice of church doctrine led him to the shore of dogmatic certitude, from which no return was possible and across which no bridge could be built. "There are two alternatives, the way to Rome and the way to Atheism."[10] Yet in his preface, Newman begs for "acquittal" from his fellow countrymen, on the charges of misplaced allegiance to mother Rome: "I had rather be an Englishman, (as in fact I am), than belong to any other race under heaven." Newman's professed Englishness lends significant overtones to his later description of Hurrell Froude: "He had a keen insight into abstract truth; but he was an Englishman to the backbone in his severe adherence to the real and the concrete." Newman himself was given intuitions of the transcendent in abundance. But he must be an *English* Roman Catholic: "I determined to be guided, not by my imagination, but by my reason. . . . Had it not been for this severe resolve, I should have been a Catholic sooner than I was."[11] Newman thus paradoxically reaches reason-defying dogma by a logically-argued and scrupulously-documented empirical record of that progress toward faith.

In the realm of fiction, Charles Dickens's *Hard Times* also articulates thesis and antithesis. The world of "facts and calculations," in which Gradgrindian utilitarian philosophers "weigh and measure any parcel of human nature," stands in desolate alienation from the fantasies and hyperbolic heroics of Sleary's Horse-riding. The materialistic men of fact and the equestrian imaginists quite literally do not speak the same language: Gradgrind's gramniverous quadruped and E. W. B. Childers's "tight-Jeff" and "slack-Jeff" exist in different linguistic universes. Yet the feckless world of Sleary's, in which father deserts child, is hardly a desirable alternative to the rationalist rigidities that entrap the infant soul. Sissy Jupe leaves the circus and comes to live with the Gradgrinds. Her "happy children" will be nurtured with "imaginative graces and delights"—but they must also live "lives of machinery and reality."[12]

The Victorian poet, too, sought synthesis in a world of antinomies. Alfred Tennyson himself insisted that *In Memoriam* incarnated a Victorian sensibility: " 'I' is not always the author speaking of himself, but the voice of the human race speaking through him."[13] The assertive optimism of the poem's "Prologue" (actually written last), "Believing where we cannot prove," is persistently undercut by the "wild and wandering cries" of the 131 lyrics that follow.[14] Tennyson's affirmations are inextricably intertwined with his deepest doubts.

The contemporary ideas that dominate the poet's reflections are among the central intellectual issues of the Victorian period. Tennyson's religious quest for belief in immortality, prompted by Arthur Hallam's untimely death, seems in direct conflict with the new materialist psychology which would argue that the essence of human nature is not soul, but merely matter:

> I trust I have not wasted breath:
> I think we are not wholly brain,
> Magnetic mockeries; not in vain,
> Like Paul with beasts, I fought with Death;
>
> Not only cunning casts in clay:
> Let Science prove we are, and then
> What matter Science unto men,
> At least to me? I would not stay.
>
> Let him, the wiser man who springs
> Hereafter, up from childhood shape
> His action like the greater ape,
> But I was *born* to other things.
> [Lyric 120]

The nebular hypothesis claimed that the earth was a product of "seeming-random forms" and "cyclic storms" (Lyric 118, ll. 9, 10) rather than divine *fiat*. Was man's appearance on the natural scene equally random? Tennyson's nightmares are haunted by "Nature, red in tooth and claw" (Lyric 56, l. 15). But ultimately it is evolution itself, translated into spiritual terms, that may provide the key to man's transcendence of the material:

> Arise and fly
> The reeling Faun, the sensual feast;
> Move upward, working out the beast,
> And let the ape and tiger die.
> [Lyric 118, ll. 25–28]

Tennyson finds further resolution in poetic form. The *abba In Memoriam* stanza skilfully brackets and unites the *"b's"* of doubt with the *"a's"* of affirmation:

Thou wilt not leave us in the dust:
Thou madest man, he knows not why,
He thinks he was not made to die,
And thou has made him: thou art just.
[Prologue, ll. 9–12]

Its elegant order and unerring constancy synthesizes the vast
range of Tennyson's contrary ideas and emotions over time
and space. The *In Memoriam* stanza is to Tennyson's poetry
what Darwin's theory of natural selection was to nature: a deceptively simple monistic principle that unifies variety yet al-
lows for infinite variation within that fundamental unity.

The Victorian thinkers in the pages to follow address themselves in prose to many of the same contemporary issues as
Tennyson: the new materialist psychology; the evolutionary
formation of the cosmos, in which man takes his place as a
member of the animal kingdom in the great chain of being.
Although in many other respects their interests were far-
removed from those of Newman, Dickens, and Tennyson, they
share—and indeed, epitomize—the Victorian frame of mind
that seeks a synthesis of the empirical and the intuitive, head
and heart. Newman had Catholic dogma; Dickens, the fantasy-
making imagination; Tennyson, poetic form. Like them, the
Victorians in my circle seek a monistic principle that will order
the universe, yoke the multiplicitous particular with the numinous general.

Although they share many general concerns of the age, I believe that these Victorians can justly be called a "circle." What
distinguishes them? They also share a common background
and a common set of ideologies. Too often, historians of ideas
are content to account for recurrent ideas by invoking a nebulous "in the air." The biographical portions of my study document the direct links by which ideas were transmitted among
them. My intellectual history will document that those ideas
share a common lineage as well.

In his classic *History of the English People in the Nineteenth Century*, Elie Halèvy argued that Evangelicalism and
Utilitarianism were the seminal forces of the Victorian age.

When Halèvy asked, "Was Utilitarianism in 1815 a growing force, Evangelicalism on the verge of decline?" his answer provided him with "the fundamental paradox of English society": "the partial junction and combination of these two forces theoretically so hostile." This paradox became the thesis of his study: "The Methodist revival . . . was after all less unfavorable to the scientific spirit than would appear at first sight"; in fact, "the emotional piety of Evangelical religion and the hunger for experimental knowledge developed at the same time, with the same intensity, and in the same social milieu."[15] Halèvy's *milieu* is precisely that of this Victorian circle: the new industrial cities to the north of London, steeped in nonconformity—the England of provincial philanthropist George Combe, heir to Scotch Presbyterian Calvinism; of Herbert Spencer, offspring of the hosiery towns of the north Midlands, with an ancestry of Methodism and Quaker-Socinian rationalism; of George Eliot, who moved with relative ease from the Evangelical pieties of her girlhood to the Biblical rationalism and scientific enthusiasms of Charles Bray and his Coventry circle in the early 1840s. When they left the provinces for a broader intellectual arena, all carried with them the emotional fervor of that Evangelical heritage, combined with the utilitarian spirit.

Certain ideologies recur like *leitmotifs* throughout all their work: positivism, phrenology, the pre-Darwinian development hypothesis, necessitarianism, "force." It will be the central task of my study to delineate the common denominators among this panorama of systems. They occur abundantly on a literal level. For example, phrenology provided Auguste Comte with the epitome of his positivist goals: the application of scientific method to the realm of psychology, previously the province of philosophers and theologians. But in larger terms, I am interested in the shape of this Victorian universe, the shared cosmology implicit in positivism, necessitarianism, evolutionary theory.

The shape of my study, like that of the ideologies it investigates, will often of necessity be circular; for many of the ideas

I discuss were held simultaneously rather than discovered sequentially. The linear structure of this book must thus be to some extent an artificial one. The nine Victorians in this circle defy simple categorization. In many ways each of them addresses all of the major themes of the study. They will visit each other's chapters frequently. All were prolific writers; in most cases I limit myself to a representative major text within the historical period during which their common ideas came to fruition.

After introducing Coleridge's *Theory of Life* as a romantic prelude to central Victorian themes, I begin with the foundations, or methodological assumptions, shared by this group, as epitomized in Mill and Comte. I then trace two different applications of this methodology: in natural science (Combe's phrenology and Chambers's evolutionary theory); and in matters of belief, philosophical and religious (Bray's necessitarianism and Martineau's mesmerism). Lewes and Spencer are, as Spencer would have phrased it, the ultimate "synthetic philosophers"; within the distinctive terms of their shared interests, their work draws upon and shapes all of the ideas, explicit and implicit, in preceding chapters. My "Finale" is intended to suggest that the ideologies that animate abstract philosophical debate can be given vivid incarnation in fictional form. This Victorian frame of mind was most fortunate in having George Eliot as its literary genius.

1. George Eliot, *Middlemarch*, ed. Gordon S. Haight (1871–72; rpt. Boston, 1956), p. 359.

2. Jerome Hamilton Buckley, *The Victorian Temper* (New York, 1951), p. 1.

3. John Stuart Mill, *Autobiography*, ed. Jack Stillinger (1859; rpt. Boston, 1969), pp. 3, 142.

4. Walter E. Houghton, *The Victorian Frame of Mind* (New Haven, 1957), p. 50.

5. Walter Jackson Bate, *From Classic to Romantic* (1946; rpt. New York, 1961), p. 111.

6. M. H. Abrams, *The Mirror and the Lamp* (1953; rpt. Oxford, 1971), pp. 308–9.

7. Abrams, *Mirror*, p. 335.

8. Jerome B. Schneewind, "Moral Problems and Moral Philosophy in the Victorian Period," *Victorian Studies*, supplement to vol. 9 (1965), rpt. in *English Literature and British Philosophy*, ed. S. P. Rosenbaum (Chicago, 1971), pp. 185–207. William Whewell and James Martineau are chief among the intuitionists. Significantly, Schneewind presents George Eliot as a Victorian who fails to fit comfortably into either category: "It is in her attempt to work out a satisfactory portrayal of human freedom that George Eliot comes closest to dealing in her novels with the conceptual tension between an Intuitionist attitude toward morality and a determinist attitude toward the universe" (p. 204). Schneewind argues that the synthesis of empiricism and intuitionism came to England via Germany in the 1870s, and that Eliot discovered it in reading Bradley and Sidgwick. My study will demonstrate many earlier, native models for her characteristic blend of intuitionist morality and utilitarian determinism.

9. Wendell V. Harris, *The Omnipresent Debate: Empiricism and Transcendentalism in Nineteenth-Century English Prose* (DeKalb, Ill., 1981), p. 17.

10. John Henry Newman, *Apologia Pro Vita Sua* (1864; rpt. New York, 1956), pp. 208, 291.

11. Newman, *Apologia*, pp. 8, 32, 100.

12. Charles Dickens, *Hard Times*, ed. George Ford and Sylvère Monod (1854; rpt. New York, 1966), pp. 2, 9, 3, 24, 226.

13. Alfred Tennyson, quoted in *The Poems of Tennyson*, ed. Christopher Ricks (London, 1969), p. 859.

14. Alfred Tennyson, *In Memoriam*, ed. Robert H. Ross (1850; rpt. New York, 1973), "Prologue," ll. 4, 41. Further references will be cited in the text.

15. Elie Halèvy, *England in 1815*, trans. E. I. Watkin and D. A. Barker (1924; rpt. London, 1960), pp. 585, 524, 559.

MAKING IT
WHOLE

Polarities: Samuel Taylor Coleridge's
Theory of Life (1817–1818)
as Victorian Cosmology

*Contemplations of nature and of bodies in their simple form
break up and distract the understanding, while contemplations of nature and bodies in their composition and configuration overpower and dissolve the understanding: a distinction
well seen in the school of Leucippus and Democritus as compared with the other philosophies. For that school is so busied
with the particles that it hardly attends to the structure; while
the others are so lost in admiration of the structure that they
do not penetrate to the simplicity of nature. These kinds of
contemplation should therefore be alternated and taken by
turns; that so the understanding may be rendered at once pen-
etrating and comprehensive.—Bacon,* Novum Organum

Party is Nature too, and you shall see
By force of Logic how they both agree:
The Many in the One, the One in the Many;
All is not Some, nor Some the same as Any:
Genus holds species, both are great or small:
One genus highest, one not high at all:
Each species has its differentia too,
This is not That, and it was never You,
Though this and that are AYES, and you and he,
Are like as one to one, or three to three.—George Eliot, epi-
graph to chapter 51, Middlemarch

"The only Wisdom is that of Ideas, their correlatives (Laws) being the only important things in the Universe," George Henry Lewes noted in the margin of his copy of Coleridge's "Essays on Method" in *The Friend.*[1] Lewes could not have been more in agreement with Coleridge himself, who wrote in his notebooks of "the incalculable *Value* of Ideas . . . in *all* departments of Knowledge . . . to the Naturalist no less than to the Theologian, to the Statesman no less than to the Moralist—in Philosophy, in Organology, in Psychology, as *subjective*, and in physiological Anatomy as *Objective*, Analytique, in Chemistry as the constructive Science de Minimis and Astronomy as the correspondent science de Maximis."[2] In this vision of the whole, embracing science and religion, subject and object, analysis and synthesis, the smallest molecule ("de Minimis") and the entirety of the cosmos ("de Maximis"), Coleridge provides a characteristically proleptic vantage point on a monistic Victorian *Zeitgeist.* Whether "subjective" or "objective," Coleridge's Ideas inhabit the realm of Platonic Absolutes. But Lewes wrote an 800-page *Biographical History of Philosophy* (1845–46) in order to disprove the validity of all metaphysics, proclaiming the inevitable demise of philosophy at the hands of positivism. He staunchly supported the fundamentals of British empiricism: "Modern philosophy stated its pretensions on the one question: *Have we any ideas independent of experience?* . . . The answer always ends in a negative."[3] Lewes may thus at first seem an unlikely champion of the Platonic Idea. It is of just such apparent contradictions that the stuff of my history is to be made.

George Henry Lewes and the other thinkers to be introduced in these pages are heirs to the great tradition of British empiricism and its progenitor Francis Bacon. Like Bacon, they found themselves in an exciting new age of scientific exploration: "It will be disgraceful if, while the regions of the material globe . . . have been in our times laid widely open and revealed, the intellectual globe should remain shut up within the narrow limits of old discoveries."[4] These Victorian Columbuses were to sail previously uncharted regions: the new sciences of physiological psychology and evolutionary biology, realms intimately (and controversially) linked with a vision of human nature untrammelled by the orthodox identification of mind with spirit, or the creative Deity of Genesis. "How eminently a scientific spirit is shown in Bacon's separation of Science from Theology," Lewes writes in the *Biographical History*.[5] To effect their scientific expeditions, they eagerly embraced the Baconian method, with its marriage of the empirical and the rational. "A Method is the vital principle of all science," proclaims Lewes; "from Bacon [comes] the whole school of scientific men."[6] Empirical tenets of observation and experience were ideally suited to the new Victorian view of man. In particular, the fascinating new science of physiological psychology was to apply scientific method to the mind, previously exclusively the domain of philosophic introspection. In his "Analysis of the Mental Faculties," Charles Bray writes: "The more perfect becomes our analysis of the mental constitution . . . the more we become struck with the truth of Lord Bacon's celebrated aphorism, as the foundation of all reasoning, that 'Man can only understand and act in proportion as he observes the order of nature.' "[7] Herbert Spencer concurs in his study of *The Principles of Psychology*: "It was not until Bacon lived, that the generalization of experience was erected into a method. Now, however . . . all educated men are in a sense Bacon's disciples."[8]

Bacon, argues Lewes, is "justly . . . entitled the Father of

Positive Science"; "his mind was antipathetic to all metaphysics."[9] But significantly, the nineteenth-century father of Positive Science, Auguste Comte, took issue with the Baconian
method on a central point: "All good intellects have repeated,
since Bacon's time, that there can be no real knowledge but
that which is based on observed facts. This is incontestable . . . but . . . it is equally true that facts cannot be observed without the guidance of some theory. Without such
guidance, our facts would be desultory and fruitless; we could
not retain them: for the most part we could not even perceive
them."[10] Although the positivists would discard the order of
conceptions provided by theology and metaphysics, their system was founded upon a monistic cosmology that demanded
an intuitive faith of its own. Lewes praises Bacon's conception
of scientific method, but also points to what he considers a
"radical defect": "its being *inductive*, and not also *deductive*."[11] Whether exploring the phrenological organs of the
brain or the developmental hierarchy of the natural world,
these Victorians unfailingly embraced the theoretical generalization as earnestly as the observed fact. They believed in the
importance of reasoning both inductively from the many to the
one, and deductively from the one to the many. If they are not
purely metaphysical idealists, neither are they simply rational
empiricists.

Nineteenth-century thinkers would be surprised to discover
that later academicians transformed them overnight from "Romantics" to "Victorians." The men and women in this study
began to shape their ideas in the mid-1830s; the seeds of their
synthesizing sensibility were sown within a romantic tradition. I have chosen Samuel Taylor Coleridge as the subject of
my "Prelude" to this study of a Victorian world view, for he
incarnates a frame of mind that has much in common with
that of his Victorian descendents. Although the particular
ideologies they espoused—such as positivism, or evolutionary
theory—were distinctively Victorian, the sensibility brought to
bear upon them within this circle owes much to romantic precursors.

I will devote this introductory chapter to Coleridge's *Hints*

*Towards the Formation of a More Comprehensive Theory of
Life.* From amidst Coleridge's considerable *opus,* the choice
may seem idiosyncratic. It is not my intention to claim the
Theory of Life as the simple source for a Victorian cosmology;
many of its central ideas are also embodied in other romantic
epistemologies, both German and English. But it so happens
that this small, posthumous volume drew the attention of a
number of thinkers in this Victorian circle. It thus provides a
direct frame of reference for the discussions of individual
thinkers that follow. In addition to introducing a characteristic frame of mind, it serves as an example of the literal links of
influence among these Victorians. The history of the *Theory
of Life* among them offers a fascinating demonstration of the
extent to which their world was a small one indeed. Ultimately, I wish to examine not so much influence as confluence; to ask not what they learned from the *Theory of Life,* but
why they were so attracted to it.

Above all, Samuel Taylor Coleridge wanted to make it
whole. "Is there no communion between the intellectual and
the moral?" he asked,

> Are the distinctions of the schools separate in Nature? Is there no
> Heart in the Head? No Head in the Heart? Is it not possible to find
> a *practical* Reason, a *Light* of Life, a focal power from the union
> or harmonious composition of all Faculties? . . . then we shall
> have a Philosophy, that will unite in itself, the warmth of the mys-
> tics, the definiteness of the Dialectician, and the sunny clearness
> of the Naturalist, the productivity of the Experimenter and the
> Evidence of the Mathematician.[12]

The nineteenth century was endowed with boundless intellectual energy, free from the snobbery of the specialist. In 1831
Coleridge's *hubris* foreshadowed that of the system-making
Victorians who would come after him: "My system . . . is the
only attempt I know, ever made to reduce all knowledges into
harmony. It opposes no other system, but shows what was true
in each. . . . I have endeavoured to unite the insulated fragments of truth."[13] Unfortunately, Coleridge never wrote his
"opus maximum," but his ambition "to reduce all knowledges

into harmony" was more than mere table talk. All of Coleridge's later work can be read as versions of this unifying impulse; none more so than the *Theory of Life*. Significantly, this little book was written around 1817–18,[14] but published by Reverend Seth B. Watson for an enthusiastic Victorian audience in 1848. Its Victorian history provides a prototypical example of the direct intellectual links that bound this circle of thinkers. Before turning to Coleridge's theory in some detail, I would like to trace its history among them. That history provides my first example of the characteristic manner in which a shared frame of mind unites a diverse range of ideologies into a single cosmology.

Herbert Spencer's *Autobiography* (1904) guaranteed that he would be remembered by posterity as not a little boorish in his unwillingness to acknowledge the wisdom of his predecessors: "I could not bear prolonged reading. . . . It was as though my intellectual digestive system was comparatively small, and would not take in heavy meals. Possibly also the tendency then, as afterwards, towards independent thought, was relatively so dominant that I soon became impatient of the process of taking in ideas set before me." The rich sauces of Kant's *Critique of Pure Reason*, for example, proved thoroughly indigestible: "I commenced reading, but did not go far." The reader cannot but help be somewhat awed by Spencer's honesty (how many, after all, have really chewed and digested Kant?): "Being then, as always, an impatient reader . . . it has always been out of the question for me to go on reading a book the fundamental principles of which I entirely dissent from."[15]

But Spencer's cantankerous disclaimers can be misleading if one draws the conclusion that he was impervious to the ideas of his times. The *Autobiography* also reveals that he read widely if not deeply in major thinkers of his century, and could respond positively to other men's ideas—when they were similar enough to his own. Like a spider, web-spinning followed ingestion: "Material which would be taken in and organized, or re-organized, so as to form part of a coherent structure in course of elaboration, there was always a readiness to receive."

The structure, of course, was Spencer's own grand Synthetic Philosophy: "The fabric of my conclusions had in all cases to be developed from within—refusing to be built, and insisted on growing." One book proved remarkably congenial to his assimilation, woven inextricably into the web of his philosophy for the decades to come: "I may have given attention to some serious books in 1849 and 50, though I do not remember it. One only which I looked into, left an impression. This was Coleridge's *Idea of Life*. . . . The doctrine of individuation struck me; and, as was presently shown, entered as a factor into my thinking."[16]

The *Theory of Life* figured prominently in Spencer's first book, *Social Statics* (1850). Spencer turns Coleridge's definition of life to his own purposes, as Coleridge's "tendency to individuation" becomes the basis of Spencer's central thesis in that study: the "individuality of each" must be "unfolded without limit" in a free society.[17] Spencer returned to the *Theory of Life* in his second book, *The Principles of Psychology* (1855), devoting an entire chapter of his "General Synthesis" to discussion of a "Proximate Definition of Life," along lines very similar to Coleridge's.[18] In *Social Statics* Spencer had applied Coleridge's individuation to political economy, to buttress his own general attack on Utilitarianism, which he felt was reductive in its vision of the individual man as a mere cog in the great social machine. In *The Principles of Psychology*, Coleridge's individuation is transformed into a principle of evolutionary biology: "Life is the tendency to individuation . . . as illustrated by the facts of development, or by the contrasts between lower and higher forms of life."[19] This transformation provides an example of the manner in which widely-divergent academic disciplines take on common shape, unified by a Victorian sensibility.

In the spring of 1850, Spencer met his lifelong friend, George Henry Lewes. That summer, the pair took frequent country rambles. Spencer claimed that Lewes attributed a new-found interest in "scientific inquiries" to those excursions.[20] Though Lewes's interest in Coleridge dates back to the late

1830s or early 1840s,[21] the *Theory of Life* enters his published work in the early years of his friendship with Spencer. In his essay on "Goethe as a Man of Science" in the *Westminster Review* in 1852, we find him writing that "this law of Repetition, which is the first law of organic growth, must be coupled with another law distinctly announced by Goethe in a very remarkable passage, and subsequently taken by Schelling and various other philosophers, including von Baer, whom Dr. Carpenter improperly credits with the discovery: the law we speak of is by Coleridge named the *Law of Individuation*."[22] Characteristically, Lewes modestly traces an intellectual genealogy; Spencer engulfs and assimilates. Quite unlike his hubristic friend, Lewes was widely-read, attuned to every new idea, well-versed in the history of ideas, and remarkably content, during those early years, to transmit the ideas of others rather than originate his own (perhaps one basis of a long-lived friendship with the egomaniacal Spencer?).

Yet just as Spencer could turn Coleridge to his own ends, so Lewes assimilated Coleridge's *Theory of Life* into preexisting concerns. The shared interests of the two men are again clear in Lewes's study of *Comte's Philosophy of the Sciences* (1853), as he digresses extensively from his explication of Comte's *Cours de philosophie positive* to discuss the "definition of life":

> In that very interesting posthumous essay by Coleridge, *Hints Towards a More Comprehensive Theory of Life* there is a definition which though not wholly unobjectionable, gives a point of view the student will find extremely useful if thoroughly appreciated— and the definition is this, "Life is the principle of individuation," or that power which discloses itself from within, combining many qualities into *one individual thing*. To appreciate this, however, it must be studied in the commentary.[23]

The commentary Lewes provides is that of Herbert Spencer, as Lewes then goes on to quote several pages of *Social Statics* on the *Theory of Life*. In Victorian hands Coleridge's theory accommodates itself not only to political economy (in *Social Statics*) and the development hypothesis (in the *Principles of*

Psychology); but here, to positivism: "Although wandering
from Comte by these remarks," Lewes concludes, "I am still
keeping within the necessities of an exposition of the Positive
Philosophy."[24]

George Eliot met Herbert Spencer and George Henry Lewes
in the fall of 1851; within the next two years, she was rumored
to be engaged to Spencer, and fell in love with Lewes. It was
Charles Bray and his wife Cara who had been Eliot's closest
friends during the decade prior to those auspicious new acquaintances. The intellectual hostilities between old and new
friends began as early as 1854, when Bray defended phrenology
against Lewes's attacks on the science in the *Leader*; the public
debate climaxed with Bray's acrimonious counterattack on
Lewes's second edition of the *Biographical History* (1857), in
his own revised edition of *The Philosophy of Necessity*
(1863).[25] Lewes always considered Bray on the dangerous metaphysical fringe of scientific psychology. Bray himself admitted
in his autobiography that he considered himself an idealist of
sorts: "The two apparently diverse classes of phenomena, the
mental and the physical, are only one. Mind is all, and all
things are known to us only as they exist in our consciousness."[26] Although Lewes was sympathetic with many of the
tenets of phrenology, Bray went entirely beyond the pale of
Lewes's positivistic sensibilities with his book *On Force, Its
Mental and Moral Correlates; and on That Which is Supposed
to Underlie All Phenomena; with Speculations on Spiritualism, and other Abnormal Conditions of Mind* (1866). Lewes's
letter to his spouse's oldest friend was scathing: "While I sym-
pathize with the pleasure you must have felt in weaving these
speculations, I cannot but regret that you should have wasted
money in printing anything so crude, and am quite sure you
will get no man of science to pay the slightest attention to it."[27]

Bray's "force" is a reformulation of the vitalist theory that
can be found in England as early as the first decade of the century.[28] Bray's pantheistic universe is ruled by a power variously
appearing as "Light, Heat, Electricity, Galvanism, Chemical
Affinity, Attraction and Repulsion," but all in reality "one

simple, primordial, absolute Force." Vitalism offered Bray a promised reconciliation of matter and spirit, a sort of spiritual physics. Force is an objectively quantifiable fact as well as an ethereal inspiration. Bray argues that once mind is "studied as all other forces are . . . then Metaphysics may take the place to which it is entitled at the head of all other Sciences."[29] Herein lay the seeds of a major development in nineteenth-century thought, a psychology that would transform the way man regarded mind.

Lewes's emphatically negative stand on metaphysics in the *Biographical History* would suggest little common ground between his philosophy and Bray's. But they share an intellectual genealogy. When reflecting on the genesis of *On Force* in his autobiography, Bray acknowledged his debt to James Hinton's essay on "Physiological Riddles" in the *Cornhill Magazine* (July–December 1860).[30] This little essay seemed to have caused quite a stir in the provinces: Sara Sophia Hennell, Bray's sister-in-law and a lifelong friend of George Eliot, wrote to Eliot to find out more about its author. "The writer of 'Physiological Riddles' is a Mr. Hinton," she replied, "Our attention was first drawn to [him] by an article in the British and For[eign] Medical Review which struck Mr. Lewes as quite marvelously similar in style to Mr. Spencer's writings, and which Mr. Spencer himself felt to be so alarmingly near to his own publications on Organic Form that he hastened to publish these in the same Review."[31] And what was Mr. Hinton's "physiological riddle"?: no less than "What is Life?" His answer,

> that of Coleridge, who in his Essay towards the Formulation of a more Comprehensive Theory of Life . . . seems to have anticipated . . . almost the entire advance of physiological knowledge since his day. His idea is, that physical life is a process, or a mode of organization, of the same powers which we recognize under other names, as magnetism, electricity, or chemical affinity. . . . they are grouped in a special way, the various forms of actions being so united as to constitute, out of many parts, a mutually dependent whole.[32]

"Individuation": "that power which discloses itself from

within, combining many qualities into *one individual thing,"*
wrote Lewes; "so united as to constitute out of many parts, a
mutually dependent whole," echoes Hinton. In Samuel Taylor Coleridge's own words:

> The unity will be more intense in proportion as it constitutes each
> particular thing a whole of itself; and yet more again, in propor-
> tion to the number and interdependence of the parts, which it
> unites as a whole. But a whole composed, *ab intra*, of different
> parts, so far interdependent that each is reciprocally means and
> end, is an individual, and the individuality is most intense where
> the greatest dependence of the parts on the whole is combined with
> the greatest dependence of the whole on its parts.[33]

We have no way of establishing exactly when George Eliot
read the *Theory of Life*, or even that she read it at all; though
the circumstantial evidence suggested by her proximity to
Lewes, Spencer, and Bray, would make her knowledge of the
work highly likely. But Eliot's essay on "Notes on Form in
Art" affords suggestive evidence that she was familiar with
Coleridge's theories. Thomas Pinney published this brief manuscript essay from a notebook dated 1868 for the first time in
the *Essays of George Eliot* (1963). Therein, Eliot illustrates
once again the way in which these Victorians embodied a diverse variety of content in a single form.

The same principles that Lewes and Spencer adapted to political economy, evolutionary biology, and positivism, could
also be transmuted into a formal aesthetic. Throughout this
essay, George Eliot defines literary form in terms of biological
metaphors: "The highest Form, then, is the highest organism." She does so in language that echoes unmistakably the
cadence as well as the concepts of the *Theory of Life*. Compare,
for example, the following passage from "Notes on Form" to
the passage just cited above from the *Theory of Life*:

> And as knowledge continues to grow by its alternating processes
> of distinction & combination, seeing smaller & smaller unlike-
> nesses & grouping or associating these under a common likeness,
> it arrives at the conception of whole composed of parts more &
> more multiplied & highly differenced, yet more & more absolutely

bound together by various conditions of common likeness or mutual dependence. And the fullest example of such a whole is the
highest example of Form: in other words, the relation of multiplex interdependent parts to a whole which is itself in the most
varied & therefore the fullest relation to other wholes.[34]

I shall return to "Notes on Form" in the context of George
Eliot's fiction at the conclusion of my study, when I discuss
Middlemarch as a Victorian finale, at the opposite pole of the
century from Coleridge's *Theory of Life*. This quintessentially
Victorian literary masterpiece is in a number of ways a fictional incarnation—both formally and ethically—of the Coleridgean cosmology.

But let us now look more closely at the *Theory of Life* itself,
in order to explain its appeal to these Victorians. Coleridge
writes: "I define life as the *principle of individuation*, or the
power which unites a given *all* into a *whole* that is presup-
posed by all its parts. The link that combines the two, and acts
through both, will of course, be defined by the *tendency* to individuation."[35] I begin by asking two questions suggested by
the previous discussion: first, how does Coleridge arrive at "individuation" as his definition of life, and in what ways does
this definition embody a characteristically British yoking of
empiricism and intuition? Second, how is it that Coleridge's
theory of life seems to adapt itself so readily to such apparently
disparate subjects as social theory, evolutionary biology, and
positivism on the one hand, and a quasi-mystical apprehension of pantheistic "force" on the other?

It is important to note at the outset that individuation is only
one of two key terms that recur throughout the *Theory of Life*;
the other is polarity: "We are now to seek for the highest law,
or most general form, under which this tendency [to individua-
tion] acts . . . what is its most general law? I answer—*polarity*, or the essential dualism of Nature, arising out of its productive unity."[36] In a sense individuation is a misleading term;
or rather, it is only half of the Coleridgean equation: individuality is inseparable from unity, the part defines itself in terms
of the whole. In his study of *What Coleridge Thought* (1971),

Owen Barfield draws extensively upon the *Theory of Life* as the key to the Coleridgean cosmos. In the course of his investigation, Barfield offers a crucial clarification of the unique and often misunderstood nature of Coleridgean polarity:

> Most of the much that has been written, in the last few decades, concerning the "reconciliation of opposites" in literature, and often with express reference to Coleridge as its putative father, betrays a lamentable failure to understand what "opposites" and their "reconciliation" actually signified in Coleridge's vocabulary. . . . Polarity is dynamic, not abstract. It is not a "mere balance or compromise," but "a living and generative interpenetration." Where logical opposites are contradictory, polar opposites are generative of each other—and together generative of a new product.[37]

Near the beginning of the *Theory of Life*, Coleridge offers a brief yet suggestive summary of the history of Western philosophy of science. In the process two polar schools of scientific method emerge: one we might call, in Coleridge's own terms, "ontological"; the other, "Newtonian." The ontological school is historically prior, but still existent: "In the thirteenth century the first science which roused the intellects of men from the torpor of barbarism, was as in all countries ever has been, and ever must be the case, the science of *Metaphysics* and *Ontology*." This is a science in which spirit takes supremacy over matter, reason over observation: "Men continued to invoke the oracle of their own spirits. . . . All attempts at philosophical explication were commenced by a mere effort of the understanding, as the power of abstraction; or by the imagination, transferring its own experiences to every object presented from without. . . . Thus physic became a sort of dull poetry." Four centuries later the "sublime discoveries" of Isaac Newton "placed the science of mechanism on the philosophic throne," as matter reigned supreme, giving "almost a religious sanction to the corpuscular system and mechanical theory. It became synonymous with philosophy itself. It was the sole portal at which truth was permitted to enter. The human body was treated of as an hydraulic machine." As in the *Biographia*

Literaria, with its attacks on Coleridge's early mentor, David Hartley, who combined Newtonian mechanics with Lockean psychology, it is clear from the *Theory of Life* that Coleridge, convinced of the "untenable nature of Materialism," is no Newtonian mechanist. But neither is he a spiritualist: "I distinctly disclaim all intention of explaining life into an occult quality."[38]

In the *Theory of Life*, Coleridge is seeking for a mediating position, one that combines "ontology" and "Newtonianism." It is in his own time, Coleridge believes, that new scientific discoveries were providing the dynamic unification of those two polar opposites, a "living and generative interpenetration" of spirit and matter: "The discovery of electricity . . . has electrified the whole frame of natural philosophy. . . . Henceforward the new path, thus brilliantly opened, became the common road to all departments of knowledge."[39] Electricity offered Coleridge a model and a metaphor for a power that was simultaneously both matter and spirit, quantifiable and ethereal, observable yet invisible. But Coleridge does not believe that electricity equals life (though some scientists did); rather, that it provides a vital analogy: "Whether the powers which manifest themselves to us under certain conditions in the forms of electricity, or chemical attraction, have any analogy to the power which manifests itself in growth and organization, is altogether a different question." Ultimately, according to Coleridge, we must only assume this power; the human mind cannot comprehend it. Thus the principle of organic life that is analogous to the inorganic electrical power can only be defined by reducing it "to its simplest and most comprehensive form or mode of attraction; that is, to some characteristic *instinct* or *tendency*, evident in all its manifestations."[40]

Yet as he continues to search for this tendency, Coleridge seems to suggest that the analogy between the power that rules the inorganic world and the organic world at some indefinable point becomes the identity of the two. Coleridge argues for a wider view, one that sees life evolving out of a "ladder" of minute gradations in the natural world: "This wider view . . .

fills up the arbitrary chasm between physics and physiology, and justifies us in using the former as means of insight into the latter, which would be contrary to all sound rules of ratiocination if the powers working in the objects of the two sciences were absolutely and essentially diverse."[11]

Thus Coleridge arrives at his definition of life: "The *power* which discloses itself from the principle of unity in the many"; "the *principle of individuation*, or the power which unites a given *all* into a *whole*."[42] But one might question the exact role of this power in creating life. However enthusiastically Coleridge may embrace the "physics" of nature, he remains an ontologist as well. Coleridge was a devout Christian at the time that the *Theory of Life* was written; but his theory contains no Butlerian analogies—Coleridge has virtually nothing to say about God here. In another sense the *Theory of Life* is about nothing *but* God, God active throughout the cosmos, embodied in his creation, the One in the many, the immaterial principle that unifies the material world.[43] Yet it must be stressed that it is fundamentally untrue to Coleridge to deny that the *Theory of Life* is not equally "about" science, the Coleridgean polar opposite of God.

"I cannot separate God from Nature," preaches pantheist Charles Bray in *On Force*, "our Priests must be one with our men of science, our Prophets are the Poets."[44] Likewise, neither can we separate man from nature: "In Man the centripetal and individualizing tendency of all Nature is itself concentered and individualized—he is a revelation of Nature," proclaims Coleridge.[45] Similarly, Spencer argues that man, at the apex of creation, represents the highest manifestation of individuation: "By virtue of his complexity of structure, he is furthest removed from the inorganic world in which there is least individuality." But man's individuality is inseparable from his unity with all natural creation. Spencer continues: "Yet must this highest individuation be joined with the greatest mutual dependence. Paradoxical though the assertion looks, the progress is at once toward complete separateness and complete union."[46] Spencer here echoes Coleridge, who writes:

> In social and political life this acme is inter-dependence; in moral life it is independence, in intellectual life it is genius. Nor does the form of polarity, which has accompanied the law of individuation up its whole ascent, desert it here. As the height, so the depth. The intensities must be at once opposite and equal. As the liberty, so must be the reverence for law. As the independence, so must be the service and the submission to the Supreme Will![47]

Despite their differences of opinion, Charles Bray approvingly quotes George Henry Lewes's *Biographical History of Philosophy* in *On Force*: "The simplest germination of a lichen is, if we apprehend it rightly, directly linked with the grandest astronomical phenomena. . . . Plato had some forecast of this when he taught that the world was a great animal; and others, since Plato, when they considered the universe the manifestation of some transcendent life, with which every separate individual life was related, as parts are to a whole."[48]

In the pages that follow, I will explore some of the practical implications of these starry generalizations for a circle of Victorian thinkers, the ways in which Mill, Comte, Combe, Chambers, Martineau, though they may not have made direct reference to Coleridge's cosmology, share with Spencer, Lewes, Bray, and Eliot in a larger confluence of views. Auguste Comte organizes the universe into a hierarchy of sciences, from mathematics and astronomy up to biology and "social physics," claiming as his goal the representation of "all phenomena as particular aspects of a single general fact."[49] Once the "chasm between physics and physiology" has been bridged, the universality of causality and law established throughout the organic as well as the inorganic creation, the doors have been opened to a new scientific view of man. "The doctrine of the Correlation and Persistence of Forces," writes Bray, "gives us a Science of Psychology based on Physiology, by which alone we can attain to the same command over mind, as we already have over physical force."[50] For this circle of Victorians, phrenology embodied just such a would-be science of psychology: Combe, Chambers, Bray, and Martineau were lifelong believers; Eliot, Spencer, and Comte youthful advocates; Mill and Lewes offered qualified praise for the system.

And the physiological psychologist who could view the created world as a grand whole in which the mind of man was as much a part of nature as the "simplest germination of a lichen" or "the grandest astronomical phenomenon" was intellectually prepared for the evolutionary theories that were to culminate with Darwin's *Origin of Species.* It was Robert Chambers's proclamation of the "development hypothesis" fifteen years prior to the *Origin* that made the grand synthesis. Through his close friendship with leading British phrenologist George Combe, phrenology taught Chambers how to unify physics and physiology, and he carried the analogy to the whole of the created universe, claiming that the same fundamental laws could be found at work everywhere, from the macrocosm of the formation of the solar system to the microcosm of embryological growth.

Harriet Martineau's *Letters on the Laws of Man's Nature and Development* continues these variations on the theme of "the true cosmical view of Nature": "All properties of matter are but various conditions of the same: . . . light, heat, electricity, magnetism, chemical affinity, &c., are convertible, or evolved one by the other." Martineau too provides evidence of the long shadow cast by Coleridge's *Theory of Life* over the Victorian age, when she asserts "the sense of variety in unity, and unity in variety; the whole in the parts, and the parts in the whole; all of one growth and origin . . . exhibiting the same law under various aspects, and all evolved . . . each symbolical of all, and all of each."[51]

In my preface to this study, I suggested that this Victorian circle provides a case in point of a characteristically British intermingling of intuition and empiricism. Halèvy's wedding of the evangelical and the utilitarian spirit can be reformulated in terms of the Coleridgean polarities of "ontology" and "Newtonianism," a view that imaginatively connects the parts within the vision of the whole, and one that reasons inductively from the particulars of empirical observation. In the broadest sense, we might simply call these polarities religion and science.

With a few notable exceptions, the works of this group have not become classics of religious, scientific, or philosophic thought. As a result they have not been given their due by intellectual historians. But I believe that the frame of mind they embody is highly significant for the history of ideas in nineteenth-century England. The conflict between religion and science is a truism of Victorian intellectual history. Yet the biographies and writings of these men and women do not reveal a pattern of anguished conflict; but instead, offer repeated evidence of genuinely optimistic conciliation, a true Coleridgean unification of polarities.

In his otherwise splendid chapter on "Coleridge and the Cosmology of Science," Owen Barfield speaks incorrectly when he categorically claims a "major collision between [Coleridge's] cosmology and the cosmology of science." Barfield is certainly correct when he says that "if Coleridge is right, then for cognition . . . physical process cannot be isolated from mental process, nor natural science from human and ethical psychology." ("Is there no communion between the intellectual and the moral? Are the distinctions of the schools separate in Nature? Is there no Heart in the Head? No Head in the Heart?" Coleridge asks.) Barfield's error comes from the vantage-point of disenchanted twentieth-century man, light-years away from any possibility of belief in a Coleridgean synthesis of natural science and ethical psychology: "The contrary assumption is of course implicit today in every observation, every choice of experiment, every laboratory, every scientific textbook on which the young are reared," he writes in 1971.[52] Quite the contrary was true for this Victorian circle. When the reader opens their books, he will find abundant evidence of and faith in (and for them, evidence and faith went hand-in-hand) the harmony of heart and head, and the complex ethical implications of that harmony. "There is not a more pernicious fallacy afloat in common parlance," wrote George Eliot in 1855, "than the wide distinction made between intellect and morality. Amiable impulses without intellect, man may have in common with dogs and horses; but morality, which is specifically human, is dependent on the regulation of feeling by intellect."[53] Eliot's beliefs on this subject remained consistent throughout her lifetime; twenty years later she offered the other half of the equation, copying into her notebooks a phrase from her first full-length novel, *Adam Bede* (1859): "Feeling is a sort of knowledge." "What seems eminently wanted is a closer comparison between the knowledge which we call rational and the experience which we call emotional," she goes on to say.[54] Samuel Taylor Coleridge would surely have agreed.

1. George Henry Lewes, quoted in William Baker, "G. H. Lewes's Annotations to Coleridge's *The Friend* (1837)," *Library* 3 (1976):32.

2. Samuel Taylor Coleridge, quoted in Alice D. Snyder, *Coleridge on Logic and Learning* (New Haven, 1929), pp. 135–36.

3. George Henry Lewes, *The Biographical History of Philosophy*, Library Edition (New York, 1882), p. 789.

4. Francis Bacon, *Novum Organum* (1620), in *Selected Writings of Francis Bacon*, ed. Hugh G. Dick (New York, 1955), p. 502.

5. Lewes, *Biographical History*, p. 412.

6. George Henry Lewes, "Spinoza's Life and Works," *Westminster Review* 39 (1843):384–85.

7. Charles Bray, *The Philosophy of Necessity* (London, 1841), 1:93.

8. Herbert Spencer, *The Principles of Psychology* (London, 1855), p. 341.

9. Lewes, *Biographical History*, pp. 410–11.

10. Auguste Comte, *Cours de philosophie positive* (1830–42), trans. Harriet Martineau, in *Auguste Comte and Positivism*, ed. Gertrude Lenzer (New York, 1975), p. 73.

11. Lewes, *Biographical History*, p. 429. Lewes also quotes liberally from Mill's *Logic* at this point in the *Biographical History*.

12. Samuel Taylor Coleridge, Ms. Egerton 2801. f. 101, in *Inquiring Spirit*, ed. Kathleen Coburn (London, 1951), pp. 126–27.

13. Samuel Taylor Coleridge, *Specimens of the Table Talk* (Edinburgh, 1905), 12 September 1831.

14. See J. H. Haeger, "Coleridge's 'Bye Blow': the Composition and Date of *Theory of Life*," *Modern Philology* 74 (August 1976):20–40. See also Sam H. Barnes, "Was *Theory of Life* Coleridge's *Opus Maximum*?" *Studies in Philology* 55 (1958):494–514.

15. Herbert Spencer, *An Autobiography* (New York, 1904), 1:91–92, 289.

16. Spencer, *Autobiography*, 1:277, 403.

17. Herbert Spencer, *Social Statics* (1850; rpt. New York, 1865), p. 476. See pp. 476–83 for Spencer's discussion of the *Theory of Life*.

18. Spencer, *Principles of Psychology*, p. 353.

19. Spencer, *Principles of Psychology*, p. 353. In "Coleridge and the Idea of Evolution," *PMLA* 40 (June 1925), George R. Potter notes that Coleridge's borrowings from Schelling for the *Theory of Life* bear "a distinct resemblance to part of Herbert Spencer's evolutionary biology" (395 n). Well they might; the similarity is far from coincidental.

20. Spencer, *Autobiography*, 1:436.

21. William Baker suggests that Lewes's reading of Mill's essay on Coleridge led him to *The Friend* ("G. H. Lewes's Annotations," 30 n). See also the Coleridge entries in *The George Eliot-George Henry Lewes Library*, ed. William Baker (New York, 1977).

22. George Henry Lewes, "Goethe as a Man of Science," *Westminster Review* 58 (October 1852):268.

23. George Henry Lewes, *Comte's Philosophy of the Sciences* (London, 1853), pp. 167-78. See pp. 166-72 for Lewes's discussion of the "definition of life."

24. Lewes, *Comte*, p. 171.

25. Charles Bray to George Henry Lewes, in *Leader*, 7 January 1854, pp. 20-21. Charles Bray, *Philosophy of Necessity*, 2d ed., rev. (London, 1863), p. 55.

26. Charles Bray, *Phases of Opinion and Experience During a Long Life* (London, 1884), p. 257. Hereafter cited as *Phases of Opinion*.

27. George Henry Lewes to Charles Bray, *The George Eliot Letters*, Gordon S. Haight, ed. (New Haven, 1954-55, 1978), 8:362.

28. See June Goodfield-Toulmin, "Some Aspects of English Physiology: 1780-1840," *Journal of the History of Biology* 2 (1969):283-320, for a discussion of vitalism in nineteenth-century English science.

29. Charles Bray, *On Force, Its Mental and Moral Correlatives* (London, 1866) pp. 3, iv. Hereafter cited as *On Force*.

30. Bray, *Phases of Opinion*, p. 98; James Hinton, "Physiological Riddles," *Cornhill Magazine* 2 (1860):421-30. See also pp. 9-11 of *On Force* for a lengthy quotation from "Physiological Riddles."

31. Sara Sophia Hennell to George Eliot, *George Eliot Letters*, 3:328-29. Hinton wrote critical notices for the *Fortnightly Review* under Lewes's editorship in the late 1860s. They first met in the late 1850s (*George Eliot Letters*, 3:320); Lewes notes a call from Hinton as late as May 1875 (*George Eliot Letters*, 6:142 n).

32. Hinton, "Physiological Riddles," p. 426. Not surprisingly, when Hinton wrote on "Herbert Spencer's *Principles of Biology*" he showed a special interest in Spencer's definition of life (*Chapters on the Art of Thinking, and Other Essays* [London, 1879], pp. 343-86).

33. Samuel Taylor Coleridge, *Formation of a More Comprehensive Theory of Life*, in *Selected Poetry and Prose*, ed. Donald Stauffer (New York, 1951), p. 574. Hereafter cited as *Theory of Life*. This work had been all but lost to the modern reader until Stauffer incorporated it into his Modern Library edition.

34. George Eliot, "Notes on Form in Art," in *Essays of George Eliot*, ed. Thomas Pinney (New York, 1963), p. 433. Hereafter cited as Pinney.

35. Coleridge, *Theory of Life*, p. 573.

36. Coleridge, *Theory of Life*, p. 578.

37. Owen Barfield, *What Coleridge Thought* (Middletown, Ct., 1971), pp. 35–36. See especially chapter 11, "Coleridge and the Cosmology of Science."

38. Coleridge, *Theory of Life*, pp. 564–65, 569, 567. This "ontological" state, wherein "men continued to invoke the oracle of their own spirits," has much in common with Auguste Comte's "theological" and "metaphysical" stages of development (see chapter 1), or Ludwig Feuerbach's theory of religion as a subjective psychological projection in *The Essence Of Christianity* (translated by Eliot in 1854).

39. Coleridge, *Theory of Life*, p. 566. Barfield notes Coleridge's close friendship with scientist Sir Humphry Davy, and makes some provocative speculations on the poet-philosopher's relationship to other pioneers in the science of electricity, Michael Faraday and Clerk Maxwell (*What Coleridge Thought*, pp. 37, 138).

40. Coleridge, *Theory of Life*, pp. 568, 569.

41. Coleridge, *Theory of Life*, p. 572.

42. Coleridge, *Theory of Life*, p. 573.

43. See Craig Miller, "Coleridge's Concept of Nature," *Journal of the History of Ideas* 25 (1964):77–96.

44. Bray, *On Force*, pp. 58–59.

45. Coleridge, *Theory of Life*, p. 601.

46. Spencer, *Social Statics*, pp. 481, 482.

47. Coleridge, *Theory of Life*, p. 601.

48. Lewes, quoted in Bray, *On Force*, p. 50.

49. Comte, *Cours*, p. 72.

50. Bray, *On Force*, p. iii.

51. Harriet Martineau and Henry George Atkinson, *Letters on the Laws of Man's Nature and Development* (London, 1851), p. 256.

52. Barfield, *What Coleridge Thought*, p. 135.

53. George Eliot, "Evangelical Teaching: Dr. Cumming," *Westminster Review* 64 (1855), in Pinney, p. 166.

54. George Eliot, "More Leaves from George Eliot's Notebook," ed. Thomas Pinney, *Huntington Library Quarterly* 29 (1966):364. See *Adam Bede* (1859; rpt. Boston, 1968), chapter lii, p. 425.

CHAPTER ONE

Foundations: John Stuart Mill and Auguste Comte

If man have thought so much of some one particular discovery as to regard him as more than man who has been able by some benefit to make the whole human race his debtor, how much higher a thing to discover that by means of which all things else shall be discovered with ease!—Bacon, Novum Organum

I. UNIVERSAL CAUSATION—JOHN STUART MILL:
SYSTEM OF LOGIC (1843)

This is my Idea that if we could once attain the logical perfection of all we know we should pass by easy stages to all attainable knowledge.—*George Henry Lewes, marginalia on Coleridge's Essays on Method,* The Friend

In his *Autobiography* John Stuart Mill wrote of the process whereby the prodigious young disciple of his father's bloodless Utilitarianism discovered that his education "had failed to create . . . feelings in sufficient strength to resist the dissolving impulse of analysis." Mill's crisis led him to the revivifying poetry of the romantics, in particular Coleridge, "in whom alone of all writers I have found a true description of what I felt." In the new beliefs that emerged, Mill sought to balance the claims of head and heart, utility and romanticism, the abstract needs of mankind and the demands of self. He was redeemed from the arid life of a reasoning machine by his vital discovery of "the internal culture of the individual."[1]

Mill turned again to the romantic thinker in an essay on "Coleridge's Works" for the *London and Westminster Review* as a complement to his earlier piece on Jeremy Bentham. In that 1840 essay, Mill unknowingly revealed considerable affinity with Coleridge's already-written but not-yet-published *Theory of Life*: "Contraries, as logicians say, are but *quae in eodem genere maxime distant,* the things which are farthest from one another in the same kind." Bentham epitomizes the empirical school, Coleridge the intuitive; Mill proclaims them not "enemies" but "allies": "The powers they wield are opposite poles of one great force of progression." And Mill also recognizes this polarity within the Coleridgean doctrine itself: "It is less extreme in its opposition, it denies less of what is true in the doctrine it wars against, than has been the case in any previous philosophic re-action." Coleridge, Mill argues, has much to offer the empirical successors to the psychology of Locke and Hartley: "His writings . . . are the richest mine from whence the opposite school can draw materials for what has yet to be done to perfect their own theory."[2]

There can be no doubt that Mill's essay on Coleridge had at
least one admirer among the Victorian circle that this study
depicts, particularly if one regards imitation as a sincere form
of admiration. In the essay on Coleridge, Mill offers his classic
definition of the "Germano-Coleridgean doctrine": "It expresses the revolt of the human mind against the philosophy
of the eighteenth century. It is ontological, because that was
experimental; conservative, because that was innovative; religious, because so much of that was infidel."[3] In one of his earliest essays, "Modern Metaphysics and Moral Philosophy of
France," published in the *British and Foreign Review* in 1843,
young George Henry Lewes adapts Mill's definition to Lewes's
own exploration of another reaction against the eighteenth
century, Auguste Comte's *Cours de philosophie positive*. The
echo of Mill is unmistakable: that positivist reaction, writes
Lewes, "is dogmatical and constructive, where [the eighteenth
century] was skeptical and destructive: it is spiritual where that
was material; religious where that was opposed to religion."[4]

Psychologist Alexander Bain first met George Henry Lewes
(then 25) in 1842, and recalled that "he sat at the feet of Mill,
read the *Logic* with avidity, and took up Comte with equal
avidity. These two works, I believe, gave him his start in philosophy."[5] Mill's letters to Lewes provide ample documentation of the student-teacher relationship in the early 1840s, as
Mill criticizes young Henry's fledgling essays ("I return your
Ms. with a good deal of pencil scratching at the back, for I have
been, & intend to be, *hyper*-critical"; 1 March 1841). He also
writes letters of introduction for Lewes to French *savants* (to
Victor Cousin, 27 April 1842: "Celui que je vous adresse est
beaucoup plus jeune: mais il a des connaissances et une capa-
cité qui donnent de grandes expérences"; and in a similar vein
to Auguste Comte, 9 June 1842) and British publishers (to the
editor of the *British and Foreign Review*, who published
Lewes's first essay, "Hegel's Aesthetics: Philosophy of Art," in
1842: "He is rather a good writer, has ideas (even in the Coleridgean sense) & he is a contributor worth having," 7 May
1841[6]). It was Mill who introduced Lewes to John William Parker, the publisher of his first book, the *Biographical History*

of Philosophy (1845-46), using his influence to help the unknown young writer.[7] The dates of Mill's *Logic* coincide with
the period of Lewes's discipleship: it was completed at the end
of 1841 and published—also by Parker—in the spring of 1843.[8]
In his introduction to the *Biographical History*, Lewes proclaimed it "perhaps the greatest contribution to English speculation since Locke's *Essay*."[9] He was to cite the *Logic* as an
authority again in his second book, *Comte's Philosophy of the
Sciences* (1853).[10]

The case of John Stuart Mill's *Logic* belies any simplistic
arguments to be made about the influence of Lewes on his life's
partner, George Eliot; Mill provides a strong example of the
remarkable confluence of interests that Lewes and Eliot must
have discovered when they met in 1851. George Eliot's enthusiasm for the *Logic* is evident in her letters. We have no idea
when she first read the book herself, but she was eager to share
the discovery with her closest friends. In October of 1849, she
writes to Charles Bray that her old Foleshill acquaintance,
John Sibree, had her copy, "which you will do well enough to
ask him for—he keeps books long enough to take a manuscript
copy of them." The Brays were evidently successful at retriev-
ing the *Logic* (and may have been equally remiss in returning
it), for two years later Eliot requests that Mrs. Bray "ask Mr.
Bray to let me have Mill's System of Logic, which I don't suppose he wants at present. I shall be glad to have it by me for
reference."[11] Unlike Lewes, Eliot never shared a personal
friendship with Mill; but her essays and notebooks provide further evidence of her continuing interest in the book from beginning to end of her career. Writing on "The Future of German Philosophy" for the *Leader* in 1855, Eliot's review of Otto
Friedrich Gruppe's *Gegenwart und Zukunft der Philosophie
in Deutschland* (1855) has as much to say about Mill as it does
of Gruppe, since she contends that the "gist" of Gruppe's argument is an effort "to map out the road which John Mill (to
whose work he seems to have given imperfect attention) has
actually wrought out and made available."[12]

George Eliot was introduced to Herbert Spencer in August
1851, and began to see him frequently after September of that

year. It seems likely that one reason for her request of the *Logic*
from the Brays in October was to share it with Spencer. Although he had first encountered the *Logic* shortly after its publication, in his provincial days at the Derby Philosophical Society, and remembered vaguely agreeing with Mill (largely in
sympathy with his "dissent from an orthodox doctrine"),
Spencer dated his real acquaintance with the book to sometime
in early 1852, when George Eliot presented him with a copy.
In March 1852 Spencer wrote to his father that he was beginning the *Logic* as a "first step towards preparing for my 'Introduction to Psychology' which I mean to begin vigorously by
and by."[13] Spencer was still digesting the *Logic* in the summer
of 1852, as he and Marian Evans strolled along the Kentish
coast at Broadstairs, discussing his plans for the new work.[14]
Spencer's introduction was to become the *Principles of Psychology* (1855), whose earliest formulations are to be found in
his essay on "The Universal Postulate." This essay appeared
in the *Westminster* under Eliot's editorship in 1853, and was
reprinted almost verbatim as chapters 2 and 3 of the *Principles*. Spencer claimed that it was written in large part in direct
response to the *Logic*.[15]

My readers will remember that Spencer had met George
Henry Lewes in the spring of 1850; the rapid development of
their friendship was founded on eagerly shared intellectual interests. Typically, the mutual intellectual influences among
this circle are circular rather than linear. Spencer dated the inception of his interest in psychology to a reading of the
Biographical History: "I had not, up to 1851, made the phenomena of mind a subject of deliberate study. I doubt not that
the reading of Lewes's book . . . gave me an increased interest in psychology . . . at the same time that it served, probably, to give more coherence to my own thoughts."[16] Thus
Mill's *Logic* figures both directly in Spencer's intellectual development, via George Eliot; and indirectly, mediated by
Lewes, himself inspired to the study of philosophy and psychology by Mill. In dissecting the loving friendships and
friendly love affairs of both heart and head among Spencer,
Lewes, and Eliot, it is often difficult to define cause and effect;

the role played in their lives and thought by Mill's *Logic* is typical of the strong mutuality of ideas that links them all. But the *Logic* was indisputably a shared interest, and, I will demonstrate, a consequent influence on all three.

Indeed, it was a text that provided a foundation for the frame of mind shared by all the members of this Victorian circle. When it appeared in the 1840s, John Stuart Mill's *System of Logic* set off reverberations that spread extensively beyond the philosophic academy. Looking back upon the previous century, intellectual historian A. W. Benn eloquently summarized the book's revolutionary appeal to the early Victorians. The *Logic*

> explained to English readers what they had never been taught before . . . how the vast edifice of physical science on which they had been accustomed to gaze with stupid wonder, as on a fairy palace, raised by magic arts, really owed its existence to a more systematic application of the same processes by which we find our way about in everyday life . . . by carrying into the study of mind and morals, of society and government, the same method by which the properties of space, the mechanism of the heavens, the composition of matter, and the conditions of animal life had been so successfully unravelled.[17]

Mill himself announced that the *Logic* was intended to counteract the influence of "the German, or *a priori* view of human knowledge" with "a text-book of the opposite doctrine—that which derives all knowledge from experience, and all moral and intellectual qualities principally from the direction given to the associations." The belief that truth can be known by intuition rather than through observation and experience is, Mill feels, "the great intellectual support of false doctrines and bad institutions." In the *Logic* Mill hoped to meet the intuitive philosophers on their own ground, and to offer an "explanation, from experience and association, of the peculiar character of what are called universal truths."[18] Mill's position was not, of course, an original one. Lewes's comparison of Mill and Locke in the *Biographical History* is no casual juxtaposition. Much of the *Logic* is a rewriting of Lockean philosophy in a distinctly Victorian vein.

It is not to my purposes here to scrutinize the more technical formulations of the *Logic*, or to attempt a comprehensive reading of this formidable academic classic. But the *Logic* offers much to the historian of Victorian ideas.[19] Let me begin with a notion that may seem self-evident, but that was to have far-reaching implications for Mill and his contemporary followers: a comprehensive logic can be formulated only if one believes in a world that operates according to rational, consistent, universal principles of cause and effect. Inductive reasoning, generalizations founded upon observation and experience, cannot take place unless nature's course is governed by universally applicable laws. Mill makes this point emphatically and repeatedly: "The ultimate major premise of all inductions" is "the uniformity of the course of nature."

Like Samuel Taylor Coleridge, Mill aspires to a monistic world view, searching for "separate threads of connection between parts of the great whole which we term nature." Mill finds his unification of part and whole, observed particular and reasoned generalization in the "general character of regularity" which "along with and in the midst of infinite diversity, pervades all nature." These uniformities he calls "Laws of Nature." Much like Coleridge, Mill seeks for a single law that will subsume unto itself all of the multiplicitous laws of nature. This ultimate law is "the Law of Causation": "The truth that every fact which has a beginning has a cause is so coextensive with human experience." Mill reminds his reader that this law of causation is really but "the familiar truth that invariability of succession is found by observation to obtain between every fact in nature and some other fact which has preceded it, independently of all considerations respecting the ultimate mode of production and phenomena."[20]

Mill's dry academic prose may seem far from incendiary to the twentieth-century reader. But his disregard for any "ultimate mode of production" was quickly recognized by the Victorians as a denial of the active presence of God in the world. Universal causation goes hand-in-hand, if not with atheism, then with a negation of the traditional ontological pieties, the creative God of Genesis. When George Eliot wrote her first es-

say for the *Westminster*, a review of R. W. Mackay's *The Progress of the Intellect*, in 1850, she showed herself fully aware of
the theological implications of the law of causation. Eliot
finds in Mackay a new, and quite heterodox, version of divine
revelation: "The master key to this revelation, is the recognition of the presence of undeviating law in the material
world. . . . It is this invariability of sequence which can
alone give value to experience and render education in the true
sense possible."[21] Ten years later, writing on "The Influence
of Rationalism" for the *Fortnightly Review*, Eliot reiterates
her belief in Mill's causal, ungodly universe, emphasizing "the
supremely important fact, that the gradual reduction of all
phenomena within the sphere of established law, which carries
as a consequence the rejection of the miraculous. . . . The
great conception of universal regular sequence . . . is the
most potent force at work in the modification of our faith."[22]
Similarly, Herbert Spencer claims in his *Autobiography* that
he was predisposed to Mill's logical version of heterodoxy virtually from infancy, its message inwrought with his deepest
sensibility: "The notion of causation was thus rendered much
more definite in me than in most of my age, there was established a habit of seeking for causes, as well as a tacit belief in
the universality of causation. Along with this there went absence of all suggestion of the miraculous."[23]

It is important to emphasize here, however, that although
Mill's *Logic* may have seemed inimical to conventional religious beliefs, it provided a *credo* of its own. Mill's affirmations
of faith are most clearly stated in the concluding book of the
Logic, "On the Logic of the Moral Sciences," where he makes
the first practical applications of his theoretical views on causality. In Book 6, as throughout the *Logic*, Mill is indebted to
John Locke. In the *Essay on Human Understanding*, Locke
had declared himself "confident . . . that if Men would in the
same method, and with the same indifferency, search after
moral, as they do mathematical Truths, they would find them
to have a stronger Connection one with another . . . and to
come nearer perfect Demonstration, than is commonly imagined."[24] Mill opens his discussion of the logic of the moral sci-

ences with a question: "Are the actions of men like all other natural events, subject to invariable laws? Does the constancy of causation, which is the foundation of every scientific theory of successive phenomena, really obtain among them?" The answer to this rhetorical question leads directly to the conclusion that Mill embodies in his title for chapter 3: "That There is, or May Be, A Science of Human Nature."[25]

This disarmingly simple assertion was to have profound ideological implications. If mind is subject to the same universal laws as matter, psychology more properly belongs to the scientist than to the philosopher; scientific method may be applied both to the mechanism of the individual mind and to its aggregate manifestation, society. It is in the Victorian age that psychology proper enters the realm of natural science. And also in this period that social science as we know it today is born. In a wide variety of ways, every Victorian thinker in this circle addresses himself to the implications of what Herbert Spencer calls the "universality of law—law in the realm of mind as in matter—law throughout the life of society as throughout individual life . . . [and] the correlative idea of universal causation."[26] George Eliot speaks for all her Victorian compatriots when she asserts in "The Progress of the Intellect" that "undeviating law" is present in the moral as well as the material world. She urges a plan of action to be adopted in a wide variety of ways by the Victorian sages who surround her: the "invariability of sequence which is acknowledged to be the basis of physical science" must no longer be "perversely ignored in our social organization, our ethics, and our religion."[27]

I began my discussion of the *System of Logic* with Mill's own assertion of its grounding in the British empiricist tradition. But Mill is more than a Victorian Locke; we find in this admirer of Bentham *and* Coleridge a true sense of Coleridgean polarity and a desire for that dynamic interpenetration Coleridge emphasizes in the *Theory of Life*. In "The Future of German Philosophy," George Eliot defends Mill against Gruppe's objection to his methodological emphasis on deduction: "Deduction, as Mill shows, is not properly opposed to induction but to experiment," she writes.[28] This passage, which Eliot is paraphrasing from the *Logic*, made a deep impression on George Henry Lewes as well; he quotes it in the introduction to his *Biographical History*: "The opposition is not between the terms Inductive and Deductive, but between Deductive and Experimental."[29] Mill believed that induction and deduction can, in fact, operate in tandem. Throughout the *Logic* Mill presents his reader with a series of polarities: they are titled, variously, induction and deduction, the experimental and the analytical methods of investigation, science and philosophy, the chemical and the geometrical models—but all have in common the fundamental opposition of the particular vs. the general. The scientist concerns himself with the observation of particulars; he begins with effects, and experiments in order to arrive inductively at causes. His method is "chemical," or concrete. In contrast the philosopher deals in abstract or "geometrical" propositions. He works deductively, from analysis of causes to an understanding of their effects. The scientist moves from the many to the one, the philosopher from the one to the many; the scientist's universe is Copernican, the philosopher's, Ptolemaic.

Mill hopes to reconcile these polarities through the "concrete deductive method," a method that he intends as both a science and an art: "science . . . following one cause to its various effects, while art traces one effect to its multiplied and diversified causes and conditions." This method attempts to sophisticate our notions of linear cause and effect, working "deductively indeed, but by deduction from many, not from one or a very few original premises; considering each effect as (what it really is) an aggregate result of many causes, operating sometimes through the same, sometimes through different mental agencies, or laws of human nature."[30]

The concept of a science of psychology provides Mill with a perfect model for his new method, a discipline that draws upon the skills of both philosopher and scientist. In order to achieve this balance, Mill proposes to add an entirely new science, which he calls "ethology," as a companion to psychology. Mill defines psychology as the "science of the elementary laws of mind"; ethology as the "ulterior science which determines the kind of character produced, in uniformity to those general laws, by any set of circumstances, physical and moral." Psychology is based on observation and experiment, the dissection of those "mechanic" laws whereby the individual mind functions; ethology is to be a deductive science, placing the individual within the larger social whole (it would be impossible to put heredity, environment, society under a microscope—the elements involved are too vast and too complex). The principles of ethology, writes Mill, lie somewhere between induction and deduction; they are the *"axiomata media . . .* of the science of mind: as distinguished, on the one hand from the empirical laws resulting from simple observation, and on the other from the highest generalizations."[31]

Without exception, these Victorians embraced Mill's doctrine of universal causation. It provided the cornerstone of their intellectual foundations. But unanimity of response stopped there: some felt Mill went too far with his new method; and some, not far enough. Mill's inclusion in my circle must be qualified. For all his theoretical claims of *axiomata media*, Mill finally remains firmly entrenched in Cartesian cogitations rather than donning a laboratory coat and approaching the dissection table. His assertion of law in the realm of mind as well as matter stops short of the next logical step: mind as matter. "Whilst we are destitute of senses acute enough, to discover the minute particles of Bodies, and to give us *Ideas* of their mechanical Affectations, we must be content to be ignorant of their properties and ways of Operation," wrote Locke in the *Essay on Human Understanding.*[32] Despite the intervening generations of scientific progress, Mill essentially remained in agreement with Locke, stopping short of a physiological psychology: "The successions . . . which obtain among mental phenomena, do not admit of being deduced from the physiological laws of our nervous organization."[33] Mill's "science of mind" still owes more to the philosopher

than to the biologist, to the seventeenth century than to the
nineteenth.

Both phrenologists and evolutionists were to disagree, and
take Mill's law of nature one logical step further. Phrenologist
Charles Bray, for example, bemoaned the tendency of his contemporaries to stray from "the right path of the true cerebral
physiology," and placed blame squarely on Mill as "principally responsible for turning a whole generation out of the
way."[34] Evolutionist Herbert Spencer also qualified his admiration: "Though in Mr. Mill's *System of Logic*, the doctrine of
causation receives full and critical exposition; yet by him, as
by the Utilitarians generally, there has not been that full study
of physical science at large which conduces to an ever-present
and vivid consciousness of cause."[35]

Yet when Spencer's essay on "The Universal Postulate," inspired in opposition to Mill, is juxtaposed to his above comments on the *Logic*, an apparent paradox is revealed; and in
that paradox we can recognize the distinctive nature of these
synthetic Victorian thinkers. Spencer himself would have
found no inconsistency in the fact that he could condemn Mill
in the *Autobiography* for his lack of practical scientific investigations on one hand; and, in "The Universal Postulate,"
controvert Mill's empiricism in favor of the more intuitive philosophy of William Whewell, Mill's arch-opponent in matters
philosophical.

Herbert Spencer, an early believer in phrenology and later
in the pre-Darwinian development hypothesis, sought to
know (in a scientific spirit) but also to believe (if not necessarily in accord with the Thirty-Nine Articles). He writes "The
Universal Postulate" in search of "some primordial belief of
which no proof can be given."[36] Spencer claimed to have found
that belief in Whewell's *Philosophy of the Inductive Sciences*—or rather, in reading Mill's *criticisms* of Whewell's philosophy in the *Logic*.[37] In "The Universal Postulate," Spencer
quotes Mill quoting Whewell: "A necessary truth is a proposition the negation of which is not only false but inconceiva-
ble." The "universal postulate" as defined by Spencer scarcely

differs: "*A belief which is proved, by the inconceivableness of its negation, to invariably exist, is true.*"[38]

Spencer agrees with Mill's empirically-based universal causation, but it is not adequate to satisfy him: "In passages controverting the doctrine enunciated by Dr. Whewell, he had . . . ignored that criterion of belief to which we all appeal in the last resort, and further, he had not recognized the need for any criterion." Though he has no use for God, Spencer, unlike Mill, does quest for "ultimate modes of production," some version of a final cause, a belief that transcends empirical proof: "Belief is the fact which . . . is antecedent to, and inclusive of, all other facts."[39] (Let me note here that in another turn of the Victorian screw, Spencer attempts to turn Whewell's intuition back upon empiricism by means of evolutionary biology—and herein lies the genesis of the *Principles of Psychology*, of which I shall have much more to say in chapter 4.)

In October 1853 George Eliot, the young editor of the *Westminster Review*, wrote to her friend Sara Sophia Hennell: "I hope you will be pleased with our present number. If you don't think the Universal Postulate first-rate, I shall renounce you as a critic."[40] I shall return later to the early intellectual relationship between Eliot and Spencer; but if we remember here that Eliot was a sympathetic audience for "The Universal Postulate," it will help in understanding why she chose the three epigraphs she did for her notebooks in the late 1870s, from Mill's *Logic*, Aristotle's *Ethics*, and Locke's *Essay on Human Understanding*. I reprint the three passages here in full, for they have a great deal to tell not only about George Eliot's response to the *Logic*, but also of her attitude towards a scientific psychology of the sort Mill proposes.

> The generation of one class of mental phenomena from another, whenever it can be made out, is a highly interesting fact in psychological chemistry; but it no more supersedes the necessity of an experimental study of the generated phenomenon, than a knowledge of the properties of oxygen & sulphur enables us to deduce those of sulphuric acid without specific observation & experiment. [Mill, *Logic*, 2:637]

We must not look for equal exactness in all departments of study, but only such as belongs to the subject matter of each, and in such a degree as is appropriate to the particular line of enquiry. . . . Nor again must we in all matters alike demand an explanation of the reason why things are what they are; in some cases it is enough if the fact that they are so is satisfactorily established. This is the case with first principles; and the fact is the primary thing—it *is* a first principle. [Aristotle, *Ethics*, 1.7.18]

If by the help of microscopical eyes (if I may so call them) a man could penetrate farther than ordinary into the secret composition & radical texture of bodies, he would not make any great advantage by the change, if such an acute sight should not conduct him to the market & exchange; if he could not see things he was to avoid at a convenient distance, nor distinguish things he had to do with, by those sensible qualities others do. He that was short-sighted enough to see the configuration of the minute particles of the spring of a clock, & observe upon what particular structure & impulse its elastic motion depends, would no doubt discover something very admirable; but if eyes so framed could not view at once the hand and the characters of the hour-plate, & thereby at a distance see what o'clock it was, their owner could not be much benefited by that acuteness, which while it discovered the secret contrivance of the parts of the machine, made him lose its use. [Locke, *Essay*, 2:23, par. 12][41]

Mill, Aristotle, and Locke are three philosophers who share much common ground. But it seems to me that the passages from Aristotle and Locke also provide an implicit—and corrective—commentary on the first passage, from the *Logic*.

True to the mediating impulse of the concrete deductive method, Mill emphasizes the necessary coexistence of deduction and induction, general laws (those of "psychological chemistry"), and observed particulars ("experimental study"). But his primary emphasis is on the importance of the empiricist's observation and experiment. Mill makes a case for an empirical science of psychology: we can study the "chemical" workings of the human mind just as we do the "properties of oxygen & sulphur." From her earliest days as a believer in phrenology, Eliot would remain in agreement with Mill's application of empiricism, according to the tenets of universal causation, to the study of the human mind. Long after her advocacy of phrenology had been qualified, she would remain convinced of the necessity of a truly scientific psychology.

The passages from Locke and Aristotle do not so much controvert as refine the passage from Mill. "We must not look for equal exactness in all departments of study," says Aristotle; the "whys" of the human mind are considerably more complex than the principles of a chemical equation, even if we do believe that it operates according to empirically verifiable scientific laws. And not only is the science of psychology—more particularly, when it enters the realm of ethics—an immensely difficult one to formulate with exactness, as the passage from Aristotle suggests: suppose we did have the "microscopical eyes" to give us, with perfect accuracy, every detail of observation and experiment? Locke, confident empiricist as he is, nonetheless emphasizes that a lucid view of every part does not equal the larger vision, "at a distance," of the whole; without universals we can make no sense of particulars; the detail is meaningless without the generalization. The final line of the passage from the *Essay* is particularly provocative: "That owner could not be much benefited by that acuteness, which while it discovered the contrivance of the parts of the machine, made him lose its use."

Remembering Spencer's universal postulate: knowledge must not stifle belief; one must allow for an intuitive formulation of the whole as well as a reasonable dissection of every part; scientific understanding of a man's mind must not displace a sympathetic apprehension of his heart. The opening paragraphs of Eliot's own notes that follow these three epigraphs provide variations on the same theme. Eliot's first statement asserts the necessity of a scientific study of man: "Ethics is a mixed science to which conduct is the corresponding art. From the scientific point of view you have to consider the forms of force or energy concerned. . . . Hence it seems an unfruitful attempt now to consider ethics apart from social & psychological evolution." This is followed by an apparently antithetical statement, a Coleridgean polar opposite: "A great deal of 'right action' is sure to be done . . . from sympathetic impulses." So much for a "scientific" ethics; Eliot explicitly disavows the rational Utilitarian analysis of human behavior: "Why have multitudes of mankind been tender to their mothers"?: "Not because they were contemplating the greatest happiness of the greatest number of mankind." Thus Eliot's thesis and antithesis. The synthesis follows; it is here that we find that notebook quotation from *Adam Bede* with which I closed my prelude: "Feeling is a sort of knowledge."[42] But George Eliot's emphasis here is not the supremacy of feeling over knowing; rather, their complementarity. These Victorians would find in John Stuart Mill's universal causation the "microscopical eyes" they needed for their quest; but Auguste Comte could promise the vision of the cosmic clock.

II. THE POSITIVE PLAN—AUGUSTE COMTE: *COURS DE PHILOSOPHIE POSITIVE* (1830–1842)

In that essay on "The Modern Metaphysics and Moral Philosophy of France" which echoed Mill's "Coleridge," George Henry Lewes concluded with an extended summary of Auguste Comte's recently-completed *Cours de philosophie positive* (which had appeared in six successive books: 1830, 1835, 1838, 1839, 1841, 1842). It was the first of many glowing reports that Lewes would write of the French philosopher in the decade to come, and one of the earliest English expositions of Comte.[43] Young Lewes enthusiastically predicted that Comte's *Cours* would "be the most memorable work of the nineteenth century. He will have founded a science and furnished its fundamental law. He will be at once the Bacon and the Newton of the nineteenth century." On the same page, Lewes footnotes as his authority his mentor John Stuart Mill's *Logic*: the *Cours* was "at once the most profound, the most complete, and the most masterly in its exposition of any work on the subject, and is invaluable to every cultivation of philosophy," Mill avows.[44]

Although the first public notice of Comte in England did not come until 1838, with physicist Sir David Brewster's review

of the first two volumes of the *Cours*,[45] Mill wrote privately to
John Pringle Nichol in December 1837 that "this said book is,
I think, one of the most profound books ever written on the
philosophy of the sciences. . . . I shall be much astonished if
this book of Comte's does not strike you more than any logical
speculations of our time."[46] In his *Autobiography* Mill explains that he had encountered the *Cours* while in the process
of writing the *Logic*, arriving at his own theory of induction
"by a different road," yet acknowledging that Comte's book
"was essential service to me in some of the parts which still
remained to be thought out," particularly Book 6, "On the
Logic of the Moral Sciences." Significantly, Mill claimed his
indebtedness to Comte for the important conception of the in-
verse deductive method, discussed above.[47] After Mill's discipleship waned in the early 1850s, he would return to the
French thinker in a more critical vein in two extended essays
for the *Westminster Review* (April and July 1865), which took
book form as *Auguste Comte and Positivism* in 1865. But in
the earlier blush of enthusiasm, Mill had written in his first
letter to Comte, 8 November 1841: "Je le lis et le relis avec une
véritable passion intellectuelle."[48]

Seven months later, 9 June 1842, Mill was to write Comte an
ingratiating letter of introduction on behalf of

> mon jeune ami Lewes, qui se réjoit très vivement de vous avoir vu.
> Je n'ai pas osé demander pour lui cet avantage parce que je savais
> qu'avec d'excellentes dispositions, et une certaine force d'esprit, il
> manque des bases essentielles d'une forte éducation positive. Je
> trouve très honorable à son caractère et à son intelligence la vive
> admiration qu'il éprouve pour vous, avec des moyens si imparfaits
> d'apprécier votre supériorité scientifique.[49]

Lewes quickly acquired that "education positive," and by 1848
had briefly taken Mill's place in Comte's eyes as the new apostle of positivism in England.[50] The *Biographical History of
Philosophy* (1845–46) heralded the advent of the Comtean age
in its concluding "Eleventh Epoch: Philosophy finally relin-
quishing its Place in favor of Positive Science"; Lewes expanded a series of *Leader* articles into *Comte's Philosophy of*

the Sciences: Being an Exposition of the Cours de Philosophie Positive of Auguste Comte (1853), the first full-length discussion of Comte in England, which appeared in the same year as Harriet Martineau's English translation.[51] Though by the mid-1850s, Lewes's relations with Comte had also cooled, he too returned to Comte in the next decade in a series of essays for the *Fortnightly Review.* He there confessed himself a "reverent heretic," but Lewes's later views of Comte were far less negative than Mill's.[52] One critic has even called Lewes's tempered later critique "an excess of charity": "If anything was likely to popularize Positivism, it was Lewes's two articles of 1866 in the *Fortnightly.*"[53]

Herbert Spencer's vehement disavowal of Comte's influence on his thought were loud and long; Spencer even went to the trouble of printing a lengthy fifty-year-old letter to George Henry Lewes as "Appendix B" to his *Autobiography,* chronicling an ongoing argument wherein Lewes levelled at Spencer the psychologically sophisticated accusation that his "antagonistic attitude toward Comte has tended to suppress the growth of any consciousness of indebtedness." Be that as it may, Spencer could honestly claim that the only source of Comte's ideas for him was Mill's *Logic,* which he had read two years after the "positivistic" *Social Statics* was written.[54]

In this appendix Spencer parenthetically reminds his reader that the *Logic* was lent him by George Eliot; and turning back to 1852, we find that Spencer's companion was urging the *Cours* upon him at the very same time: "In the course of the spring the name of Comte came up in conversation. She had a copy of the *Philosophy Positive,* and at her instigation, I read the introductory chapters of 'Exposition.' " Though admitting to an inadequate knowledge of French and a "neutral" attitude to Comte's doctrine of the three stages, Spencer expressed a "pronounced dissent" from the other major tenet of the *Cours,* Comte's classification of the sciences. He found young Marian Evans "greatly surprised: having, as she said, supposed the classification perfect." It was Spencer who prevailed in the debate (as he remembered it!): "She was but little given to argument; and finding my attitude thus antagonistic, she forthwith dropped the subject of Comte's philosophy, and I read no further."[55]

But George Eliot most certainly did not drop the subject in the simultaneously emergent friendship with George Henry Lewes, which turned to love during the same era in which Lewes held forth on Comte for the *Leader*. She became more intimate with both the manuscript of *Comte's Philosophy* and its author than she cared to admit publicly, chiding publisher John Chapman: "How came you to mention to Miss M. that you saw the proof of Mr. Lewes' book '*in [my] Miss Evan's room*'? I think that you must admit that your mention of my name was quite gratuitous. So far you are naughty—but never mind."[56]

The intrigue involved here was professional as well as sexual, for "Miss M.," Harriet Martineau, was engaged in something of a rival work: the translation of the *Cours*, to be published by Chapman, Eliot's coeditor at the *Westminster*. The plan for a translation had been in the works even before Eliot's editorship officially began (29 September 1851), and her early opinions of Martineau's qualifications for the undertaking were not generous.[57] However, as relations between Eliot and Martineau—and Martineau's mentor George Henry Atkinson—warmed, Eliot's position changed considerably. Martineau herself went so far as to make Eliot "joint trustee" with Atkinson of a fund for Comte's publication, in March 1852.[58] It was Eliot herself who reviewed Martineau's translation for the *Leader* (3 December 1853), and confessed (in editorial plurality) that as she read, "Our misgivings changed into approbation."[59] Comte himself thought so highly of the translation and abridgement that he had the work *re*translated into French and proclaimed it the official text of the *Cours*! Martineau's work encouraged Eliot to tackle Herbert Spencer on the subject of Comte once again; we find him writing to his father in February 1854 that "I am reading Miss Martineau's abridged translation of Comte . . . as two of my friends, Mr. Lewes and Miss Evans, were in large measure adherents of Comte's views,

I was curious to learn more definitely what these were."[60]

George Eliot's first published reference to Comte is to be found in the opening paragraph of her first essay for the *Westminster Review*, on "The Progress of the Intellect" (January 1851), in which she claims the truth of Comte's view "that the theological and metaphysical speculation have reached their limit, and . . . the only hope of extending man's sources of knowledge and happiness is to be found in positive science, and in the universal application of its principles." Eliot did qualify her agreement with the warning that positivism should not obviate the necessity of an historical viewpoint, a study of the "true process of development"—a point later to be reiterated by her evolutionary friend Herbert Spencer.[61] Eliot had concluded her review of Martineau's translation of the *Cours* with an exhortation: "May this work find its way to every sincere student of philosophy!"[62] As with her enthusiasm for Mill's *Logic*, George Eliot was a "sincere student" of Comte well before her first meeting with his English disciple, George Henry Lewes. It seems a likely possibility that her first acquaintance with Comte came through Mill's *Logic*.[63]

Having established the biographical interweaving of these two, I would now like to turn more directly to the relationship between the *System of Logic* and the *Cours de philosophie positive*, to trace both some sympathetic resonances between the two works and some very consequent areas of disagreement.[64] These Victorians were attracted to Comte's positivism for many of the same reasons they read Mill; but it is in the significant differences between the two thinkers that they found much of what was in fact most attractive to them in Comte. Like Mill's *Logic*, the *Cours* made the radical claim that the scientific method could be extended far beyond the laboratory—to psychology, ethics, social science. Unlike Mill, Comte was willing to carry the implications of this claim to their logical limits.

In *Auguste Comte and Positivism*, Mill provides an excellent starting point for any discussion of the major tenets of the *Cours*. By juxtaposing Mill's definition of the fundamental doctrine of positivism with my above discussion of the *Logic*, it becomes clear just why Mill read and re-read the *Cours* with such "passion intellectuelle":

> We have no knowledge of anything but Phaenomena; and our knowledge of phaenomena is relative, not absolute. We know not the essence, nor the real mode of production, of any fact, but only its relations to other facts in the way of succession or of similitude. These relations are constant; that is, always the same in the same circumstances. The constant resemblances which link phaenomena together, and the constant sequences which unite them as antecedent and consequent, are termed their laws. The laws of phaenomena are all we know respecting them. Their essential nature, and their ultimate causes, either efficient or final, are unknown and inscrutable to us.[65]

Comte's positivism, like Mill's logic, is predicated upon "the uniformity of the course of nature." Like Mill, Comte seeks for methodological unity in the midst of nature's diversity: Mill's universal causation is essentially one with Comte's positive law. Comte's method, like Mill's, has significant theological implications; just as Mill denies we can know the "ultimate mode of production of phaenomena," Comte disclaims "ultimate causes." Comte makes the heterodox consequences of his philosophy more explicit than does Mill, however, in asserting the fundamental positivistic law of the three stages. According to Comte, every branch of our knowledge "passes successively through three different theoretical conditions: the theological, or fictitious; the metaphysical, or abstract; and the scientific, or positive."[66] Once the positivistic apotheosis is reached, the outmoded theology and metaphysics of past ages will be easily jettisoned.

The second central tenet of the *Cours*, Comte's famous hierarchy of the sciences, is closely linked to this three-stage process. Each book of the *Cours* is devoted to one of the six sciences, in an ascending hierarchy: mathematics, astronomy, physics, chemistry, biology, and "social physics." Comte's principles of organization can be categorized in several ways: he moves along a spectrum from the most abstract (mathematics) to the most concrete (the social sciences); or from the most deductive to the most inductive; or from the inorganic to the organic. Comte believes that each science, at its own pace, must go through the three stages: again, one can range Comte's sciences along a spectrum, from mathematics, which was always purely "positive," to Comte's own newly-defined science of "social physics," which according to him had yet to emerge from the murky metaphysical realm—that is, prior to Comte. Like Mill, Comte believes that man—both individually, through a scientific psychology; and collectively, by means of "social physics" (Mill's "ethology")—can be studied according to the same "positive" or empirical experimental principles as constellations or chemical reactions.

But this brief summary must emphasize that Comte's fundamental concern is with identity rather than diversity. After all, Comte's positivist is engaged in much the same essential occupation as his theologian or his metaphysician: "to represent all phenomena as particular aspects of a single general fact"; "to find the one rational order among a host of possible systems." The difference merely lies in the monistic principle of explanation: the theologian's God has been transformed into Comte's Law. This same impulse toward unity characterizes the Comtean hierarchy: the sciences are "branches from a single trunk." Once they reach the positive stage, all science becomes one: "The only necessary unity is that of method."[67]

Induction and deduction will work together in the concrete deductive method; observed scientific particulars find true harmony with reasoned generalizations. Lewes sums up this positive promise in the *Biographical History*:

> In the present state of things the speculative domain is composed of two very different portions,—general ideas and positive sciences. The general ideas are powerless because they are not positive; the positive sciences are powerless because they are not general. The new [Positive] Philosophy . . . is destined to put an end to this anarchy, by presenting a doctrine which is *positive*, because elaborated from the sciences, and yet possessing all the desired *generality* of metaphysical doctrines, without possessing their vagueness, instability, and inapplicability.[68]

Social science stands at the apex of Comte's hierarchy; it deserves its exalted rank because it is at once the most general and the most particular of sciences. As Eliot writes in her essay on "The Natural History of German Life" (1856), "Social science, while it has departments which in their fundamental *generality* correspond to mathematics and physics, namely, the grand and simple generalizations which trace out the inevitable march of the human race as a whole . . . has also, in the departments of government and jurisprudence, which embrace the conditions of social life in their *complexity*, what may be called its Biology."[69] According to Comte, social science effects the fullest identity of organic and inorganic. It is the study of "man or humanity," in which "sociology is subordinated to the whole of organic philosophy, which discloses to us the laws of human nature," but equally addresses the "medium or environment" in which man lives, a subject that "is connected with the whole system of inorganic philosophy." Thus social science takes the *via media*, between man and his environment, organism and medium: "The study of the external world and of man is the eternal business of philosophy, and there are two methods of proceeding: by passing from the study of man to that of external nature or from the study of external nature to that of man. Wherever philosophy shall be perfect, the two methods will be reconciled."[70]

Herein, I believe, lies Comte's potent appeal to a Victorian frame of mind characterized by a strong mediating sensibility. In reconciling psychology and natural history, attempting to study man the organism within a social medium, Comte parallels Coleridge's notion of individuation, the idea that the highest form of development is that in which each individual is most uniquely himself, yet simultaneously most fully integrated into the whole: "The superiority of the social to the individual organism is . . . the more marked speciality of the various functions fulfilled by organs more and more distinct but interconnected, so that unity of aim is more and more combined with diversity of means."[71] The foundations are laid for a cosmology in which universal causation unifies the macrocosm and the microcosm within a single model.

Lewes summarizes it well in his chapter on "Passage from Inorganic to Organic" in *Comte's Philosophy*: "Thus in an ascending series of evolutions from the simple to the complex . . . we learn to gather the phenomena of the universe into one majestic Whole, and learn that all lines of demarcation are subjective only."[72]

Lewes's choice of the word "subjective" provides the clue to Mill's ultimate divergence from Comte. Mill recognized in the *Cours* a foreshadowing of the more mystical tendencies of Comte's later work, the attempt "to systematize . . . knowledge from the human or subjective point of view, the only one, he contends, from which a real synthesis is possible." Mill objects on two grounds: to the subjectivity, and to the synthesis, both of which are entirely too near a monistic mysticism for Mill's reasoned empiricist taste. Mill finds Comte's "ethical science" dangerously "metaphysical." He even goes so far as to claim that Comte relies on the "*a priori* philosophy," "erecting a mere creation of mind into a test or *norma* of external truth."[73]

Significantly for my purposes here, Mill detects a fundamental sympathy with Comte's departure from *a posteriori* empirical reasoning in Herbert Spencer's "Universal Postulate." In *Auguste Comte* Mill bemoans this peculiar hybrid—what we might call a positivist metaphysics—as it manifests itself, not in "those who still adhere to the old opinions," but in "one of the most vigorous as well as the boldest thinkers . . . full of the scientific spirit, Mr. Herbert Spencer"; and, "following in his steps," that "able expounder of the positive philosophy . . . Mr. Lewes," both of whom contend "that the ultimate test of the truth of a proposition is the inconceivableness of its negative." Mill ruefully concludes that "when those from whom it was least to be expected" turn from the objective to subjective grounds of proof, "we must admit that the metaphysical mode of thought still rules in higher philosophy, even in the department of inorganic nature, and far more in all that relates to man as a moral, intellectual, and social being."[74]

Thus John Stuart Mill finally remains more fundamentally Benthamite than Coleridgean, strongly committed to the association psychology of his empiricist predecessors. Comte's position is quite different: when he turns to the "Intellectual and Moral, or Cerebral Functions" in the *Cours*, he launches a direct attack on the "fundamental principles of interior observation" of the association psychologists; "the absurdity of the supposition of a man seeing himself think." Furthermore, says Comte, this approach to psychology has another "radical fault": "a false estimate of the general relations between the affective and the intellectual faculties." Comte contends that all prior approaches to psychology have erred in making "the intellect . . . almost exclusively the subject of their speculations." To the contrary, Comte asserts, "daily experience shows that the affections, the propensities, the passions, are the great springs of human life."[75] The opposition between Comte and Mill on this point is striking: "To say that men's intellectual beliefs do not determine their conduct, is like saying that the ship is moved by the steam and not by the steersman," counters Mill.[76]

Let me pause here. I have traveled some distance from the point at which this discussion of the *Cours de philosophie positive* began: Mill's summary of the fundamental doctrine of positivism, with its reasoned, constant sequences of antecedent and consequent, its positivist laws that had so much in common with Mill's universal causality, its promise of the positivistic millennium in which the scientific or experimental method will rise newborn from the dead husks of outmoded theology and metaphysics. Yet are not the "affections," "propensities," and "passions" more at home in the sanctuary of the Christian theologian or the metaphysical speculations of the romantic nature-worshipper?

This same potential confusion can be found in Comte's critics. After accusing Comte of "concessions to the metaphysical method," "follow[ing] Kant" in admitting the unknowable, "essences beyond our comprehension," A. W. Benn then goes on to claim positivism as nothing new to England, but rather "resuscitating old ideas originally peculiar to this island and afterwards discredited by the religious revival." Benn finds Comte's philosophy presaged in Hume's *Essay on Human Understanding* and Brown's *Treatise on Cause and Effect,* and considers positivism an offshoot of eighteenth-century empiricism rather than romantic transcendentalism.[77] Conversely, in defining positivism for *The Encyclopedia of Philosophy,* Nicola Abbagnano begins by stating that "it opposes any kind of metaphysics and . . . any procedure of investigation that is not reducible to scientific method," but goes on to point out that positivism has affinities with the "absolute idealism" of the nineteenth century, and "belongs with it in the general range of romanticism."[78] As early as 1860, Lewes summed up the characteristic confusion of the Comtean critic: "Comte is frequently written against by those who know him only at second hand, as offensively dry, hard, materialistic, and irreligious; while by those who have more or less acquainted themselves with his writings, he is frequently condemned as a mystical, sentimental, and despotically moral pontiff."[79] What is Comte?—a pantheistic idealist, or an empirical logician—or both?

Let me first present the simple solution, which has had considerable currency among both Comte's contemporaries and later historians, disciples and critics alike. This explanation could be termed "the two Comtes." It accounts for the divergence temporally: the early Comte of the *Cours,* with its emphasis on science and philosophy, and the later Comte of the *Politique Positive* (1851-54) and beyond, the "moral pontiff" of the "Religion of Humanity" (a religion replete with all the ceremonial trappings, including prayers to the new "Father"—Auguste Comte!).[80] W. M. Simon has recounted the inbred warfare among Comte's English disciples after the first wave of philosophical and scientific Comteans, led by Mill and Lewes, gave way to the more "religious" leadership of Richard Congreve. The religion of humanity is "Catholicism minus Christianity," sneered T. H. Huxley; on the contrary, retorted Congreve: it is "Catholicism *plus* science."[81]

There was, undeniably, a considerable distance between the *Cours* and Comte's later, more messianic, thought. Lewes provides an apt analogy from the annals of the Oxford movement to suggest the wide range of applications for the term "positivist": "It is as if the disciples of Dr. Newman who refused to follow him to Rome, were confounded with the disciples who followed him everywhere."[82] Lewes may have been an early believer in the *via media*, but he never went over to Rome. Yet as early as 1852, reviewing the recently-published *Système de Politique Positive* for the *Westminster Review*, Lewes himself suggested that the seeds of the "second" Comte were already present in the "first": "This regeneration, though extremely important, is only a *development*, not a *change* of view: all that he now preaches he preached before. . . . In his [Cours de] 'Philosophie Positive,' he elaborated from the sciences a philosophy of science; in his 'Politique Positive,' he aspires to convert that philosophy into a religion." Although his objections to the more literal realizations of Comte's religion were legion, Lewes praised the *Système* for its consistent reiteration of the same view of human nature to be found in the *Cours*: "that intellect is not the highest aspect of humanity, and that it must be the servant, not the lord, of the heart."[83]

Indeed, Auguste Comte was capable of inspiring an emotional conversion experience long before his post-*Cours* proclamations of positivist priests and prophets. In 1851 Harriet Martineau finished her *Letters on the Laws of Man's Nature and Development*, a book predicated on "the grand conception,—the inestimable recognition,—that science, (or the knowledge of fact, inducing the discovery of laws) is the sole and the eternal basis of wisdom—and therefore of human morality and peace." Thus predisposed she opened the *Cours de philosophie positive* for the first time. As she recounts the "rapture" she experienced in the process of her translation, Martineau provides a case in point of Comte's affective supremacy: "Many a passage of my version did I write with tears falling into my lap." Writing to Maria Weston Chapman, Martineau states explicitly that her positivism was a product of faith, not doubt: "Positive philosophy is at the opposite pole to skepticism . . . it issues in the most affirmative (not dogmatical) faith in the world, and excludes unbelief as absolutely as mathematical principles do . . . positive philosophy is, in short, the brightest, clearest, strongest, and only irrefragable state of conviction that the human mind has ever attained."[84] In her preface to the translation, Harriet Martineau speaks directly to the emotional needs fulfilled by the *Cours* in an age "alienated for ever" from the old faiths, finding in Comte a tonic "to retrieve a vast amount of wandering, of unsound speculation, or listless or reckless doubt, and of moral uncertainty and depression." Yet Martineau's preface reveals at the root of this emotive salvation a set of beliefs as intellectual, as rational, as logical as Mill's universal causality could require. The redemption that Comte offers Martineau takes a distinctly reasoned tone: "We find ourselves suddenly living, not under capricious and arbitrary conditions, unconnected with the constitution and movements of the whole, but under great, general, *invariable laws*, which operate on us as part of the *whole*," she writes.[85]

Thus the appeal of the *Cours* to these Victorians in the 1840s and early 1850s was on one hand identical with that of the *Logic*: the promise that regular, rational laws rule the universe and that thus the methods of natural science could be extended to new human sciences. This new positive plan would account for the particularity of the individual at the same time that each individual could be viewed as part of the larger whole— both the whole of society, and even more important, the whole of inorganic and organic creation. But Auguste Comte does not so much controvert John Stuart Mill as he goes one step further: where Mill, like Comte, seeks to reconcile deductive with inductive methods, experiment and observation with abstract reasoning, particular with general, Comte extends the mediating impulse even further, to attempt a more fundamental reconciliation of intellect and emotion.

Comte's philosophy was as likely to be repudiated by the scientist as by the theologian. "Men of science will reject with a sneer the subordination of the Intellect to the Heart,—of Science to Emotion," writes Lewes, "and the unscientific, feeling the deep and paramount importance of our Moral Nature, will be repelled from a philosophy which rests solely upon a scientific basis." It is Comte, not Mill, who is finally the true heir to the Coleridgean communion of intellectual and moral. "Logic and Sentiment—to use popular generalizations—have long been at war, and men reject Comte's system, because it seeks to unite them," asserts Lewes in his preface to *Comte's Philosophy*.[86] Coleridge's description of *his* ideal system could be grafted neatly onto Comte's: "a Philosophy, that will unite in itself, the warmth of the mystics, the definiteness of the Dialectician, and the sunny clearness of the Naturalist, the productivity of the Experimenter and the Evidence of the Mathematician."

Basil Willey has written that "Comte is, in a sense, the century in epitome, so that to study him is to find the clue to much that the *Zeitgeist . . .* was doing."[87] Mill's universal causation articulated a fundamental premise upon which this Victorian world view was founded. But Auguste Comte both qualifies and extends that premise. In so doing he provides the prototype of both the temperamental and the intellectual foundations for the applied science, new faiths, and synthetic philosophies shared by this Victorian circle.

1. John Stuart Mill, *Autobiography*, pp. 84, 86.

2. John Stuart Mill, "Coleridge's Works," *London and Westminster Review* 33 (1840), rpt. in *Mill on Bentham and Coleridge*, ed. F. R. Leavis (London, 1950), pp. 101, 140, 108, 117. See Leavis's excellent introductory essay to the two essays.

3. Mill, "Coleridge's Works," p. 108.

4. George Henry Lewes, "Modern Metaphysics and Moral Philosophy of France," *British and Foreign Review* 15 (1843):354-55. See William Baker, "G. H. Lewes's Annotations to Coleridge's *The Friend* (1837)," *Library* 31 (March 1976):31-36 for a discussion of Lewes's reading of Coleridge. Baker suggests that it was Mill who first led Lewes to the sage of Highgate.

5. Alexander Bain, quoted in Anna Kitchel, *George Lewes and George Eliot* (New York, 1933), p. 42.

6. John Stuart Mill, *The Earlier Letters of John Stuart Mill, 1812-48*, vol. 13 of

Collected Works, ed. Francis E. Mineka (Toronto, 1963), pp. 466, 517. 527, 475-76. Hereafter cited as *Earlier Letters*.

7. Mill, *Earlier Letters*, 13:628. Mill writes Parker, "I have a very high opinion of Mr. Lewes's qualifications for undertaking it."

8. See Mill, *Earlier Letters*, 13:628; also *Autobiography*, p. 133.

9. Lewes, *Biographical History*, p. xxi.

10. See Lewes, *Comte's Philosophy*, pp. 20, 105, 210.

11. George Eliot to Mr. and Mrs. Charles Bray, *George Eliot Letters*, 1:310, 363. Her letters reveal that Eliot was to re-read the *Logic* at least once more, in 1866, and to write in 1875 that she had studied it "with much benefit" (4:233; 5:163).

12. George Eliot, "The Future of German Philosophy," *Leader*, 28 July 1855, rpt. in Pinney, p. 150.

13. Spencer, *Autobiography*, 2:568; 1:453.

14. See Haight, *George Eliot*, pp. 114-15.

15. See Spencer, *Autobiography*, 1:482. The "Universal Postulate" appeared in the *Westminster Review* 60 (October 1853):513-50. As Eliot read "The Universal Postulate," she volunteered a "better form for the axiom which is the basis of the syllogism as explained by Mill"; Eliot told Sara Sophia Hennell that Spencer responded to her suggestion with "intense delight," claiming "how important [it] was to him in his work on Psychology" (George Eliot to Sara Sophia Hennell, *George Eliot Letters*, 2:145). He acknowledged the assistance of this "distinguished lady—the translator of Strauss and Feuerbach" in *The Principles of Psychology* itself (p. 162 n; see also Haight, *George Eliot Letters*, 1:145 n).

16. Spencer, *Autobiography*, 1:439.

17. Alfred William Benn, *The History of English Rationalism in the Nineteenth Century* (London, 1906), 1:431-32. Benn's lucid and valuable work is the only study that discusses all the members of this Victorian circle.

18. Mill, *Autobiography*, p. 135. This is what Spencer also claims to do in *The Principles of Psychology*.

In her essay on "The Future of German Philosophy," George Eliot similarly claims that "a system of logic . . . which assigns the first place to general ideas . . . inverts the true order of things"; "universality" has its "origin purely in the observations of the senses" (in Pinney, p. 151).

19. John Bicknell's comment in a recent bibliography of Victorian prose research provides a good case in point of the *Logic*'s neglect by students of the Victorian period: "Few even philosophically inclined readers will be anxious to work through John Stuart Mill's *Logic*" ("The Unbelievers," in *Victorian Prose: A Guide to Research* [New York, 1973], p. 472).

20. John Stuart Mill, *A System of Logic*, ed. J. M. Robson, in *Collected Works* (Toronto, 1973), 7:309, 315, 326-27. Robson uses the 8th edition (1872), with all textual variants of earlier editions given. See in general chapter 4, "Of Laws of Nature."

21. George Eliot, "The Progress of the Intellect," *Westminster Review* 54 (1851), in Pinney, p. 31.

22. George Eliot, "The Influence of Rationalism," *Fortnightly Review* 1 (1865), in Pinney, p. 413.

23. Spencer, *Autobiography*, 1:101.

24. John Locke, *An Essay Concerning Human Understanding*, ed. Peter Nidditch (1690; rpt. Oxford, 1975), p. 552.

25. Mill, *Logic*, in *Collected Works*, 8:835, 844.

26. Spencer, *Autobiography*, 1:241.

27. Eliot, "Progress of the Intellect," in Pinney, p. 31.

28. Eliot, "Future of German Philosophy," in Pinney, p. 152.

29. Lewes, *Biographical History*, p. xxi. See Mill, *Logic*, book 2, chapter 4, p. 142.

30. Mill, *Logic*, in *Collected Works*, 8:948, 894.

31. Mill, *Logic*, in *Collected Works*, 8:869, 870.

32. Locke, *Essay on Human Understanding*, p. 556.

33. Mill, *Logic*, in *Collected Works*, 8:851.

34. Charles Bray, *Phases of Opinion*, p. 66. Similarly, Henry George Atkinson writes of Mill's "lamentable" "inability to discern the value of physiology as the necessary and essential basis of mental science" (letter to Charles Bray, in *On Force*, p. 164).

35. Spencer, *Autobiography*, 2:102-3.

36. Spencer, "The Universal Postulate," pp. 520-21.

37. This conversion by contraries was characteristic of Spencer. Similarly, he was converted to Lamarckism by reading Lyell's attack on Lamarck (see *Autobiography*, 2:7).

38. Spencer, "The Universal Postulate," 521, 530.

39. Spencer, "The Universal Postulate," 482, 519.

40. George Eliot to Sara Sophia Hennell, *George Eliot Letters*, 2:118.

41. Eliot, "More Leaves," 363. Pinney dates these essays between 1872-73, but I would suggest it more likely that they were written around December 1876, the date in Eliot's copy of Locke's *Essay*; they abound with references to Locke. I print here the Rackham translation from the Loeb Classical Library; in Eliot's Ms. the passage is in the original Greek.

42. Eliot, "More Leaves," p. 364.

43. See W. M. Simon, *European Positivism in the Nineteenth Century* (New York, 1963), p. 173. William Smith wrote the first review of the complete *Cours* for *Blackwood's* in 1843.

44. Lewes, "Modern Metaphysics," 402; Mill, quoted in Lewes, "Modern Metaphysics," 402 n.

45. See Simon, *European Positivism*, pp. 172-73.

46. Mill, *Earlier Letters*, 13:363.

47. Mill, *Autobiography*, p. 125. See pages 125-27 for Mill's discussion of the *Cours*. A. W. Benn writes: "The first edition of Mill's 'Logic' contained admiration for the 'Philosophie Positive' and its author, well calculated to attract public attention and to win reader for that cyclopaedic work" (*History of English Rationalism*, 1:427).

48. Mill, *Earlier Letters*, 13:489.

49. Mill, *Earlier Letters*, 13:527.

50. See Simon, *European Positivism*, p. 197.

51. See Simon, *European Positivism*, chapter 7, "England: the Ambience of John Stuart Mill." pp. 172-201 for a thorough historical discussion of positivism among the Victorian *intelligentsia*.

52. George Henry Lewes, "Auguste Comte," *Fortnightly Review* 3 (1865-66):404.

53. Simon, *European Positivism*, pp. 200-201.

54. Spencer, *Autobiography*, 2:567-68. For an extended comparison of Spencer and Comte, see John C. Greene, "Biology and Social Theory in the Nineteenth Century: Auguste Comte and Herbert Spencer," in *Critical Problems in the History of Science*, ed. Marshall Clagett (Madison, 1962), pp. 419-46; also Simon, *European Positivism*, pp. 217-18. For Spencer's own explicit disavowal of Comtean influence, see his essay on "The Genesis of Science," *British Quarterly Review* 20 (July 1854):108-62.

55. Spencer, *Autobiography*, 1:461.

56. George Eliot to John Chapman, *George Eliot Letters*, 2:132. See also 2:126 n; Eliot's copy of Lewes's *Comte* is inscribed "Marian Evans from G. H. L."

57. "It is true that Harriet Martineau's style is admirably adapted for the people, clear, spirited, idiomatic, but I should have less confidence in the equal fitness of her calibre of mind for rendering a trustworthy account of Comte's work" (George Eliot to John Chapman, *George Eliot Letters*, 1:361).

58. George Eliot to Mrs. Charles Bray, *George Eliot Letters*, 2:17.

59. George Eliot, "Miss Martineau's Translation of Comte," *Leader*, 3 December 1853, p. 1,171 (See *George Eliot Letters*, 2:123 n for verification of Eliot's authorship).

60. Spencer, *Autobiography*, 1:517; though Spencer ultimately proved no more receptive, concluding that "the only indebtedness I recognize is the indebtedness of antagonism" (ibid.). Eliot did write to Bray that Spencer, "who never praises but upon compulsion," had at least acknowledged Martineau's translation "perfectly lucid" (*George Eliot Letters*, 2:140).

61. Eliot, "The Progress of the Intellect," in Pinney, p. 28.

62. Eliot, "Miss Martineau's Translation," p. 1,172.

63. In her journal for 7 June 1865, Eliot mentions she is reading Mill's "second article on Comte, to appear in the Westminster," lent her by Herbert Spencer (*George Eliot Letters*, 4:196). Although my study is limited to the *Cours*, let me note here that her interest in Comte was lifelong (see *George Eliot Letters*, 7:326, 335, 341). Only weeks before her death, she was reading Bridges' translation of the *Politique* aloud with husband John Walter Cross, who was to write afterwards: "For all Comte's writings she had a feeling of high admiration, intense interest, and very deep sympathy. I do not think I ever heard her speak of any writer with a more grateful sense of obligation and enlightenment" (quoted in Simon, *European Positivism*, p. 211).

In addition to Simon's chapter, "England: Sympathizers and Others" (especially pp. 207-13), see James F. Scott, "George Eliot, Positivism, and the Social Vision of 'Middlemarch,'" *Victorian Studies* 16 (1972):59-76; T. R. Wright, "George Eliot and Positivism: A Reassessment," *Modern Language Review* 76 (1981): 257-72.

64. In his *History of Rationalism*, Benn discusses the *Logic* and the *Cours* side-by-side, asserting the significance of their convergence in "rescuing the physical sciences from pietistic or hypocritical specialists" (1:449).

65. John Stuart Mill, *Auguste Comte and Positivism*, 4th ed. (London, 1891), p. 6. Hereafter cited as *Auguste Comte*.

66. Comte, *Cours*, p. 71. Mill renames these three stages "volitional," "ontological," and "experimental" (*Auguste Comte*, p. 10).

67. Comte, *Cours*, pp. 72, 93, 259, 85.

68. Lewes, *Biographical History*, p. 779. Eliot echoes Lewes in her essay on "The Natural History of German Life": "In the various branches of social science there is an advance from the general to the special, from the simple to the complext, analogous with that which is found in the series of sciences, from mathematics to biology" (*Westminster Review* 66 [1856]), rpt. in Pinney, 289–90.

69. Eliot, "Natural History," in Pinney, p. 290; my emphasis.

70. Comte, *Cours*, pp. 253–54.

71. Comte, *Cours*, pp. 163, 270. Note the similarity here to Coleridge's "individuation."

72. Lewes, *Comte's Philosophy*, p. 161.

73. Mill, *Auguste Comte*, p. 72.

74. Mill, *Auguste Comte*, pp. 72, 73.

75. Comte, *Cours*, pp. 184, 185.

76. Mill, *Auguste Comte*, p. 104. Mill's assertion seems naive to the post-Freudian reader!

77. Benn, *History of English Rationalism*, 1:417–18.

78. Nicola Abbagnano, "Positivism," *Encyclopedia of Philosophy*, (New York, 1967), 8:414–15.

79. Lewes, "Auguste Comte," pp. 401–2.

80. "Great Teacher and Master, Auguste Comte, Revealer of Humanity to all her children, Interpreter of her Past, Prophet of her Future, Founder of her Religion, the one, the Universal Religion" (quoted in Simon, "Auguste Comte's English Disciples," p. 167).

"In fact," observed one Comtean worshipper at Congreve's services, "it was just like a church: there was Lord Houghton fast asleep" (Spencer, *Autobiography*, 2:110–11).

81. Quoted in Simon, "Auguste Comte's English Disciples," p. 162.

82. Lewes, "Auguste Comte," p. 400.

83. George Henry Lewes, review of Auguste Comte, *Système de Politique Positive*, in "Contemporary Literature of France," *Westminster Review* 57 (January 1852):347.

84. Harriet Martineau, *Autobiography*, 2:232, 391, 3:323–24.

85. Harriet Martineau, "Preface" to Auguste Comte, *Cours de philosophie positive* (London, 1885), 1:v, x.; my emphasis.

86. Lewes, *Comte's Philosophy*, p. 5.

87. Basil Willey, *Nineteenth Century Studies* (1949; rpt. New York, 1966), p. 188. Appropriately, Willey's description of Comte is a direct echo of his words on Coleridge: "Coleridge's literary and spiritual insight placed him upon a point of vantage from which he could overlook the nineteenth century in front of him, and reply in advance to all that the *Zeitgeist* would thereafter bring forward" (p. 40).

CHAPTER TWO

Applied Science—Phrenology and Evolution: George Combe and Robert Chambers

I form a history and tables of discovery for anger, fear, shame, and the like; for matters political; and again for the mental operations of memory, composition and division, judgment and the rest; not less than for heat and cold, or light, or vegetation, or the like.—Bacon, Novum Organum

"*Agir par affection, et sentir pour agir*: such is the motto of [Comte's] system, which indicates the predominance given to the emotive over the merely intellectual—in opposition to the old psychology which always subordinated the emotions to the intellect." George Henry Lewes singled out this aspect of Comte's philosophy as its most potent appeal. The emotive bias that suffused Auguste Comte's thought from its earliest exploration of positivistic method to the later manifestations of messianic fervor originated in and was founded upon a scientific source: the phrenological system of Franz Joseph Gall.

Lewes argued that Gall provided Comte with "a bias and point of departure."[1] In the *Cours de philosophie positive* itself, Comte makes abundantly clear his debt on the subject of affective supremacy to Franz Joseph Gall, whose *Recherches sur le système nerveux en général et sur celui du cerveau en particulier* (Paris, 1809-11), coauthored with Johann Caspar Spurzheim, became the first textbook of the science of phrenology:

> A full contemplation of Gall's doctrine convinces us of its faithful representation of the intellectual and moral nature of Man and animals. All the psychological sects have misconceived or ignored the preeminence of the affective faculties, plainly manifest as it is in all the moral phenomena of brutes, and even of Man; but we find this fact placed on a scientific basis by the discovery that the affective organs occupy all the hinder and middle portions of the cerebral apparatus, while the intellectual occupy only the front portion, which, in extreme cases, is not more than a fourth, or even a sixth part of the whole. The difference between Gall and his predecessors was not in the separation of the two kinds of faculties, but that they assigned the brain to the intellectual faculties alone.[2]

Contemporary critics of the *Cours* made no secret of their disapproval of Comte's affiliations with the new cerebral psychology. W. H. Smith's 1843 essay on Comte, the first on the complete *Cours* to appear in England, bemoaned the fact that Comte was a phrenologist. Smith's orthodox piety was mightily offended by the heretical implications of the science: what was to become of the soul if mind was reduced to mere matter?—such regions were better left a sacred mystery: "Upon the dial of a watch the hands are moving, and a child asks why? Child! I respond, that the hands *do* move is an ultimate fact."[3] Two decades later, in *Auguste Comte and Positivism*, John Stuart Mill responded with equal disapprobation: "And what Organon for the study of 'the moral and intellectual functions' does M. Comte offer, in lieu of the direct mental observation which he repudiates? We are almost ashamed to say, that it is Phrenology!" But the bias of Mill's objection is antithetical to Smith's: "The later course of physiological observation has not tended to confirm, but discredit, the phrenological hypothesis."[4] It was to be phrenology's fate, as it was positivism's, that it antagonized both men of religion and men of science; its heterodoxy was equally theological and physiological.

But there were many in the intellectual vanguard who approached phrenology with respect. Mill himself in 1842 had taken up Gall's second major work, the six-volume *Sur les fonctions du cerveau* (1825), at Comte's instigation: "J'ai commencé l'étude de Gall: il me paraît un homme d'un esprit supérieur. Je le lis avec plaisir et j'espère aussi avec fruit." A month later Mill submitted a lengthy progress report on his study, confessing his difficulty with Gall's physiological specifications, and finding his map of the brain premature, "vague et anti-scientifique." But yet a month later, Mill wrote again, and tempered his earlier objections: "Pour parler maintenant de Gall, je crain de vous avoir donné une idée exagérée de mon éloignement actuel de sa doctrine. Je suis bien loin de ne pas la trouver digne d'être prise, selon votre propre expression, en sérieuse considération; bien au contraire, je crois qu'elle a irrévocablement ouvert la voie à un ordre de recherches vraiment positives, et de la première importance."[5]

Mill had introduced his young friend Lewes to Comte in the same letter in which he criticized phrenology. The juxtaposition of the two subjects was more than casual, for Lewes too was intrigued by the new science. When Lewes himself turned to a series of essays on "Phrenology and Phrenologists" in the *Leader* between December 1853 and January 1854, he echoed Mill's reservations as well as his praise of phrenology for introducing "positive" researches into the human mind. "We believe in Phrenology, but not in the Phrenologists. . . . We believe in Phrenology and Physiology, both as sciences having a positive basis," asserts Lewes; "we admit the tentative [claims] made by Gall as the first and greatest step towards the positive psychology."[6]

Psychology was to be the proving-ground of positivism; or, as Comte put it, "the last battleground, in the popular view, between the positive philosophy and the ancient."[7] Man's beliefs about his "intellectual and affective phenomena" were the final stronghold of the theologians—with their talk of soul—and the metaphysicians—with their notions of consciousness. Comte believed that he had found in Gall's phrenology the perfect organon of a purely positive psychology. He wrote in the *Cours*:

> It was not till our own time that modern science, with the illustrious Gall for its organ, drove the old philosophy from this last portion of its domain and passed on in the inevitable course from the critical to the organic state. . . . Neither enmity nor irrational advocacy has hindered the continuous spread, in all parts of the scientific world, of the new system of investigation of intellectual and moral man. All the signs of the progressive success of a happy philosophical revolution are present in this case.[8]

Phrenology's premier English advocate, George Comte, echoes Comte in his ecstatic vision of the positivist millennium: "Before the appearance of Drs. Gall and Spurzheim . . . the science of Mind was very much in the same state as that of the heavenly bodies prior to the times of Copernicus and Newton."[9]

The founder of phrenology, Franz Joseph Gall, was born in Baden in 1758; about 1800, he began his physiological researches, dissecting human and animal brains with his student and disciple, Johann Caspar Spurzheim. Official displeasure led to their departure from Vienna in 1805, whence they embarked on a successful lecture tour of Europe, settling in Paris in 1807; their jointly-authored *Recherches* appeared in 1809. The two parted ways when Spurzheim added philosophy to Gall's physiology and broke with the master in 1814. Gall, unlike his follower, was wary of emphasizing ideology over anatomy. In that same year, Spurzheim arrived in England to preach the new gospel, touring and lecturing extensively throughout the British Isles until his death in 1832.[10]

Franz Joseph Gall summarized the four chief tenets of this new positive psychology in the *Anatomie et physiologie*: "The moral and intellectual dispositions are innate; their manifestation depends on organization; the brain is exclusively the organ of the mind; the brain is composed of as many particular and independent organs, as there are fundamental powers of the mind;—these four incontestable principles form the basis of the whole physiology of the brain."[11] Of Gall's four principles, it is the fourth that has remained in the memory of the twentieth century as "phrenology": the "crainioscopy" practiced by the phrenologists, bump-reading, the art of divining character by the contour of the skull (fig. 1.1). Admittedly, among a certain segment of the populace (particularly in the English provinces and in America), this aspect of phrenology had a large and popular following. But among the more intellectual observers of phrenology, adversaries and advocates alike were critical of the cruder populist applications of the science. Writing on "Phrenology in France" for *Blackwood's* in 1857, George Henry Lewes scoffed, "As the general public knows not fear, it buys treatises, attends lectures, collects skulls, and manipulates heads."[12] On this point, at least, ardent phrenologist Charles Bray was in agreement: "The public, however, consider that manipulating the head is phrenology, and we cannot too much reprobate the practice of those persons who aid thus to deceive them, and who have brought the science into disrepute by their presumptions and confident assumption of accuracy which has not yet been attained," Bray wrote in an open letter to Lewes published in the *Leader*.[13]

Despite his reservations about phrenology as a fad, Lewes

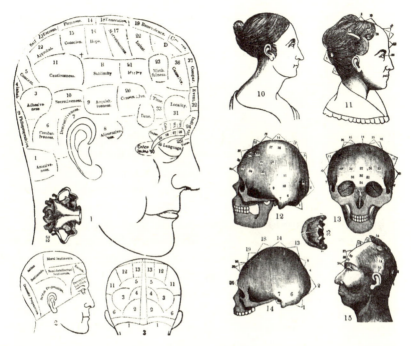

Fig. 1. From O. S. Fowler, *Fowler's Practical Phrenology*, 22d ed. (New York, 1845).

was fascinated by it as a science. In his *Biographical History of Philosophy*, he made an eloquent plea for phrenology as a seminal influence on the development of physiological psychology:

> The day for ridiculing Gall has gone by. Every impartial compe-
> tent thinker, whether accepting or rejecting Phrenology, is aware
> of the immense services Gall has rendered to Physiology and Psy-
> chology, both by his valuable discoveries, and by his bold, if ques-
> tionable hypothesis. He revolutionized Physiology by his method
> of dissecting the brain, and by his bold assignment of definite
> functions to definite organs. To verify or refute his hypotheses,
> vast researches were undertaken . . . and now there is no phys-
> iologist who openly denies that mental phenomena are directly
> connected with nervous structure.[14]

Gall's first three principles may not seem particularly original, or even controversial—so much were they shared by the luminaries of later nineteenth-century psychology, and to such an extent as they are scientifically accepted today. But in Victorian England, it was these aspects of phrenology that were, in fact, the most truly controversial and profoundly significant. To British intellectuals of the 1830s and 1840s, the heirs of philosophical psychology, for whom mind meant a Lockean *tabula rasa* and for whom the psychologist was a meditative Cartesian cogitator, the ideological implications of phrenology were radical, whether or not one agreed with the specifics of Gall's cerebral localization (such as the exact location of the "organ" of "amativeness" or "veneration").

Despite the inadequacies and inaccuracies of Gall's system, his contribution to psychology was extremely significant: not in terms of the physiological specifics of brain structure (where he erred grossly), but rather as a new *method* for studying the mind, a method that liberated psychology from the confining discipline of philosophy. Gall believed in psychology as a physical science, not a branch of epistemology.[15] Quite simply, phrenology claimed that since the brain is the organ of the mind, mind is matter. As such, it can be subjected to the same scientific methods that might apply in investigating any other human organ—or any organic being—or inorganic nature as well. According to the Comtean hierarchy, the method of biology becomes that of psychology, just as the method of chemistry became that of biology; and so on, back to the cosmology of astronomy and the pure laws of mathematics. Universal causation reigns supreme throughout organic and inorganic creation.

For my purposes it is the broader assumptions informing the phrenological world-view that are of greater interest than the specific scientific strengths or weaknesses of phrenology's "organology." In his 1835 preface to *The Constitution of Man*, the most widely-read British gospel of this new philosophy, phrenologist George Combe himself admitted that his work "may be instructive even to those who contemn Phrenology as unfounded," insofar as it demonstrates the more fundamental assertion that "we are physical, organic, and moral beings, *acting under the sanction of general laws*, whether the connection of different mental qualities with particular portions of the brain, as taught by Phrenology, be admitted or denied."[16] Comte's statement suggests that phrenology would have a potent ideological appeal to the Victorian intellectual immersed in Mill's universal causation and Comte's positivism.

Under Spurzheim's missionary tutelage, phrenological enthusiasm had flourished; by the year of his death, there were twenty-nine phrenological societies in Great Britain. From its earliest arrival in England, phrenology intrigued many thinking men and women. Appropriately, we find Spurzheim taking a phrenological reading of Samuel Taylor Coleridge at Highgate in 1816; a year later, the poet proclaimed him "beyond all comparison the greatest Physiognomist who ever appeared," praising "the undoubted splendor and originality of his and Gall's Anatomical Discoveries to the Structure of the Brain."[17] Spurzheim's lecture tours in the provinces were to have a seminal effect on Herbert Spencer as well; he recalls in his *Autobiography* that in about 1830 "Gall's disciple, Spurzheim . . . went about the country diffusing knowledge of the system. Derby was among the towns he visited. Being then perhaps 11 or perhaps 12, I attended his lecture." Despite the "considerable repugnance" the lad felt for the "grinning skulls" that accompanied Spurzheim, young Herbert "became a believer, and for many years remained one." Spencer continued to take considerable interest in the science throughout the 1840s: phrenologist J. Q. Rumball came to Derby in 1842 and made a reading of Spencer's head, which Spencer published in full in the *Autobiography*. In 1843 and 1844, Spencer published phrenological essays in the *Zooist*, a journal devoted to phrenology and mesmerism: "Partially dissentient though I was concerning special phrenological doctrines, I continued an adherent to the general doctrine." Ultimately, after he began new psychological inquiries in the late 1850s, Spencer was led "to conclude that, though the statements of phrenologists might contain adumbrations of truths, they did not express the truths themselves."[18] Yet Gall's theories were to have a profound influence on Spencer's later thought.

Phrenology was eagerly received by the aspiring intellectuals of the provinces, removed from traditional centers of learning and hungry for the latest knowledge. Despite the fact the phrenologists had little praise for the female brain—"Women do not extend their reasonings beyond the range of the visible world," noted the *Phrenological Journal*, "nor do they make any great or daring excursions into the regions of fancy"—over half the audience for these provincial lectures was often female.[19] A visiting phrenologist provided the educationally disenfranchised woman with a rare opportunity for instruction in the natural sciences. One such woman was Marian Evans, twenty years before she became novelist George Eliot: the mind of a genius in the body of a Warwickshire spinster, housekeeper for an ailing father, a woman with no formal education beyond provincial "dame" schools; a mind that devoured any of the all-too-scarce ideas (or "reasonings beyond the range of the visible world") afloat in the provinces. George Eliot's first reference to phrenology—"my organs of ideality and comparison"—comes in one of her earliest extant letters, in November 1838.[20] Her correspondent was teacher Maria Lewis, an ardent Evangelical (as was Eliot herself at that time); their interest in the science gives proof to the claim of many phrenologists that phrenology and religion were not necessarily mutually exclusive (I will have more to say on that subject in my discussion of George Combe). The two women continued to share this keen interest: "It was very kind of you to remember my requests about phrenology," Eliot writes a year later; "I have not at this moment any phrenological thoughts but when I have I will endeavour to tell you fully all I have been able to opine on the matter." Phrenological references recur in Eliot's letters of 1840 to Martha Jackson: the "superior development of a certain region of your brain"; the "paucity of my cerebrum in a certain part."[21]

Her meeting in 1841 with Charles Bray, ribbon manufacturer and resident philosopher of Coventry, was certainly central to George Eliot's continuing interest in and advocacy of phrenology. In his autobiography Charles Bray described the "free and easy mental atmosphere, harmonizing with the absence of all pretension and conventionality" that prevailed at his Rosehill home, with its "peculiar charm" for all who visited there. "Every one who came to Coventry with a queer mission, or a crochet, or was supposed to be a 'little cracked,' was sent up to Rosehill," he mused.[22] Welcome above all were advocates of phrenology, a science that Bray saw as the sole basis of "the Natural Laws of Mind," and "surely the most interesting of all studies." Phrenology provided the foundation for all of Bray's pet reforms and for his philosophy of necessity. Even in the final years of his life, he devoted a large proportion of his autobiography to a defense of the science, asserting that his discovery of phrenology had changed his life.[23]

Phrenology must have been an immediate bond between the Coventry circle and Marian Evans; within three months of her first meeting with the Brays, she writes Maria Lewis: "Having had my propensities sentiments and intellect gauged a second time, I am pronounced to possess a large organ of 'adhesiveness,' a still larger one of 'firmness,' and as large of conscientiousness." It is probable that both readings were made by Bray himself; later that year Eliot writes of her "lessons from the arch-phrenologist." Bray too was an eager pupil, for in February 1844 Cornelius Donovan, principal of the London Phrenological Institution, gave both Bray and George Eliot some phrenological tutelage. That summer Eliot accompanied Bray to London to have her head cast by phrenologist James Deville.[24]

In 1851 George Eliot left the provinces for London, to begin her career as editor of the prestigious and radical *Westminster Review*. But she did not leave phrenology behind in Coventry; nor did she desert the friends of her youth. On 29 August 1851, the Brays introduced George Eliot to the heir to phrenology's English throne, George Combe, who stopped frequently at their Rosehill home en route to Scottish proselytizing.[25] The intellectual attraction between Combe and Eliot was instantaneous, strong, and mutual. Combe immediately pronounced Eliot "the most extraordinary person of the party," on the basis of their conversation on religion, economy, and politics. He went on to a detailed phrenological description of her brain.[26]

A warm friendship quickly ensued: "The Combes are coming again on Tuesday!" Eliot noted enthusiastically in a letter to John Chapman on 14 September 1851. She traveled to visit the Combe family in Edinburgh in October of the following year (a visit that was also to take her to new friend Harriet Martineau's Ambleside home), and enthused to Sara Sophia Hennell: "Yes, he is an apostle. An apostle, it is true, with a back and front drawing room, but still earnest, convinced, consistent, having fought a good fight and now peacefully enjoying the retrospect of it. I shall leave these good friends on Wednesday evening with regret." Emotion and intellect were inseparable for Marian Evans; her mentors—Spencer, Lewes, and Combe—were always, in some sense, her lovers, the recipients of her emotions as well as her ideas. "I often think of you," she effuses to Combe, "when I want some one to whom I could confess all my difficulties and struggles with my own nature, as the person, among all I have known, who is, as Madame de Staël said of her friend, the most completely 'de son avis'—having a profound faith in his principles and acting them out."[27]

A rash of phrenological descriptions in her letters to the Brays coincides with the most intense period of Eliot's friendship with George Combe: of W. R. Greg (27 April 1852): "His brain is large, the anterior lobe very fine and a moral region to correspond"; of Charles Dickens (5 May 1852): "His appearance is certainly disappointing—no benevolence in the face and I think little in the head—the anterior lobe not by any means remarkable"; of William George Spencer (Herbert's father) (23 June 1852): "a large-brained, highly informed man, with a certain quaintness and simplicity"; and finally, the report from George Henry Lewes of a conversation with Professor Robert Owen, "in which the latter declared his conviction that the cerebrum was not the organ of the mind [contrary to

Comte's belief] but the cerebellum rather! . . . The professor has a huge anterior lobe of his own. What would George Combe say if I were to tell him?"[28]

In fact, George Combe was to have a great deal to say over the next few years on the subject of George Henry Lewes's phrenological heresies, and of the seduction of his prize pupil from what he considered the true path of cerebral physiology. For Combe was not the only cause of Eliot's renewed interest in phrenology in the early 1850s. Within a month of her first meeting with Combe, George Eliot was introduced to George Henry Lewes; her friendship with Combe was to wane as her love for Lewes grew. The explanation of this is perhaps as much intellectual as it is emotional.

Lewes was a "reverent heretic" on the subject of phrenology as well as positivism. His own acquaintance with phrenology began as early as July 1836, the date he inscribed on his copy of George Combe's *System of Phrenology*.[29] Lewes's study of Comte's *Cours* in the early 1840s would again have brought phrenology to his attention. But significantly, it was not until the early 1850s and the blossoming of his friendships with Spencer and Eliot that Lewes took a greater and more controversial interest in the science. His critique of phrenology in the 1850s climaxed with his new chapter on the subject in 1857 revised edition of the *Biographical History*. Although he there gave Gall his due for having revolutionized physiology, he also had harsher words for phrenology's premature conclusiveness and its methodological weaknesses: "We find Physiology confessing its incompleteness . . . whereas Phrenology claims to be complete, equipped, full-statured!"; "If Phrenology is the Physiology of the nervous system, it must give up Gall's approximative method for a method more rigorously scientific."[30]

I would suggest that George Eliot's elopement to Germany with Lewes in 1854 was as offensive intellectually as it was morally to her phrenological friends. The editorial policies of the *Westminster Review* towards phrenology and mesmerism between 1851–54 became the focal point of increasing acri-

mony between Eliot and Combe.[31] But her personal relationship with the apostle remained on apparently amicable terms;
as late as 9 June 1854, she was politely refusing Combe's invitation to visit him in Kingston. The very next month, she did
indeed choose to travel—to Weimar, alone, with the married
George Henry Lewes. A heated correspondence on the subject
ensued between the Brays and the Combes. Although Charles
Bray loyally defended Eliot's conduct, George Combe was un-
appeased: "I should like to know whether there is insanity in
Miss Evans's family; for her conduct, with *her* brain, seems to
me like morbid mental aberration."[32]

Combe's moral indignation was as much a product of intellectual rivalry as it was of outraged morality. For as George
Eliot's relationship with Lewes continued, she began to qualify her acceptance of phrenology along lines similar to his. On
10 July 1855, Bray's visit to the pair led to an ugly argument
with Lewes, in which Eliot, to the dismay of her old mentor,
sided with her new mate. Bray, outraged, accused her of desert-
ing the cause.[33] Her ensuing apologetic letter of 16 July quickly
grew into a staunch defense of Lewes:

> Mr. Lewes begs me to say that he never meant to deny that size was
> a measure of power [in the brain], *all other things being
> equal.* . . . I am not conscious of falling off from the 'physio-
> logical basis." I have never believed more profoundly than I do
> now that character is based on organization. . . . But I do not,
> and I think I never shall, consider every man shallow or uncon-
> scientious who is unable to embrace all Mr. Combe's views of or-
> ganology and psychology.[34]

George Eliot still retained her interest in the organization of
the brain that phrenology had inspired; but Lewes was introducing her to methods of physiological investigation that were
more firmly based on scientific fact than the crainioscopy of
the phrenologists.[35]

In concluding this biographical summary, however, I
would stress the continuity of Eliot's and Lewes's commitment
to the essential methodology and doctrine behind the science
of phrenology, their conviction that Gall was fundamentally

correct in claiming psychology as a natural science. A few months after the unhappy visit from Charles Bray, noted above, George Eliot writes to Sara Sophia Hennell: "We are reading Gall's Anatomie et Physiologie du Cerveau, and trying to fix some knowledge about plexuses and ganglia in my soft mind!"[36]

In October 1854 Eliot wrote an essay on "Women in France" for the *Westminster Review*. "I think [it] would please you much," Bray conciliatorily pointed out to Combe, "as having the 'physiological basis.'"[37] In that essay George Eliot provides ample documentation of her belief in Gall's tenets that the moral and intellectual dispositions are innate, their manifestation dependent on organization:

> What were the causes of this earlier development and more abundant manifestation of womanly intellect in France? The primary one, perhaps, lies in the physiological characteristics of the Gallic race: the small brain and vivacious temperament which permit the fragile system of woman to sustain the superlative activity requisite for intellectual creativeness; while, on the other hand, the larger brain and slower temperament of the English and the Germans are, in the womanly organization, generally dreamy and passive. . . . Throughout the animal world, the higher the organization the more frequent is the departure from the normal form.[38]

But it was not merely the "physiological basis" that drew Victorians to phrenology; it was a world view, with powerful appeal to a Victorian sensibility.

II. THE THIRD APOSTLE AND HIS TWO GOSPELS:
GEORGE COMBE'S *THE CONSTITUTION OF MAN
IN RELATION TO EXTERNAL OBJECTS* (1835)

*And had we such a Knowledge of the Constitution of Man,
from which his Faculties of Moving, Sensation, and Reasoning, and other Powers flow; and on which his so regular shape
depends, as 'tis possible Angels have, and 'tis certain his Maker
has, we should have quite other Idea of his Essence, than what
now is contained in our Definition of that Species, be it what*

it will: and our Idea *of any individual* Man *would be as far different from what it now is, as is his, who knows all the Springs and Wheels, and other contrivances within, of the famous Clock at* Strasburg, *from that which a gazing Countryman has of it, who barely sees the motion of the Hand, and hears the Clock strike, and observes only some of the outward appearances.—Locke,* Essay Concerning Human Understanding

At the time of Johann Caspar Spurzheim's death in 1832, Scotsman George Combe "was left as the sole chief of phrenology," writes his biographer. As the heir apparent to Gall and Spurzheim, he was "the last of its three first apostles."[39] Among a prolific outpouring of tracts and treatises throughout his lifetime, *The Constitution of Man* was unquestionably the received gospel of phrenology's creed. Harriet Martineau's memoir of Combe for the *Daily News* opened: "A man must be a conspicuous member of society who writes a book approaching in circulation to the three ubiquitous books in our language—the Bible, 'Pilgrim's Progress,' and 'Robinson Crusoe.' "[40] This was not simply the hyperbole of the eulogist. As a point of comparison, it took over fifteen years for Darwin's *Origin of Species* to sell 16,000 copies in England; *The Constitution of Man* sold 2,000 copies in ten days. Combe's biographer, Charles Gibbon, prints some of the astounding publishing statistics for the book: the first edition, published in June 1828, sold a mere 1500 copies; by October 1836, 11,000 copies of the first through fourth English editions of the book had been printed. "The People's Edition" at ls. 6d. sold 59,000 copies (including a "school edition") in England between November 1835 and October 1838.[41]

The Constitution of Man was firmly grounded in the science of phrenology, but it was much more than a mere handbook of the science. Its appeal clearly extended to an audience beyond the phrenological faithful. "Upon the physiological studies of Gall had been erected a mighty superstructure, variously termed a social science, a universal philosophy, a guide to reform life itself," writes historian John D. Davies;[42] phrenology contained "a scientific philosophy applied to the whole progress of man," David deGiustino concurs.[43] *The Constitution of Man* was the textbook of that philosophy, and its Victorian students were legion. Having established the strong ties between this Victorian circle and the science of phrenology, I would now like to explore the more specialized appeal of its philosophy to a group of intellectuals steeped in the universal causation of John Stuart Mill and the positivistic promise of Auguste Comte.

Combe's gospel of phrenology was to have a seminal influence on some of the finest scientific minds of the century. In the early 1840s, Alfred Russel Wallace—a decade later to "discover" evolution at the same time as Charles Darwin (and I shall address myself later to the close relationship between phrenology and evolution)—read Comte's *Constitution of Man* and other works on phrenology. Wallace remained a lifelong believer; when he looked back upon his times in 1899 in *The Wonderful Century*, he heralded "The Neglect of Phrenology" as the premier failure of the age, avowing it to be "a Science of whose substantial truth and vast importance I have no more doubt than I have of the value and importance of any of the great intellectual advances already recorded," and commending Combe as "the best English advocate of the science, and probably one of the best practical phrenologists of any country."[44] Similarly, Alexander Bain, leading psychologist of the mid-Victorian age, whose work represented the culmination of association psychology and the beginnings of respectable physiological psychology, studied the *Constitution* at the Mechanics' Mutual Instruction Class in Aberdeen from 1835–38. In his extensive discussion of Bain's work in *Mind, Brain, and Adaptation*, Robert M. Young persuasively presents evidence of phrenology as an important early source of Bain's interest in physiological psychology.[45]

We have both direct and indirect evidence that the *Constitution* was well-known to the Victorian circle that this study delineates. Writing to George Henry Lewes on 15 December

1853 (a letter that Lewes published in the *Leader*), Charles
Bray declared Combe's *Constitution of Man* "a more perfect
system of psychology than any other."[46] The opening sentence
of Bray's 1841 preface to his *Philosophy of Necessity* contains
an unmistakable echo of Combe: "The object of the present
Work is to inquire into the nature of the constitution of man;
to ascertain his place in creation, the object and aim of his existence, and the boundaries of his mind."[47] In light of Herbert
Spencer's conversion during the 1830s, it seems likely that he
was well-versed in the leading gospel of phrenology's third
apostle.[48] And what of George Eliot? I have documented her
eager belief in phrenology throughout the 1840s and her personal friendship with Combe in the early 1850s. As with Herbert Spencer, it seems unthinkable that she would not have
known the *Constitution* well, although her only direct reference to the book is a casual one, in an extended and fairly technical letter to Combe dated 22 January 1853, on the subject of
Biblical criticism (perhaps its very casualness belies her com-
fortable acquaintance with the work): "By the bye, I wonder if
you have read a clever work on 'Jésus-Christ et sa doctrine,' by
Salvador, a free-thinking Jew, in which the writer attempts to
shew that the Mosaic system presented the quintessence of political and social wisdom, and that, morally, it was an adum-
bration of the doctrine contained in 'The Constitution of
Man'."[49] *The Constitution of Man* is a work extremely significant to this Victorian frame of mind. Mill, Comte, Combe,
Chambers, Bray, Martineau, Lewes, Spencer, Eliot: one of the
key common denominators among them all was some degree
of interest in the science of—and more important, the philosophy that grew out of—the study of phrenology. And George
Combe's *Constitution of Man* was the Bible of this new faith.

After the fanfare of the preceding pages, let me state at the
outset of this discussion that I do not intend to claim the *Constitution* as a neglected masterpiece of Victorian intellectual
prose. In fact, one suspects that it was its considerable weak-
ness as a work of philosophy that was paradoxically the source
of its immense popularity with the general reading public. In

her sketch for the *Daily News,* Harriet Martineau had an accurate fix on both the limitations and the value of Combe's work: "If he did not advance his own department of science, but rather hindered its development by his own philosophical incapacity, he prepared for its future expansion by opening the minds of millions to its conception."[50] Later critics were to be less charitable: "Combe, benignly rhetorical, had only partially reached a scientific synthesis, and could not compass a philosophic one," wrote John M. Robertson in the *History of Free Thought in the Nineteenth Century.*[51] George Eliot herself said what perhaps is the most that can be said on Combe's behalf, in the course of offering the phrenological philosopher her editorial commentary on his *Relation of Religion of Science* in 1853. Her comments there apply equally well to the *Constitution of Man:* "We wish to know the moral and religious views of a thoughtful, experienced and distinguished man, not because we expect him to tell us something new on these subjects, but because he is himself a new fact—a new mind which has gone through the steps of the great problem."[52]

And indeed, much of *The Constitution of Man* is nothing new. We will find its message in the rational divines of the eighteenth century—Paley, Bishop Butler—whom Combe quotes generously throughout the book: "The system of sublunary creation, so far as we perceive it, does not appear to be one of optimism, yet benevolent design, in its constitution, is undeniable."[53] Whatever is, is right; this is the best of all possible worlds; the hand of God is to be seen in his creation. *The Constitution of Man* offered deism for the masses; a populist Victorian version of tenets once held by an eighteenth-century intellectual elite. There is considerable irony implicit here: the heterodoxy of one century was to become the best-selling orthodoxy of the next; to find God in nature rather than in the sacraments might be shocking to the eighteenth century; to many Victorians, it was a comfort to find him *anywhere.* J. D. Y. Peel writes in his study of Herbert Spencer that *The Constitution of Man* "furnished a bridge between traditional

religion and purely secular amelioration . . . a deistic, this-
worldly, natural religion . . . it was one of the agencies of
popular secularization."[54]

But once we strip away the comforting trappings of Butler
and Paley, just how religious is *The Constitution of Man?*
This is a question that aroused considerable controversy.
Among the pious conservatives, phrenology was inextricably
associated with atheism. If one believed that mind was matter,
surely little room was left for an immortal soul or divine inspiration. But George Combe himself would not have agreed. In
fact, he opens with the unequivocal pronouncement that
"there is not one practical result of the natural laws expounded
in the subsequent pages, which does not harmonize precisely
with the practical aspects of the New Testament." Yet Combe
closes with a provocative (and characteristically egotistical)
comparison of himself to Galileo. In any clash between the
Church and Nature, the latter will win, says Combe, "because
the evidence of physical nature is imperishable and insupera-
ble, and cannot give way to any authority whatever. The same
consequence will evidently happen in regard to phrenology. If
it were possible that any facts in physiology did not actually
and directly contradict any interpretation of Scripture, it is not
difficult to perceive which must yield."[55] So much for the
Church!

In fact, *The Constitution of Man* consists of two arguments
that have little to do with each other. What I will call its first
gospel, the pious deistic veneer, the optimistic "handbook of
natural religion," undoubtedly accounted for the book's mass
appeal. What it offered that seemed new and attractive to the
Victorian reader was this: Combe apparently places eighteenth-century deism within the context of nineteenth-century
science, a new, positivistic world-view; exemplified for Combe
by phrenology. *The Constitution of Man* teased the Victorian
reader with the assurance that the old religion could continue
to exist side-by-side with the new science.

But a closer look at the *Constitution* reveals that Robertson
was absolutely correct in his accusation that Combe failed to

achieve a philosophic or scientific synthesis. Combe never offers any convincing arguments to explain *how* phrenology and faith coexist. He persistently shirks the Galilean clash between religion and science, avoiding any real explanation of the religious implications of his second gospel: that is, the genuinely radical view of human nature and the relation between man and his environment predicated on the science of phrenology.

"I do not intend to teach that the natural laws, discerned by unassisted reason, are sufficient for the *salvation* of man without revelation," equivocates Combe. Actually, he will eschew the other-worldly altogether: "To enjoy this world, I humbly maintain, that man must discover and obey the natural laws." Combe's real subject in *The Constitution of Man* has nothing to do with religion at all: "My object, I repeat, is to investigate the natural constitution of the human body and mind, their relations to external objects and beings *in this world*, and the causes of action that, in consequence, appear to be beneficial or hurtful *in this life*.[56]

It would remain for the two thinkers to whom I turn in the next chapter, Charles Bray and Harriet Martineau, to confront more honestly the theological and ethical implications of these natural laws; to face uncomfortable words like "determinism"; and to receive (in contrast to the mass popularity that greeted Combe's *opus*) outraged accusations of atheism.[57] But here I wish to look more closely at Combe's second gospel, his investigation of "the natural constitution of the human body and mind, their relations to external objects and beings in this world." This was the book, I believe, that was read by and had a significant influence on this circle of Victorian intellectuals; not Combe's vague and optimistic rehash of eighteenth-century deism.

As I have suggested above, Combe had little of real interest to say about religion, or about the relationship between science and belief. But he did have a great deal that was more revolutionary to offer on the subject of man's place "in this world." I will shortly argue that through the work of Combe's close

friend Robert Chambers, who possessed in abundance just
what Combe lacked—a brilliant ability to synthesize—
Combe's notions of "the constitution of the human body and
mind" and their implications for man's place in nature would
pass into the mainstream of Victorian evolutionary thought.

But first, let me explicate Combe's second gospel. Chapter 1
of *The Constitution of Man* is entitled "Of Natural Laws"; it
contains much that should strike the reader as familiar after
Mill and Comte. Combe begins with the premise that the laws
of nature "are universal, unbending, and invariable in their
operation." These laws "have formed an interesting subject of
inquiry to philosophers of all ages," admits Combe; "but, so
far as I am aware, no author has hitherto attempted to point
out, in a combined and systematic form, the relations between
those laws and the constitution of man."[58] Reviewing Combe's
book *On The Relation Between Science and Religion* for the
Westminster Review in 1857, H. B. Wilson offers a good summary of the phrenologist's logical progression from "laws of
mind" to "universal law": "If it could indeed be sufficiently
established, that there exists an uniform relation between certain ascertained forms of the brain, in its parts, and certain intellectual and moral powers . . . this would certainly furnish
an *illustration* of the general laws of uniformity, order, and
mediate action in the universe."[59] The final bastion has fallen:
mind too is subject to universal causation. For Combe, as for
Auguste Comte, a science of psychology is the last battle-
ground, the ultimate proof that law reigns *everywhere*.

The Constitution of Man can be read as a practical exercise
in Mill's ethology or Comte's social physics: "The present Essay," writes Combe, "is an attempt, (a very feeble and imperfect one indeed), to arrive, by the aid of phrenology, at a demonstration of *morality as a science*." "We are physical, organic,
and moral beings, acting under general laws," he asserts. Like
Comte, Combe organizes his system hierarchically: "The organic law rises above the physical, and the moral and intellectual law above the organic."[60] We can translate for Combe's
"physical" Comte's astronomy and chemistry; for "organic,"

biology; for "moral and intellectual," "social physics." But like Comte, Combe stresses the fundamental *unity* of this hierarchy: it is the same law that rules on all levels. Man himself embodies the living proof of this unity: at the apex of creation, he is a walking synthesis of the physical, the organic, and the moral. Like Comte, Combe desires to unite the parts into the whole, to formulate the grand synthesis, in which the many become the one: "Hence it is only after ultimate principles have been discovered, their relations ascertained, and this knowledge systematized, that science can attain its full character of utility."[61] Combe's claim that phrenology will do for the human sciences what Copernicus and Newton did for the physical sciences may seem almost comically hubristic; but this systematizing and unifying impulse is absolutely central to the phrenological philosophy.

And after all, what better model for the many in the one, the one in the many than phrenology's chart of the human brain, "that unhappy continent on which Gall had already put more federated faculties than there are states in the German Bund," as James Martineau once sarcastically observed.[62] In *The Constitution of Man* Combe offers the classical phrenological outline of the human mind (fig. 2.1). There are two "orders": "feelings" (significantly first) and "intellectual faculties"; the former broken down into two "genus(es)": "propensities" and "sentiments," containing a total of eighteen separate "organs," from "amativeness" and "philoprogenitiveness" through "veneration" and "hope," to "conscientiousness" and "firmness"; the latter, into four "genus(es)": "external senses," "intellectual faculties" (of two sorts), and "reflecting faculties"; the four breaking down into a total of fifteen different "organs." But ultimately, of course, we are talking about a single human mind, that living personality that is the sum of its many parts.

And thus we come to the other pole of the phrenological philosophy, that aspect of the science that entitles it with certainty to rank as a Victorian yoking of polar opposites. For as surely as phrenology was a monistic cosmology, it was also a science

80

Order I. FEELINGS.

Genus I. PROPENSITIES—*Common to Man with the Lower Animals.*

1. AMATIVENESS ; Produces sexual love.
2. PHILOPROGENITIVENESS.—*Uses :* Love of offspring.—*Abuses :* Pampering and spoiling children.
3. CONCENTRATIVENESS.—*Uses :* It gives the desire for permanence in place, and for permanence of emotions and ideas in the mind.—*Abuses :* Aversion to move abroad ; morbid dwelling on internal emotions and ideas, to the neglect of external impressions.
4. ADHESIVENESS.—*Uses :* Attachment ; friendship, and society result from it.—*Abuses :* Clanship for improper objects, attachment to worthless individuals. It is generally large in women.
5. COMBATIVENESS.—*Uses :* Courage to meet danger, to overcome difficulties, and to resist attacks.—*Abuses :* Love of contention, and tendency to provoke and assault.
6. DESTRUCTIVENESS.—*Uses :* Desire to destroy noxious objects, and to kill for food. It is very discernible in carnivorous animals.—*Abuses :* Cruelty, desire to torment, tendency to passion, rage, harshness and severity in speech and writing.
7. CONSTRUCTIVENESS.—*Uses :* Desire to build and construct works of art.—*Abuses :* Construction of engines to injure or destroy, and fabrication of objects to deceive mankind.
8. ACQUISITIVENESS.—*Uses :* Desire to possess, and tendency to accumulate articles of utility, to provide against want.—*Abuses :* Inordinate desire for property ; selfishness ; avarice.
9. SECRETIVENESS.—*Uses :* Tendency to restrain within the mind the various emotions and ideas that involuntarily present themselves, until the judgment has approved of giving them utterance ; it also aids the artist and the actor in giving expression ; and is an ingredient in prudence.—*Abuses :* Cunning, deceit, duplicity, lying, and, joined with Acquisitiveness, theft.

Genus II. SENTIMENTS.

I. *Sentiments common to Man with the Lower Animals.*

10. SELF-ESTEEM.—*Uses :* Self-interest, love of independence, personal dignity.—*Abuses :* Pride, disdain, overweening conceit, excessive selfishness, love of dominion.
11. LOVE OF APPROBATION.—*Uses :* Desire of the esteem of others, love of praise, desire of fame or glory.—*Abuses :* Vanity, ambition, thirst for praise independent of praiseworthiness.
12. CAUTIOUSNESS.—*Uses :* It gives origin to the sentiment of fear, the desire to shun danger, to circumspection ; and it is an ingredient in prudence.—*Abuses :* Excessive timidity, poltroonery, unfounded apprehensions, despondency, melancholy.
13. BENEVOLENCE.—*Uses :* Desire of the happiness of others, universal charity, mildness of disposition, and a lively sympathy with the enjoyment of all animated beings.—*Abuses :* Profusion, injurious indulgence of the appetites and fancies of others, prodigality, facility of temper.

II. *Sentiments proper to Man.*

14. VENERATION.—*Uses :* Tendency to worship, adore, venerate, or respect whatever is great and good ; gives origin to the religious sentiment.—*Abuses :* Senseless respect for unworthy objects consecrated by time or situation, love of antiquated customs, abject subserviency to persons in authority, superstition.
15. HOPE.—*Uses :* Tendency to expect and to look forward to the future with confidence and reliance ; it cherishes faith.—*Abuses :* Credulity, absurd expectations of felicity not founded on reason.

16. IDEALITY.—*Uses :* Love of the beautiful and splendid, the desire of excellence, poetic feeling.—*Abuses :* Extravagance and absurd enthusiasm, preference of the showy and glaring to the solid and useful, a tendency to dwell in the regions of fancy, and to neglect the duties of life.

WONDER.—*Uses :* The desire of novelty, admiration of the new, the unexpected, the grand, and extraordinary.—*Abuses :* Love of the marvellous, astonishment.—*Note.* Veneration, Hope, and Wonder, combined, give the tendency to religion ; their abuses produce superstition and belief in false miracles, in prodigies, magic, ghosts, and all supernatural absurdities.

17. CONSCIOUSNESS.—*Uses :* It gives origin to the sentiment of justice, or respect for the rights of others, openness to conviction, the love of truth. *Abuses :* Scrupulous adherence to noxious principles when ignorantly embraced, excessive refinement in the views of duty and obligation, excess in remorse, or self-condemnation.
18. FIRMNESS.—*Uses :* Determination, perseverance, steadiness of purpose.—*Abuses :* Stubbornness, infatuation, tenacity in evil.

Order II. INTELLECTUAL FACULTIES.

Genus I. EXTERNAL SENSES.

FEELING or TOUCH. TASTE. SMELL. HEARING. LIGHT.	*Uses :* To bring man into communication with external objects, and to enable him to enjoy them. *Abuses :* Excessive indulgence in the pleasures arising from the senses, to the extent of impairing the organs and debilitating the mind.

Genus II. INTELLECTUAL FACULTIES—*which perceive existence.*

19. INDIVIDUALITY—Takes cognizance of existence and simple facts.
EVENTUALITY—Takes cognizance of occurrences and events.
20. FORM—Renders man observant of form.
21. SIZE—Renders man observant of dimensions, and aids perspective.
22. WEIGHT—Communicates the perception of momentum, weight, resistance, and aids equilibrium.
23. COLOURING—Gives perception of colours.

Genus III. INTELLECTUAL FACULTIES—*which perceive the relations of external objects.*

24. LOCALITY—Gives the idea of space and relative position.
25. ORDER—Communicates the love of physical arrangement.
26. TIME—Gives rise to the perception of duration.
27. NUMBER—Gives a turn for arithmetic and algebra.
28. TUNE—The sense of Melody arises from it.
29. LANGUAGE—Gives a facility in acquiring a knowledge of arbitrary signs to express thoughts—a felicity in the use of them—and a power of inventing them.

Genus IV. REFLECTING FACULTIES—*which compare, judge, and discriminate.*

30. COMPARISON—Gives the power of discovering analogies and resemblances.
31. CAUSALITY—To trace the dependencies of phenomena, and the relation of cause and effect.
32. WIT—Gives the feeling and the ludicrous.
33. IMITATION—To copy the manners, gestures, and actions of others, and nature generally.

The first glance at these faculties suffices to show, that they are not all equal in excellence and elevation ; that some are common to man with the lower animals ; and others peculiar to man. In comparing the human mind, therefore, with its external condition, it becomes

FIG. 2. From George Combe, *The Constitution of Man* (New York, 1835).

of human nature that took into account, more fully than any previous attempts at such a science had done, the intense particularity of the individual personality. Just as seriously as phrenology proclaimed the deductive abstraction, it investigated the empirical detail.

Each individual, according to phrenology, is a highly variable and absolutely unique combination of these multiple "propensities," "sentiments," and "faculties." Phrenology was the first psychology to focus on individual differences rather than normative faculties; Gall is thus "the first modern empirical psychologist of character and personality." With phrenology, psychology took a giant step toward the science as we know it today; Gall and his followers found evidence for their theories not in the library, or even entirely in the laboratory, but also in the living world of human society, as they turned "away from speculations and toward common society, family life, schools, the jails and asylums, medical cases, the press, men of genius, and the biographies of great or notorious men."[63] If phrenology was biology, it was also natural history.

Needless to say, this vision of human nature had a wealth to offer the would-be novelist, George Eliot, who wrote on "The Natural History of German Life" for the *Westminster Review* in 1856 in scorn of the tendency created by "the splendid conquests of modern generalization, to believe that all social questions are merged in economic science, and that the relations of men to their neighbours may be settled by algebraic equations," championing instead the same "natural history" she would herself employ as a novelist: "a real knowledge of the People, with a thorough study of their habits, their ideas, their motives."[64] Nothing could seem more rational than the elevated abstractions of the phrenological cosmology; yet as we have already seen, phrenology placed emotion above intellect (topologically as well as ideologically!). "In my view," writes George Combe, in words worthy of sympathetic novelist George Eliot, "knowledge by itself is comparatively worthless and impotent, compared with what it becomes when vivified by elevated emotions. It is not enough that Intellect is informed; the moral faculties must simultaneously cooperate."[65]

One other aspect of the phrenological view of human nature is also worth noting here: "No faculty is bad, but, on the contrary, each has a legitimate sphere of action." The infinite variables into which the mental faculties could combine, and the infinite shadings of the use and abuse of each (no faculty is necessarily good, either), in conjunction with phrenology's emphasis on the primacy of emotion and the "moral faculties," led to a philosophy with a rich potential for exploration of the intricacies of human nature without the reductive onus of good and evil to inhibit the investigation.

"This is the doctrine of Phrenology exactly: that the *endowments* of men are unequal; and that, as their *circumstances* vary, their faculties for the cultivation of their powers, vary also; and consequently, that their responsibility varies."[66] With this statement Combe introduces a new and crucial variable into the investigative process: *circumstances.* Thus far I have focused my discussion on the first half of Combe's title: "the constitution of man." But with the second half of the title of this work, "in relation to external objects," Combe removes phrenology from the eighteenth-century realm of static, innate mental endowment where it had begun with Gall, and places it within the changeful Victorian cosmos.

I conclude by returning to the distinction with which my discussion of *The Constitution of Man* began: the two gospels of George Combe; one, of the eighteenth century, the other, of the nineteenth. This dichotomy reappears when we turn to the question of the relation between "the constitution of man" and "external objects." I will indulge in a vast generalization for the purposes of sorting out Combe's two arguments: from the eighteenth-century viewpoint, the static world is benevolently adapted to "the constitution of man," "it is constituted in harmony with the whole faculties of man"; in the nineteenth-century view, man is adapted to the constitution of the world: "It is obvious that the very scheme of creation which I have described, implies that man is a progressive being."[67] As the remainder of this chapter will illustrate, phrenology and the pre-Darwinian development hypothesis were to prove remarkably compatible.

III. MORE THAN METAPHOR: PHRENOLOGY AS MENTAL GEOLOGY

The Bedesman ought to profit by such a journey; whether any glimpse of beauty will irradiate my Physiology may be more confidently questioned. It was so very amusing to find myself thinking of 'nerve cells' amid the grand mountains, and of physiological processes on the shores of a lake. But after all the two went perfectly well together.—G. H. Lewes to John Blackwood, Dresden, 19 July 1858

Although she was to chide Aristotle for his praise of metaphor, indulging in a "lamentation that intelligence so rarely shows itself in speech without metaphor that we can so seldom declare what a thing is except by saying it is something else," George Eliot herself was an inveterate employer of metaphors long before she put them to brilliant novelistic use.[68] In Eliot's letters of the late 1830s and 1840s, the young and self-conscious phrenological enthusiast repeatedly describes the human mind in physical, chemical, biological, and geological metaphors.

Since George Eliot here speaks vividly for herself, let me simply list some examples. Physics: "The poor girl's brain is fast loosing its little specific gravity and is flying off to Milton's limbo."[69] Chemistry: "He is evidently a character made up of natural crystallization, instead of one turned out of a mould" (1:98); "My brain is a very wishy-washy material . . . the ideas are like the imperfect crystallizations from thin salt and water" (1:210); "Yours was a sort of alkali nature which would detect the slightest hint of falsehood" (1:243); "My thoughts are all aqueous—they will not crystalize—they are as fleeting as ripples on the sea" (1:274). Biology and "natural history": "I take too much mental food to digest" (1:47); "I should like to send you an abstract of his argument. I have gulped it (pardon my coarseness) in a most reptile-like fashion; I must *chew* it thoroughly to facilitate its assimilation with my mental frame" (1:64); "The intellectual errors which we once fancied were a mere incrustation have grown into the living body and . . . we cannot . . . wrench them away without destroying vitality" (1:162); "I have been in a sort of molluscous-animal state without voluntary motion" (1:172); "I have been a horrid stagnant pool where you can hear nothing but croakings of miserable batrachian reptiles" (1:244); "I have gone through a trial of the same genus as yours, though rather differing in species." (1:260).

Eliot similarly frames a number of brief geological metaphors: "a few struggling animals of the new formation in the early strata of the new [mental life]" (1:144); the "extinct volcanoes of one's spiritual life" (1:282). But the most extended, elaborate, and fully-developed of all George Eliot's mental metaphors drawn from the natural sciences grounds itself in the vocabulary of contemporary geology. In a letter to Maria Lewis, dated 4 September 1839, she writes:

> My mind, never of the most highly organized genus, is more than usually chaotic, or rather it is like a stratum of conglomerated fragments that shews here a jaw and rib of some ponderous quadruped, there a delicate altorelivo of some fernlike plant, tiny shells, and mysterious nondescripts, encrusted and united with some unvaried and uninteresting but useful stone. My mind presents just such an assemblage of disjointed specimens of history, ancient and modern, scraps of poetry picked up from Shakespeare, Cowper, Wordsworth, and Milton, newspaper topics, morsels of Addison and Bacon, Latin verbs, geometry entymology and chemistry, reviews and metaphysics, all arrested and petrified and smothered by the fast thickening every day accession of actual events, relative anxieties, and household cares and vexations. May I hope that some pure metallic veins have been interjected, that some spiritual desires have been sent up, and spiritual experience gained? (1:29)

"It was very kind of you to remember my requests about Phrenology," George Eliot goes on to say in this same letter; "I have not at this moment any phrenological thoughts but when I have I will endeavour to tell you fully all I have been able to opine on the matter" (1:30).

In these early letters, George Eliot reveals herself an enthusiastic student of physics, chemistry, biology, and geology. But it is phrenology, I would suggest, that provides a rationale for her metaphor-making; a more than casual, or purely imaginative, basis for analogy between psychology and the natural sciences of the day. In her mental metaphors, Eliot implicitly reveals her adherence to phrenology's claim to be a science of mind which is fully analogous to the other sciences, both inorganic and organic.

"Phrenology is a science of observations as truly as is geology itself," wrote Alfred Russel Wallace;[70] Wallace, significantly, was an ardent believer in phrenology at the same time that he developed his theory of evolution. John Stuart Mill added an extended expository footnote to a later edition of the *Logic*, offering two examples of the concept "hypothesis," in what may prove more than a random juxtaposition: "The attempt to localize in different regions of the brain the physical organs of our different mental faculties and propensities was, on the part of its original author, a legitimate example of a scientific hypothesis"; "Mr. Darwin's remarkable speculation on the origin of species is another unimpeachable example of a legitimate hypothesis."[71] Over a century later, historian Robert M. Young makes the identical point: "The analogy between the theory of evolution and that of crainiology is instructive. . . . Logically [evolution] was in the same position as phrenology for most of the nineteenth century. It rested on naturalistic observations and a mass of anecdotes collected more or less systematically. Doubt remained whether the causal relations proposed by the theory were real, or only mistaken references from correlations reflecting the union of chance circumstances."[72]

But I will go one step beyond Wallace, Mill, and Young, to claim that the analogy between phrenology and geology or natural history was not merely formal or logical; similar methods were to lead to similar conclusions. Phrenologist Charles Bray made the point with an appropriate metaphor in *The Education of the Feelings* (1849): "As geologists show the formation of the earth to have been gradual, layer after layer being added, more perfect plants, and animals of a higher order of feeling and intelligence appearing, as the world was prepared for them, so has the mind of man been developed, region added to region."[73] The phrenologist could excavate that "stratum of conglomerated fragments" that constitute the human brain and arrive at the same developmental conclusions as the geologist with fossil in hand.

For all his assertions of the world's benevolent adaptation to the constitution of man, George Combe is finally as much of a Victorian in his views of nature as he is in his religious beliefs (or lack thereof). Combe's cheerful assertion of man's capability of determining his own "progression" ("Intelligent beings are capable of observing nature and of modifying their actions") is only the reasonable eighteenth-century half of the picture. As early as page four of *The Constitution of Man*, Combe reveals that he has been reading the geological speculations of Sir Humphrey Davy, Charles Lyell, and Dr. Buckland: "Physical nature itself has undergone many revolutions, and apparently has constantly advanced. Geology seems to show a distinct preparation of it for successive orders of living beings, rising higher and higher in the scale of intelligence and organization, until man appeared."[74] I would suggest that new discoveries in geology did not so much reveal to Combe the existence of the evolutionary process, as harmonize perfectly with the evolutionary notions already implicit in the science of phrenology.

Phrenology stressed man's physical and organic as well as his moral nature; his oneness with the natural world was implicit in phrenology's assertion that mind was also matter. Although the "intellectual faculties" on phrenology's chart were man's alone, all thirteen faculties of the first genus of "feelings," entitled "propensities," come under the heading "Common to Man with the Lower Animals"; half of the second genus, "sentiments," are similarly categorized. Darwin might suggest how man was related to the ape, but *that* he was so related should come as no surprise to the phrenologist.[75]

"The physical world [is] gradually *improved* and *prepared for man*," blurbles Combe in a bit of Butlerian balderdash.[76] But George Combe had also read Malthus as early as 1805,[77] and made a statement based on phrenology's credo, three decades before *The Origin of Species*, that was uncannily prophetic of the conclusions to which Malthus combined with geology and natural history would lead Charles Darwin: "Man is to a certain extent an animal in his structure, powers, feelings, and desires, and is adapted to a world in which death reigns, and generation succeeds generation."[78]

George Combe opens *The Constitution of Man* not with *homo sapiens*, but with a discussion of contemporary geology: "The crystalline rocks, or, as they are called by geologists, the primary rocks, which contain no *vestiges of a former order* of things, were the result of the first consolidation on its surface"; "Five successive races of plants, and four successive races of animals, appear to have been created and swept away by the physical revolutions of the globe, before the system of things became so permanent as to fit the world for man." This geological history is a necessary backdrop for *The Constitution of Man's* more original subject: "Let us now contemplate Man himself." Phrenology complements geology: "The order of creation seems not to have been adapted at his introduction:—he appears to have been adapted to it. He received from his Creator an organized structure, and animal instincts." Phrenology recognizes both man's similarity to the animal kingdom—the continuity of creation— and man's higher cerebral development. Hence the conclusion: "Man is evidently a progressive being; . . . the Creator having designed a higher path for him than for the lower creatures. . . . Time and experience are necessary to accomplish these ends, and history exhibits the human race only in a state of progress towards the full development of their powers."[79]

In 1844 an anonymous amateur scientist, man of letters, and synthetic philosopher was to explore these "vestiges of a former order of things," in a work animated by unmistakable similarities to the progressive optimism of *The Constitution of Man*: "There is, nevertheless, a general adaptation of the mental *constitution of man* to the circumstances in which he lives, as there is between all parts of nature to each other."[80] The author of these words was Edinburgh publisher Robert Chambers; the book, *Vestiges of the Natural History of Creation*. I reserve my wider analysis of the *Vestiges* for the following section of this chapter. But here, I would like to stress the important links between phrenology and geology in this classic Victorian evolutionary cosmology.

Chambers proclaims Franz Joseph Gall's system of mind "the only one founded upon nature." He goes on to summarize phrenology's chart of the mental faculties, and in that chart, finds evidence of evolution: "Bound up as we thus are by an identity in the character of our mental organization with the lower animals we are yet, it will be observed, strikingly distinguished from them by this great advance in development." Citing studies from the *Phrenological Journal*, Chambers gives evidence that "when the human brain is congenitally imperfect or diseased, or when it is in the state of infancy, we see in it an approach towards the character of the brains of some of the inferior animals." The author of the *Vestiges* finds this resemblance not degrading to man, but rather elevating evidence of the "wonderful unity of the whole system, the grades of mind, like the forms of being, are mere stages of development." This "wonderful unity" does not limit itself to the structure of the brain. Like Combe, Chambers finds analogous evidence of progressive development in the macrocosm as well as the microcosm: "Geology and physiology exhibit *lively vestiges or traces of that* [usual natural order in the organic creation] *having actually been followed.*"[81]

George Combe and Robert Chambers have both been chronicled by twentieth-century historians: Combe, in David deGiustino's *Conquest of Mind* (1975); Chambers, in Milton Millhauser's full-length study, *Just Before Darwin: Robert Chambers and the Vestiges* (1959). But it is regrettable that they were not better-acquainted with one another's subject matter. Millhauser's book is a wide-ranging exploration of the *Vestiges* itself, its role in Victorian evolutionary thought, and its public reception, all within the context of main currents of Victorian biology, zoology, geology. But Millhauser knows little of the science of phrenology, and suffers from embarrassment that the discussion above should have shown to be unnecessary. As a result he seriously underestimates the importance of phrenology to the *Vestiges*: "Chambers would have liked to draw upon phrenology for further evidence as to the materiality of mind. He does not quite do so (recognizing, no doubt, that his 'science' was not highly regarded by his contemporaries); he does however, refer to it in passing, and he cites some of the more technical studies of the great Dr. Franz Joseph Gall."[82] Conversely, deGiustino is equally dismissive and bemused on the subject of geology: "Later editions of *The Constitution of Man* provided a definition of geology (which Combe spelled with a capital 'g') and quotations from contemporary geologists. Everyone was fascinated by the study of natural history in the 1830s and forties, and the phrenologists were no exception."[83] But I would argue that phrenology plays far more than a passing role in the *Vestiges of Creation*; the link between phrenology and geology is more than a faddish simultaneity.

Outraged contemporary critics of the *Vestiges* had no difficulty in recognizing the connections between that book and phrenology: "If all the mental phenomena in man result from organization, in the same way as they do in animals, of what is the author's 'immortal spirit' to consist? . . . As to where such a philosophy could come from few men can have little doubt," insinuates the *British Quarterly Review*.[84] "For the sake of his argument, we cannot but regret the stress which [Chambers] has laid on the details of Gall's and Spurzheim's phrenology," mourns Francis Newman in *The Prospective Review*.[85] The most infamous and vituperative reviewer of them all, Adam Sedgwick of the *Edinburgh Review*, spends seven full pages of attack on the phrenological basis of the *Vestiges*:

> He believes that he is a great metaphysician—that mind and soul (as our fathers understood the word) are all a dream—that material organs are all in all—that he can weigh the mind as a butcher does a joint, by a steelyard . . . that Gall and Spurzheim are the only mental philosophers since the days of Plato—that he can swallow their whole system without any grumblings among his digestive organs. . . . He believes that the human family may be (or ought

to be) of many species, and all sprung from apes—that while he bestializes men and humanizes beasts, he is a great moralist.

Sedgwick concludes: "We turn away from the material and phrenological jargon of this author with feelings somewhat like those which would be raised within us by the impertinencies of a guide who could talk only of ladders and scaffolds, hammers, chisels, and mortar-hods, while we were first gazing at one of the most glorious monuments of human art."[86]

Robert Chambers's acquaintance with phrenology was much closer than Franz Joseph Gall and Johann Caspar Spurzheim. George Combe's biographer, Charles Gibbon, counts Chambers among Combe's "intimate friends."[87] Publisher Chambers was converted by Comte to phrenology in 1834, and claimed that sales soared after he covertly introduced the doctrines of *The Constitution of Man* into *Chambers' Edinburgh Journal.*[88] Gibbon offers direct evidence of the conversion in process (or rather, the proselytization in process), printing an 1833 letter from Combe to Chambers, in which Combe enumerates "the leading principles of 'The Constitution of Man,'" its promise of a truly "scientific" "moral philosophy," its exhortation that men must "modify their conduct systematically to adapt it to external nature." Combe was eager to enlist the powerful publisher of the popular *Chambers' Journal* on his side: "I am induced to express myself thus freely to you on account of the immense power which you wield over opinion."[89]

Chambers's role in disseminating the new philosophy did prove an important one. Gibbons notes that Chambers took a strong interest in the *Constitution*: the first four editions of the book sold only 11,000 copies between 1828-36; it was Chambers's more accessible "People's Edition" that sold 59,000 copies between 1835-38. ("Oh Mr. Chambers, how *can* you print that abominable book?" cried one distressed citizen; "If you had only heard our minister on it last Sunday you would have burned it!"[90])

Chambers's own venture into the constitution of man, *Ves-*

tiges of the Natural History of Creation, was published anonymously (by Chambers's friend and fellow-phrenologist, Alexander Ireland) in anticipation of its scandalized reception. Among the *least* likely authors suggested by a curious public was Prince Albert (!); among the more likely, George Combe himself.[91] The *Constitution of Man* helped prepare Victorian readers for the controversial *Origin of Species*; but it also laid the foundations for the *Vestiges*. "There were many in fact who felt justified in seeing an antireligious conspiracy; they were now quite certain that Combe's great essay of 1828 was consciously designed as a prelude to the evolutionary ideas of the *Vestiges*."[92]

But Combe was not the only member of this Victorian circle with whom Robert Chambers was acquainted. Nor was the *Vestiges of Creation* simply an evolutionary reformulation of the *Constitution of Man*. George Combe had failed to unify his two gospels. Unlike him, Robert Chambers moved irrevocably into the nineteenth century, to build a confident Victorian cosmology that truly "made it whole."

IV. "ONE MAJESTIC WHOLE":
ROBERT CHAMBERS'S *VESTIGES OF CREATION* (1844)

The Development Hypothesis is an inevitable deduction from the Monistic conception of the world.—G. H. Lewes, "Mr. Darwin's Hypothesis"

Robert Chambers was a lifelong friend of George Henry Lewes. After Lewes's scandalous elopement with George Eliot to Weimar in 1854, Chambers was one of the few to whom he wrote to explain his actions.[93] His brief but dramatic entrance in George Eliot's biography rests in part on the basis of his friendship with George Combe. Combe, as we have seen, was aghast at the liaison, and John Chapman attempted to placate Combe's moral outrage by "commission[ing] Mr. Robert Chambers to say a few words to you concerning Miss Evans." Chapman also wrote to Chambers himself, begging that their more intimate knowledge of Eliot's situation "be regarded as strictly confidential," and indulging in a little moral hand-wringing of his own: "I think [Lewes] much the most blame-worthy in the matter. Now I can only pray, against hope, that he may prove constant to her; otherwise she is *utterly* lost."[94]

But Chambers's role in this circle as a harbinger of new ideas was destined to be far more consequent than his entrance as a bearer of bad tidings. The *Origin of Species* came as little sur-prise to George Eliot; she viewed it simply as a more intellec-tually respectable but less compellingly readable version of *The Vestiges of Creation*:

> We have been reading Darwin's book on the 'Origin of Species' just now: it makes an epoch, as the expression of his thorough adhesion, after long years of study, to the Doctrine of Develop-ment—and not the adhesion of an anonym like the author of the 'Vestiges,' but of a long-celebrated naturalist. The book is ill-writ-ten and sadly wanting in illustrative facts. . . . This will prevent the work from becoming popular, as the 'Vestiges' did.[95]

The subject of Herbert Spencer's first conversation with George Henry Lewes was to set the tone of their shared inter-ests in the early 1850s (although Spencer, characteristically, re-acted to Lewes's advocacy of Chambers in much the same way he had received George Eliot on Comte's hierarchy of the sci-ences): "One of our topics was the development hypothesis; and I remember surprising Mr. Lewes by rejecting the interpre-tation set forth in the *Vestiges of The Natural History of Cre-ation*: he having supposed that that was the only interpreta-tion."[96] But just as Herbert Spencer could never quite detach himself from Comte, so subsequent critics of Spencer have sug-gested that Chambers's evolutionary philosophy ultimately has more in common with Spencer than it does with Darwin.[97]

Spencer's own earliest pronouncements on "The Develop-ment Hypothesis" were published in the 20 March 1852 *Leader*, under Lewes's editorship. Although it was not Spen-cer's first essay, he later reprinted it at the head of *Essays Sci-entific, Political, and Speculative*, "because it came first in or-der of thought, and struck the keynote of all that was to follow."[98] Chambers initiated Herbert Spencer's interest in evolutionary psychology, which culminated in *The Principles of Psychology*.

George Henry Lewes's shared fascination with the subject at this time was carried on in print as well as in private conversation. When Lewes wrote on "A Precursor of the *Vestiges*" for *Fraser's* in November 1857, he claimed to "have been long collecting materials for the history of this and similar conceptions."[99] Always the historian of ideas, Lewes traced the development hypothesis through "Lyell and Owen on Development" (*Leader*, 18 October 1851) and "Von Baer on the Development Hypothesis" (*Leader*, 25 June 1853). But even in those essays, he had words in defense of the *Vestiges of Creation*: "There are faults in that delightful work; errors both in fact and philosophy; but compared with the answers it provoked, we cannot help regarding it as a masterpiece."[100] Lewes's evolutionary essays climaxed with a series of four articles for the *Leader* on the *Vestiges* itself, on the occasion of the tenth edition of the work.[101] Despite his characteristic reservations about the "metaphysical" dimensions of Chambers's philosophy, Lewes was still able to find, nine years after its first publication, "novelty to startle, grandeur to enlarge and satisfy the intellectual longings of meditative minds."[102] Even this early in his career, long before writing on "Mr. Darwin's Hypothesis" in the *Forthnightly Review* (1868), Lewes was becoming known as a champion of the controversial concept of evolution.[103]

In an essay on "The Argument for Organic Evolution Before the *Origin of Species*, 1830-1858," A. O. Lovejoy claims that much of the disrepute into which the *Vestiges* retrospectively fell among historians of science can be traced to T. H. Huxley's attacks on the book. Lovejoy is attuned to the rich ironies that the history of ideas can offer: Huxley was later to champion Darwin on many of the same grounds for which he earlier attacked Chambers. Lovejoy argues that in the early 1850s Huxley's real objections to the *Vestiges* were more emotional than intellectual, a product of "religious tradition or temperamental conservatism." Furthermore, Huxley overlooked the forest for the trees; he was "so shocked by minor breeches of scientific propriety in the *Vestiges*," writes Lovejoy, "that he forgot the weightier matters of the law of scientific method. In his irritation at Chambers's incidental slips in zoology, he became blind to the importance and suggestiveness of the general outline of the writer's reasoning."[104]

Lovejoy's analysis of Huxley's attack comes very close to Robert Chambers's self-defense in the 1846 "Explanations" that he offered his critics as a "sequel" to the *Vestiges of Creation*.[105] Admittedly, much of Chambers's amateur biology and zoology appeared as outlandish in his time as it does today. Furthermore, Chambers's critics, like Darwin's, were immediately wont to fasten with alarm on the ghastly theological implications of man's brotherhood with lower forms of life.[106] Yet the *Vestiges of Creation*, explains Chambers, was not primarily intended to be a work of scientific fact; the accuracy of particular details finally does not undermine its broader thesis. The true precursors of the *Vestiges* are not to be found in treatises of the naturalists or geologists of the day, but in works like Auguste Comte's *Cours de philosophie positive* and John Stuart Mill's *Logic*. Darwin is above all a scientist; Chambers is a philosopher. Chambers's book seeks to incarnate a Victorian world view; its evolutionary theory is subservient to a larger monistic *credo*:

> I must start with a more explicit statement of the general argument of *Vestiges*, for this has been extensively misunderstood. The book is not primarily designed, as many have intimated in their criticisms, and as the title might be thought partly to imply, to establish a new theory respecting the origin of animated nature. . . . The object is one to which the idea of an organic creation in the manner of natural law is only subordinate and ministrative, as likewise are the nebular hypothesis and the doctrine of a fixed natural order in mind and morals. This purpose is to show that the whole revelation of the works of God presented to our senses and reason is a system, based on what we are compelled, for want of a better term, to call LAW.[107]

For Robert Chambers organic creation in the manner of natural law, the nebular hypothesis, and a fixed natural order in mind and morals are unified under one principle: "LAW." These three phrases contain the essence of Chambers's monistic synthesis. The nebular hypothesis (the formation of the universe) stands at one pole of creation: the macrocosm, inorganic nature. The fixed natural order in mind and morals (embodied for Chambers in the science of phrenology) is the other pole: the microcosm of the human mind, organic nature in its highest form. As a student of Mill and Comte, George Henry Lewes understood Chambers's intentions perfectly: "Life, and life in its most complex form, society, are as amenable to rigorous Law as any of the phenomena of the inorganic world," he wrote in summary of the *Vestiges*.[108] All of Chambers's science—his astronomy, geology, zoology, embryology, psychology—is quite frankly borrowed (and much of it is of dubious worth). What was revolutionary and unique in the *Vestiges of Creation* was its methodological synthesis: "The book, as far as I am aware, is the first attempt to connect the natural sciences into a history of creation," Chambers accurately claims.[109]

The *Vestiges* opens with a consecutive account of creation, from "the Bodies of Space," formation of the earth, beginnings of organic life, to the "commencement of the present species." Chambers argues that all these processes, this endless creative variety, are manifestations of a single mode: "One set of laws overspread them all with life. The whole productive or creative arrangements are therefore in perfect unity."[110] Like Mill and Comte, Chambers believed that the same scientific method that informed geology could be applied to biology. As might be expected, Chambers is an enthusiastic reader of Mill's *Logic*: "There is . . . no more interesting or valuable testimony to universal causation than that presented in the System of Logic of Mr. Stuart Mill."[111] His advocacy of phrenology led Chambers to agree with Mill that universal causation reigned in mind as well as matter. In the *Vestiges* Chambers simply extended the notion to the whole of natural creation. Like Darwin, Chambers saw the conceptual link between geological uniformitarianism and biological evolutionism. Lewes summarized Chambers's radical insight: "the novelty consists in linking on the hypothesis of Laplace [the nebular hypothesis] to a modification of Lamarck [biological evolution], thus bringing the inorganic and organic worlds under one magnificent generalization of progressive development."[112] Phrenology, the geology of the mind, helped Chambers make this vital connection between the inorganic and the organic.[113]

It should be readily apparent, even from this brief summary of the *Vestiges*, that Chambers's attempt "to connect the natural sciences into a history of creation" would harmonize readily with the interconnected Comtean hierarchy of the sciences, from astronomy through biology and "social physics." On 18 July 1845, John Stuart Mill sent Auguste Comte Sedgwick's review of the *Vestiges* from the *Edinburgh Review*, and introduced the French philosopher to a man who was in many ways his British counterpart: "Sous le titre de 'Vestiges of the Natural History of Creation' il tache de deviner une sorte de cosmogonie positive," Mill writes Comte. Though Mill was no more a convert to Chambers's development hypothesis than he was to Gall's phrenology, he was sympathetic with its larger implications: "Quoique d'une valeur purement négative, cet ouvrage n'a pas laissé de faire ici une sensation assez prononcée, et je crois qu'il tend a préparer un peu les esprits pour le positivisme."[114]

In this review of the *Vestiges*, Sedgwick passes directly from his discussion of phrenology to an attack upon the nebular hypothesis. The transition is a logical one: the nebular hypothesis is to the cosmos as phrenology is to the mind; it is the other pole of a positivistic creation. Though it owed its genesis to Kant and Swedenborg, and was further developed by Laplace and Comte, the nebular hypothesis became inextricably linked in the public mind with Robert Chambers.[115] George Eliot demonstrates this association when she ridicules Dr. Cumming in her essay on "Evangelical Teaching" (1855), in defense of the *Vestiges of Creation*:

> He tells us that "the idea of the author of the 'Vestiges' is, that man is the development of a monkey, that the monkey is the embryo man, so that *if you keep a baboon long enough, it will develope*

itself into a man." How well Dr. Cumming has qualified himself to judge of the ideas in "that very unphilosophical book," as he pronounces it, may be inferred from the fact that he implies the author of the "Vestiges" to have *originated* the nebular hypothesis.[116]

Herbert Spencer examined the nebular hypothesis "that stars, and their attendant planets, have been formed by the aggregation of nebulous matter" in his essay "The Nebular Hypothesis" (1858). Spencer opens this abstruse and technical essay with a statement that clearly places his scientific interest in the subject within the larger context of a Victorian cosmology: "Science has been proving uniformities of relation among phenomena which were before thought either fortuitous or supernatural in their origin. . . . Each further discovery of Law has increased the presumption that Law is everywhere conformed to. And hence, among other beliefs has arisen the belief that the solar-system originated, not by *manufacture* but by *evolution.*"[117]

"And hence . . . evolution." Chambers added something revolutionary to Mill's universal causation and Comte's hierarchy of the sciences, and Herbert Spencer and George Henry Lewes took the conceptual leap with him. In discussing Mill and Comte, I attempted to suggest how the notion of universal law leads inevitably to positivism, a universal method; and to show how phrenology became a proving-ground for such a method, what Mill called its "ultimate point": a law of human volitions. Such a universal method in turn suggests an interconnected hierarchy of the sciences. That hierarchy provides a model for a unified natural creation, inorganic and organic, the one in many. What Chambers makes explicit is the necessary *process* that attends the unifying method: development.

"The doctrine of the universality of natural causation, has for its inevitable corollary the doctrine that the Universe and all things in it have reached their present form through successive stages physically necessitated," writes Spencer in his *Autobiography.*[118] Spencer and Lewes were to find more reliable biology or geology in other scientists of the day (Lyell, Owen, Lamarck); but it was Chambers who first provided the ideological synthesis. In my discussion of Coleridge's *Theory of Life*, I pointed out that Lewes sustained a digression on the subject of the *Theory of Life* in the midst of his explication of Auguste Comte's *Cours*. Recall Lewes's fascination there with Coleridge's "definition of life": " 'The principle of individuation,' or that power which discloses itself from within, combining many qualities into *one individual thing*."[119] If we remember that Lewes was writing on Comte in the summer of 1852, in the midst of his series of essays on the development hypothesis, we can appreciate the fact that Coleridge was not the only inspiration for Lewes's exposition of positivism: "Thus in an ascending series of evolutions from the simple to the complex . . . we learn to gather the phenomena of the universe into one majestic Whole, and learn that all links of demarcation are subjective only. In a word, we learn that Life is an evolution, not a separate creation."[120] "Thus the whole is complete on one principle," Chambers concludes similarly in the *Vestiges of Creation*,

> the masses of space are formed by law; law makes them in due time theatres of existence for plants and animals; sensation, disposition, intellect are all in like manner developed and sustained in action by law. It is most interesting to observe into how small a field the whole of the mysteries of nature thus ultimately resolve themselves. The inorganic has one final comprehensive law, GRAVITATION. The organic . . . rests in like manner on one law, and that is— DEVELOPMENT. Nor may even these be after all twain, but only branches of one still more comprehensive law, the expression of that unity which man's wit can scarcely separate from Deity itself.[121]

It was that hovering Deity behind Chambers's creation, a Deity essentially one with George Combe's eighteenth-century Artificer, that persistently bothered Lewes. The "primary error" of the *Vestiges*, wrote Lewes in 1853, "is the quiet assumption of Nature's growth and development being a pre-ordained 'Plan.' " Such an assumption, Lewes believed, seduced Chambers into "treacherous metaphysics."[122] But Lewes characteristically advocates a conciliatory middle ground between matter and spirit: "While Lamarck is too much of a 'materialist,' the author of the *Vestiges* is too much of a 'metaphysician'; one lays the whole stress of his argument on 'external circumstances,' the other on a pre-ordained plan."[123]

Fifteen years later Lewes was still chastizing Chambers for "the helplessness of such metaphysical explanations," in his *Fortnightly Review* essay "Mr. Darwin's Hypothesis." Yet Lewes there affirms a more fundamental affinity between himself and Chambers: "The Development Hypothesis is an inevitable deduction from the Monistic conception of the world; and will continue to be the battle-ground of contending schools until the opposition between Monism and Dualism ceases. For myself, believing in the ultimate triumph of the former, I look on the Development Hypothesis as one of the great influences which will . . . hasten that triumph."[124] No work of nineteenth-century thought better exemplifies a monistic conception of the universe than the *Vestiges of the Natural History of Creation.*

Before he turns more specifically to "Mr. Darwin's hypothesis," Lewes offers a provocative definition of what he calls the Monistic "Weltanschauung": "It reduces all phenomena to community, and all knowledge to unity. This conception, under its various forms of Pantheism, Idealism, Materialism, Positivism, is irreconcilable with the rival, or Dualistic, conception, which in phenomena separates and opposes Force and Matter, Life and Body, and which in knowledge destroys unity by its opposition of physical and final causes."[125] With this deceptively simple categorization, Lewes offers an important key to a Victorian cosmos that may at times seem self-contradictory: the reconciling principle behind Auguste Comte's simultaneous idealism and positivism, or George Combe's and Robert Chambers's pantheism and materialism. They are embraced within a larger monistic synthesis of "Force and Matter," "Life and Body"—the same synthesis that was to be the subject of Lewes's own psychological *magnum opus, Problems of Life and Mind* (1874–79)—which could take a Protean variety of forms, yet still retain its essential monistic identity.

It is with this in mind that I turn briefly in conclusion to a later chapter of Robert Chambers's intellectual biography. On 10 February 1867, Chambers wrote to Alfred Russel Wallace: "It gratifies me much to receive a friendly communication from the Mr. Wallace of my friend Darwin's 'Origin of Species' and my gratification is greatly heightened on finding that he is one of the few men of science who admit the verity of the phenomena of spiritualism. I have for many years *known* that these phenomena are real."[126] At the end of *Just Before Darwin*, Milton Millhauser lifts the veil from Chambers' authorship in the 1850s and 60s of a series of anonymous articles and an unpublished manuscript on the subject of spiritualism. Millhauser suggests that the manuscript's inaccessibility accounts for its scholarly neglect. He offers a tantalizing hint of its contents, and argues that it is not an aberration, but a significant development in Chambers's thought.[127]

On the face of it, Chambers's conversion in the 1850s to spiritualism was a radically disjunctive shift from his earlier materialistic scientific study of geology, zoology, psychology: "His conversion left the Chambers of 'Testimony' at the opposite pole from the Chambers of *Vestiges*."[128] Millhauser conveniently employs the Coleridgean metaphor of polarity, and counters with a conclusion that interprets Chambers's later beliefs as a reconciliation of polar opposites, suggesting that Chambers's conversion from scientific theory to mesmeric mysticism was an evolution rather than a revolution. "My idea is that the term 'supernatural' is a gross mistake," Chambers wrote Wallace. "We have only to enlarge our conceptions of the natural and all will be right."[129] Chambers believed that his later spiritualism was just as "scientific" as his earlier materialism; he continued to publish later editions of the *Vestiges* after his conversion, and saw no conflict between old and new beliefs ("Into how small a field the whole of the mysteries of nature thus ultimately resolve themselves").

In both the *Vestiges of Creation* and the later spiritualistic manuscript, Chambers concerns himself with "the general upward progress" of the "great chain of nature." Electricity and magnetism were the bridge between the simple laws of matter and the more complex rules of spirit.[130] In the true spirit of Victorian monism, Chambers's spiritualism is the logical counterpart of his materialism, since force and matter are fundamentally one, subject to the same physical laws; life and mind are inseparable. And, of course, these are the same assumptions that inform the science of phrenology, simply taken to their ultimate logical conclusion.

It should thus come as no surprise that phrenology was to wed magnetism, mesmerism, and "electro-biology" in the 1840s, and that many phrenologists were as likely to be found at a seance as in a laboratory. In my next chapter, I turn to two other converts, Charles Bray and Harriet Martineau. Like Robert Chambers, their conversions were really continuities, as they walked a conciliatory line between matter and spirit.

1. Lewes, *Comte's Philosophy*, p. 217.

2. Auguste Comte, *The Positive Philosophy of Auguste Comte*, trans. Harriet Martineau (London, 1875), 1:388.

3. W. H. Smith, "Comte," *Blackwood's* 53 (1843):406-7.

4. Mill, *Auguste Comte*, p. 65.

5. Mill, *Earlier Letters*, in *Collected Works*, 13:519, 525-26, 531.

6. George Henry Lewes, "Phrenology and Phrenologists," *Leader*, 10 December 1853, pp. 1,192-93. See also "Noble on Insanity" (*Leader*, 24 December 1853, pp. 1,240-42) and "Phrenology and Physiology" (*Leader*, 7 January 1854, pp. 20-21).

7. Comte, *Cours*, in Lenzer, p. 181.

8. Comte, *Cours*, in Lenzer, p. 183.

9. George Combe, *The Constitution of Man*, 6th American ed. from the 2d English ed., Corrected and Enlarged (Boston, 1838), pp. 335-36. The original date of this edition was 1835.

10. I am indebted for this summary to David deGiustino, *Conquest of Mind* (London, 1975), chapter 2, "A Science of Mind," pp. 12-31. See also Leslie Hearnshaw, *A Short History of British Psychology* (London, 1964), p. 18.

11. Franz Joseph Gall, *Sur les fonctions du cerveau* (Paris, 1825), rpt. in *A Source Book in the History of Psychology*, ed. Richard J. Herrnstein and Edwin G. Boring (Cambridge, Mass., 1965), p. 219.

12. George Henry Lewes, "Phrenology in France," *Blackwood's* 82 (1857):666. See John D. Davies, *Phrenology: Fad and Science* (New Haven, 1955) for a discussion of the populist aspects of the science. Social historian David deGiustino focuses on the influence of phrenology in the realm of penal and educational reform in Great Britain,

in his study *Conquest of Mind*. Robert M. Young approaches phrenology from the history of science in *Mind, Brain, and Adaptation in the Nineteenth Century* (Oxford, 1970). He admits that he "originally studied Gall because his work was the starting-point of empirical localization, and I planned to spend only a few weeks on phrenology . . . the result is quite far from what I had anticipated. . . . I should acknowledge an important debt to Gall. The perspective on later work which his writings have provided has done more than any other single factor to shape my own view of the domain and aims of biological psychology" (p. xi).

More recent articles include R. J. Cooter, "Phrenology: the Provocation of Progress," *History of Science* 14 (1976); Angus McLaren, "Phrenology: Medium and Message," *Journal of Modern History* 46 (1974); T. M. Parsinnen, "Popular Science and Society: The Phrenology Movement in Early Victorian England," *Journal of Social History* 7 (1974); Steven Shapin, "*Homo Phrenologicus*: Anthropological Perspectives on an Historical Problem," in *Natural Order: Historical Studies of Scientific Culture*, ed. Barry Barnes and Steven Shapin (Beverly Hills, 1979).

13. Charles Bray to George Henry Lewes, *Leader*, 15 December 1853, p. 20.

14. Lewes, *Biographical History*, pp. 752-53.

15. Young writes: "The thesis that behavior and the functions of the brain . . . are amenable to objective observation" was given its modern impetus with the work of Gall. "Before Gall psychology was a branch of the philosophic discipline of epistemology, and division of the brain into functional regions had never been empirically related to behavior" (*Mind, Brain, and Adaptation*, p. 12).

16. Combe, *Constitution*, p. viii; my emphasis.

17. Samuel Taylor Coleridge, *The Notebooks of Samuel Taylor Coleridge*, vol. 3 (1808-19), ed. Kathleen Coburn (Princeton, 1973), entry 4,355. Intriguingly, in this small nineteenth-century world, it was George Eliot's later mentor Dr. R. H. Brabant who introduced Coleridge to phrenology (see Coleridge, *Collected Letters* [1815-19], ed. Earl Leslie Griggs [London, 1959], 14:613).

18. Spencer, *Autobiography*, 1:228, 231, 261, 282-83. Spencer's articles in the *Zooist* were "On the Situation of the Organ of Amativeness," no. 6, July 1844, and "A Theory Concerning the Organ of Wonder," no. 7, October 1844. Spencer dabbled in the practical as well as the theoretical: in 1846, he designed a "cephalograph," a machine for making exact measurements of the skull and brain (his draftsmanlike drawings constitute appendix H of the *Autobiography*, 1:634-38).

19. *Phrenological Journal*, quoted in deGiustino, *Conquest*, p. 72. Mill (who wrote *On the Subjection of Women* in 1860) took issue with phrenology's antifeminist bent, arguing against Comte over phrenology's claim that female brains are inferior (see *Earlier Letters*, 13:604-11).

20. George Eliot to Maria Lewis, *George Eliot Letters*, 1:11. See N. N. Feltes, "Phrenology from Lewes to George Eliot," *Studies in the Literary Imagination* (1968), pp. 13-22 for a brief outline of Eliot and phrenology. In his recent study of *George Eliot and the Visual Arts* (New Haven, 1979), Hugh Witemeyer includes a fascinating discussion of the phrenological aspects of Eliot's physical descriptions of her characters (pp. 48-52).

21. George Eliot to Martha Jackson, *George Eliot Letters*, 1:29, 36, 38.

22. Bray, *Phases of Opinion*, p. 70.

23. Bray, *Phases of Opinion*, p. 23. See especially chapter 4, "Phrenology and the Natural Laws of Mind," pp. 20-46.

24. George Eliot to Maria Lewis, *George Eliot Letters*, 1:126; George Eliot to Mrs. Charles Bray, *George Eliot Letters*, 1:167, 193; Haight, *George Eliot Letters*, 1:178 n.

25. "Mrs. Bray writes me word how valuable your sympathy and encouragement are to Mr. Bray in his solitary labours at backward Coventry" (Eliot to Combe [*George Eliot Letters*, 8:74]).

26. George Combe Journal, *George Eliot Letters*, 8:27. In two new volumes of the *George Eliot Letters*, Gordon Haight publishes the extensive correspondence between Combe and Eliot during the early 1850s. Eager young Marian Evans must have provided a delightful change from Combe's own "devoted wife," Cecilia Siddons (daughter of actress Sarah), who, Bray ruefully reminisces, "did not surprise us sometimes when . . . [she] dropped asleep in the middle of his discourse, her head inclined towards him in a reverent attitude of attention!" (*Phases of Opinion*, p. 71).

27. George Eliot to Sara Sophia Hennell, *George Eliot Letters*, 2:61; George Eliot to George Combe, *George Eliot Letters*, 8:37.

28. George Eliot to Mr. and Mrs. Charles Bray, *George Eliot Letters*, 2:21, 23; George Eliot to Charles Bray, *George Eliot Letters*, 2:37, 56.

29. See William Baker, ed., *The George Eliot-George Henry Lewes Library*, p. 42. Their library contains several works by Combe, although not the *Constitution of Man*.

30. Lewes, *Biographical History*, pp. 761, 765. Bray was infuriated, and counterattacked in his 1865 edition of *The Philosophy of Necessity*: "This is so elementary a principle in phrenology that we must in all candour have supposed Mr. Lewes as well acquainted with the subject as every one who has read a sixpenny book upon the subject" (2d ed., p. 146).

31. From the start Eliot was caught between the *Westminster*'s editor John Chapman and the scientific radicals with whom she had allied herself in the 1840s. "I wish to keep the Westminster in *our* hands—viz: in yours and mine and Miss Evans's et hoc genus omne," (Bray to Combe in 1852 [*George Eliot Letters*, 8:58]). Combe complained to Chapman that the *Review* was "about to become a very staid and decorous journal, conducted with due regard to the prejudices of the times" (8:38). Chapman counters that the journal will remain "the bold and uncompromising exponent of the most advanced and philosophical views," but that mesmerism is not numbered among them: "I am aware that Miss Martineau is not likely to approve . . . but since I cannot regard as verities all the articles of her *last formed* faith, it is not likely that I should allow the Review to endorse them" (8:38). Eliot's subsequent letter to Combe reveals that phrenology is also at issue: "The assertions that 'it will not admit even an incidental allusion, if respectful, to such subjects as Mesmerism and Phrenology' . . . is false. But I think you will agree with me that the great majority of 'investigations' of mesmerism are anything but 'scientific' " (8:41).

But Eliot was politic, agreeing to publish an article on "Mental Physiology" if Combe could find a suitable author (8:41). Nonetheless, phrenology became an increasing source of acrimony between Combe and the *Westminster*. In June of 1853, Eliot agreed to accept an article from Combe on "Prison Discipline" (an article riddled with references to phrenology). It did not appear until April 1854, after a series of acrimonious exchanges between Chapman and Combe, with Eliot as referee. Combe

even presented Eliot with a statement of "medical support" signed by leading physiologists, with the request that she pass it along to science editor T. H. Huxley. Eliot's
refusal is graceful, emphatic, and somehow less than sincere: "Being a woman and
something less than half an editor, I do not see how the step you propose could be
taken with the naturalness and *bienseance* that could alone favour any good result"
(8:90).

On 17 November 1853, Combe sent Eliot a copy of "Prison Discipline." Had he
begun to doubt the phrenological loyalties of Eliot herself?: "You and Mr. Chapman
may feel quite at ease about rejecting it, if found too phrenological and technical, for
I shall print it as a pamphlet and distribute it, if you reject it" (8:86). Combe contra-
dicts this Olympian stance by a manifest display of annoyance at a "loud paragraph
of conglomerated nonsense . . . on Phrenology" which he had just read in the
Leader (November 12, pp. 1,095-96). "I do not know *who* is now the Editor of the
Leader," Combe confesses, deploring its "bending backwards on the science through
which only certain and self-consistent progress in all interests emanating from and
resting on the mind of man, can be made" (8:87). The culprit was, of course, G. H.
Lewes, whose romantic intimacy with Eliot had begun (unknown to Combe) the previous January. Eliot's reply is interesting: she skirts any mention of Lewes, and appears to support Combe: "I agree with you that it is sufficiently shallow and shows
profound ignorance of the 'Crainiology' which he undertakes to pronounce upon"
(8:88).

32. George Eliot to George Combe, *George Eliot Letters*, 8:111; George Combe to
Charles Bray, *George Eliot Letters*, 8:129.

33. See Haight, *George Eliot*, p. 183.

34. George Eliot to Charles Bray, *George Eliot Letters*, 2:210; see also, George Eliot
to Sara Sophia Hennell, *George Eliot Letters*, 2:401-2.

35. The final chapter in the relationship between Lewes and Combe is amusing. In
1856 Lewes published an essay on "Dwarfs and Giants" in *Fraser's*. "A curious thing
happened the other day," Eliot wrote Sara Sophia Hennell: "A few days ago, came a
letter from George Combe addressed to G. H. L. Esq., care of the Editor of Frazer [sic],
expressing very high admiration of the physiological essay. . . . He didn't seem to know
that G. H. L. was G. H. Lewes! . . . I fear Mr. Combe would be rather disappointed
to find out whom he had been praising, Mr. Lewes being his favourite aversion, as a
'shallow, flippant man'!" (*George Eliot Letters*, 2:264). How Lewes must have relished his
reply to Combe: "Your approbation of my article . . . is very flattering. . . . With respect to the method of comparative physiology to which you allude I am profoundly
convinced that GALL was on the right track and that he laid down the basis of a positive
psychology, but . . . I think our knowledge of the nervous system generally is still incomplete for more than approximate conclusions" (8:162).

36. George Eliot to Sara Sophia Hennell, *George Eliot Letters*, 2:220.

37. Charles Bray to George Combe, *George Eliot Letters*, 8:127.

38. George Eliot, "Women in France," *Westminster Review* 62 (1854), in Pinney,
p. 55.

39. Charles Gibbon, *The Life of George Combe* (London, 1878), 1:276.

40. Harriet Martineau, "George Combe," in *Biographical Sketches, 1852-1868*, 3d
ed. (London, 1870), p. 265. Combe's tombstone identified him as "Author of 'The
Constitution of Man' " (Gibbon, *Life*, 2:368).

41. See deGiustino, *Conquest of Mind*, p. 3; Gibbon, *Life*, 2:262-63. There were also translations into French, German, and Swedish: The *National Union Catalogue* lists fifty-five different American imprints between 1828 and 1856.

42. Davies, *Phrenology*, p. 80.

43. deGiustino, *Conquest of Mind*, p. 33. He is interested in the phrenological philosophy's appeal to a mass audience: "It was logical and slightly mysterious, precise but hopeful. It meant amusement and improvement, common sense and social liberation" (p. 74).

44. Alfred Russel Wallace, *My Life* (New York, 1905), 1:234; *The Wonderful Century: Its Successes and Its Failures* (New York, 1899), pp. 160, 162. See chapter 16, "The Neglect of Phrenology."

45. Young, *Mind, Brain, and Adaptation*, p. 119. Young points out that Elizabeth Haldane claims in the *DNB* that Bain was "led by Mill to make a special study of the philosophy of George Combe" (p. 123). Young can find no evidence of this in Bain or Mill, but notes that "Mill introduced Bain to Comte's writings (which contained an enthusiastic treatment of Gall)," and that Bain's book *On the Study of Character, Including an Estimate of Phrenology* (1861) "follows almost exactly the programme laid down by Mill" in Book 6 of the *Logic*, where Mill calls for a science of ethology (pp. 123-24).

46. Bray, *Leader*, 7 January 1854, p. 20.

47. Bray, "Preface," *Philosophy of Necessity*, p. iii.

48. Young notes: "The phrenological work which corresponds most closely to Spencer's position is George Combe's Essay on the Constitution of Man" (*Mind, Brain and Adaptation*, p. 158 n).

49. George Eliot to George Combe, *George Eliot Letters*, 8:69-70. Eliot's first published letter dates from January 1836. Since the popularity of the *Constitution* crested with the "People's Edition" between November 1835 and November 1836, Eliot was likely to have encountered the book in the mid-1830s.

50. Martineau, "George Combe," p. 276.

51. John M. Robertson, *History of Free Thought in the Nineteenth Century* (London, 1929), 1:25.

52. George Eliot to George Combe, *George Eliot Letters*, 8:85.

53. Combe, *Constitution*, p. 37. See also pp. 30, 41, 282-84.

54. Peel, *Herbert Spencer*, p. 11.

55. Combe, *Constitution*, pp. 24, 323. As recently as 1965, A. Cameron Grant wrote a very Victorian essay on "Combe on Phrenology and Free-Will: A Note on XIXth-Century Secularism" (*Journal of the History of Ideas* 26 [1965]:141-47) in which he argued, as did Combe's contemporary critics, that Combe's "system denied religion" (147). George Eliot apparently had little difficulty distinguishing between Combe's rhetoric and his reality: "You sometimes use phrases such as 'approaching the Throne of God' which are irreconcilable with your opinions elsewhere expressed. But I do not find any difficulty in ascertaining the views you really inculcate. The inconsistency arises probably from a momentary sympathy with views you are describing or alluding to" (*George Eliot Letters*, 8:85). Eliot speaks of Combe's *Relation of Religion to Science* (1857), but her words could apply equally to the *Constitution*.

56. Combe, *Constitution*, pp. 37, 38; my emphasis.

57. This is not to imply that the *Constitution* was not as controversial as it was popular. Gibbon reports that when the book first appeared, "bewilderment, horror, and indignation took possession of many of [Combe's] best friends. Earnest appeals were addressed to him . . . to suppress the whole series as subversive of Christianity and false to phrenology" (*Life of Combe*, 1:181).

58. Combe, *Constitution*, pp. 33, vii.

59. H. B. Wilson, review of Combe's *Constitution of Man*, in "Contemporary Literature," *Westminster Review* 68 (July 1857):237.

60. Combe, *Constitution*, pp. 200, vii, 189.

61. Combe, *Constitution*, p. 335.

62. James Martineau, "Mesmeric Atheism," *Prospective Review* 7 (1851):227.

63. Young, *Mind, Brain, and Adaptation*, pp. 18, 19.

64. Eliot, "Natural History of German Life," *Westminster Review* 66 (1856), in Pinney, p. 272.

65. Combe, *Constitution*, p. 96. See also pp. 113, 361 on a phrenological view of the relation between intellect and emotion.

66. Combe, *Constitution*, p. 373.

67. Combe, *Constitution*, pp. 39, 99.

68. George Eliot, *The Mill on the Floss*, ed. A. S. Byatt, (1860; rpt. Harmondsworth, Middlesex, England, 1979), p. 209.

69. George Eliot to Maria Lewis, *George Eliot Letters*, 1:108. Further references in this section to be cited in the text.

70. Wallace, *Wonderful Century*, p. 182.

71. John Stuart Mill, *Logic* in *Collected Works*, 7:498-99.

72. Young, *Mind, Brain, and Adaptation*, p. 44.

73. Charles Bray, *The Education of the Feelings*, 2d ed. (London, 1849), p. 162.

74. Combe, *Constitution*, pp. 29, 4.

75. See Combe, *Constitution*, pp. 50-53, and chapter 2, section 1: "Man Considered as a Physical Being," section 2: "Man Considered as an Organized Being," section 3: "Man Considered as an Animal—Moral—and Intellectual Being," pp. 41-50.

76. Combe, *Constitution*, p. 6.

77. "George Combe's reading of Malthus in 1805 came as a 'flash of light'" (deGiustino, *Conquest*, p. 9).

78. Combe, *Constitution*, p. 6. Angus McLaren writes: "In addition to introducing the artisan to materialistic doctrine, phrenology was preparing his mind for an acceptance of the revolutionary biological theories of the second half of the century. Phrenological charts comparing the skulls of monkeys and men could not fail to popularize a crude conception of evolution." He notes that "the role played by phrenology in early evolutionary theory has not been fully appreciated" ("Phrenology: Medium and Message," 93, 94 n).

79. Combe, *Constitution*, pp. 5-6, 11-12; my emphasis.

80. Chambers, *Vestiges of Creation*, p. 181; my emphasis.

81. Chambers, *Vestiges of Creation*, pp. 175, 179, 178, 215.

82. Milton Millhauser, *Just Before Darwin* (Middletown, Ct., 1959), p. 109.

83. deGiustino, *Conquest*, p. 49.

84. Review of Chambers's *Vestiges of Creation*, *British Quarterly Review* 1 (1845):510.

85. Francis Newman, Review of Chambers's *Vestiges of Creation*, *Prospective Review* 1 (1845):77.

86. Adam Sedgwick, Review of Chambers's *Vestiges of Creation*, *Edinburgh Review* 82 (1845):11, 17. The *Edinburgh* had a longstanding reputation as a foe of phrenology (see Dr. John Gordon, "The Physiognomical System of Drs. Gall and Spurzheim," *ER* 25 [1815]:227-268).

87. Gibbon, *Life*, 2:261. Similarly, Millhauser: "Possibly [Chambers's] closest friends were the Combes, phrenologists and philosophical materialists" ("though [*The Constitution of Man*] did not touch on evolution," he says inaccurately) (*Just Before Darwin*, p. 83).

88. See deGiustino, *Conquest*, p. 32. He doubts whether phrenology was really the source of the *Journal*'s success.

89. George Combe to Robert Chambers, in Gibbon, *Life*, 1:296-97.

90. Quoted in Gibbon, *Life*, 1:331. In 1843 W. & R. Chambers also published an "outline of Phrenology" as numbers 59-60 of their *Information for the People*: "We deem it right . . . to mention that Phrenology appears to us as beforehand likely to be true, in as far as it assigns a natural basis to mind . . . its leading doctrines have acquired a title to very respectful attention" (quoted in Gibbon, *Life*, 2:160-61).

91. See deGiustino, *Conquest*, p. 53.

92. deGiustino, *Conquest*, p. 53.

93. See Haight, *George Eliot Letters*, 2:176 n; Carlyle was another in whom Lewes confided.

94. John Chapman to George Combe, *George Eliot Letters*, 8:122; John Chapman to Robert Chambers, *George Eliot Letters*, 8:126.

95. George Eliot to Mme. Eugene Bodichon, *George Eliot Letters*, 3:227.

96. Spencer, *Autobiography*, 1:399-400.

97. See Benn, *History of English Rationalism*, 2:9; and Millhauser, *Just Before Darwin*, p. 86.

98. Herbert Spencer, "The Development Hypothesis," *Leader*, 20 March 1852, rpt. in *Essays, Scientific, Political, and Speculative* (New York, 1904), p. 1.

99. George Henry Lewes, "A Precursor of the Vestiges," *Fraser's* 56 (1857):527. Lewes's precursor was J. B. Robinet's *De la Nature* (1761). A. O. Lovejoy substantiates Lewes's thesis: "The principle of continuity . . . compelled him to postulate a single model for all animate and even inanimate natural individuals. Thus Robinet, though not the originator, was (so far as I know) the first elaborater and enthusiastic champion of that notion of an *Urbild*" (*Great Chain of Being* [1936; rpt. New York, 1960], p. 279).

100. George Henry Lewes, "Lyell and Owen on Development," *Leader*, 18 October 1851, p. 996.

101. George Henry Lewes, "The Development Hypothesis of the 'Vestiges,'"

Leader, 13 August 1853, pp. 784–85; 20 August 1853, pp. 812–14; 27 August 1853, pp. 832–34; 10 September 1853, p. 883.

102. Lewes, "Development Hypothesis," p. 785.

103. Much to George Eliot's dismay, the new science editor of the *Westminster*, young T. H. Huxley, wrote a lacerating notice of Lewes's book on Comte. He was particularly antagonistic on the subject of evolution: "Mr. Lewes is a warm advocate of the Development Hypothesis, a speculation to which, *as an hypothesis merely*, . . . we have no objection whatsoever" ("Science," *Westminster Review* 61 [1854]:255–56; see also Haight, *George Eliot Letters*, 2:132 n). Huxley had similarly skewered Chambers four months earlier in the *British and Foreign Medico-Chirugical Review* (13 [1854]:425–39). When Eliot filled Lewes's column in the *Leader* that spring (see *George Eliot Letters*, 2:150 n), she noted acerbically: "A writer who evidently delights in wielding the scalpel in more senses than one has chosen the 'Vestiges' as a subject, and dissects it with immense gusto" (April 15, p. 354).

104. Arthur O. Lovejoy, "The Argument of Organic Evolution Before 'The Origin of Species,' 1830–1858," in *Forerunners of Darwin*, ed. Bentley Glass, Oswei Temkin, William Strauss (Baltimore, 1959), pp. 360, 362.

105. Lovejoy writes that Chambers's "Explanations" is "little known," yet "in some respects superior to the original work" ("Argument of Organic Evolution," p. 375 n).

106. This alarm is implicit in Huxley's review of Lewes's *Comte*: "We cannot pass over such statements as the following without offering them to be unworthy of a place to be in any work claiming to be on a level with the science of the present day." Lewes's offending statement?: "Everyone knows how the animal and vegetable kingdoms are inextricably interlaced at their boundaries" (Huxley, "Science," p. 256).

107. Chambers, "Explanations," in *Vestiges*, p. 202.

108. Lewes, "The Development Hypothesis of the 'Vestiges,' " p. 784.

109. Chambers, "Note Conclusory" to the *Vestiges*, p. 199.

110. Chambers, *Vestiges*, pp. 5, 70, 86.

111. Chambers, "Explanations," in *Vestiges*, p. 275.

112. Lewes, "The Development Hypothesis of the 'Vestiges,' " p. 785.

113. Loren Eiseley numbers himself among the few who have recognized the originality of Chambers's contribution: Chambers "actually put the separate pieces of the lost chart of Hutton, Cuvier, and Smith together and came up with the idea that organic as well as cosmic evolution was a reality" (*Darwin's Century* [1958; rpt. New York, 1961], p. 136).

114. Mill, *Earlier Letters*, in *Collected Works*, 13:678.

115. Millhauser, *Just Before Darwin*, p. 79.

116. George Eliot, "Evangelical Teaching: Dr. Cumming," *Westminster Review* 64 (1855), in Pinney, pp. 175–76.

117. Herbert Spencer, "The Nebular Hypothesis," *Westminster Review* 70 (1858), in *Essays*, pp. 111, 109.

118. Spencer, *Autobiography*, 2:7.

119. Lewes, *Comte's Philosophy*, pp. 167–68.

120. Lewes, *Comte's Philosophy*, p. 161.

121. Chambers, *Vestiges*, p. 185.

122. Lewes, "The Development Hypothesis of the 'Vestiges,' " pp. 883, 884.

123. Lewes, "The Development Hypothesis of the 'Vestiges,' " p. 832.

124. George Henry Lewes, "Mr. Darwin's Hypothesis," *Fortnightly Review* 3 (1868):356, 355.

125. Lewes, "Mr. Darwin's Hypothesis," p. 354.

126. Chambers, quoted in Wallace, *My Life*, 2:303.

127. Millhauser, *Just Before Darwin*, pp. 181–82.

128. Millhauser, *Just Before Darwin*, pp. 176, 184. The only one of these spiritualistic essays to which Chambers gave his name was "Testimony: Its Posture in the Scientific World," *Edinburgh Papers* (1859) (Millhauser, p. 178).

129. Chambers, quoted in Wallace, *My Life*, 2:303.

130. See Millhauser, *Just Before Darwin*, p. 184.

CHAPTER THREE

New Faiths—The Philosophy of
Necessity, "Force," and Mesmerism:
Charles Bray and Harriet Martineau

*The chain of causes cannot by any force be loosed or broken,
nor can nature be commanded except by being obeyed.*
—*Bacon,* Novum Organum

They must necessarily reject all Principles of Vertue, *who can-*
not put Morality and Mechanism together; *which are not very*
easy to be reconciled, or made consistent.—Locke, Essay on
Human Understanding

On 12 August 1838, young Charles Darwin read Sir David
Brewster's review of the first two books of Auguste Comte's
Cours de philosophie positive, the first public notice of
Comte's work in England; the response he recorded in his notebooks was as much visceral as it was cerebral: "At the Athenaeum Club was very much struck with an intense headache . . . which came on from reading (review of) M. Comte
Phil." I suggest that this headache was a product of the considerable mental turmoil that Comte aroused in Darwin. Darwin
was both intrigued and appalled by certain implications of M.
Comte's philosophy. He clearly recognized both the theological and the psychological implications of Comte's universal
causality: "Now it is not a little remarkable that the fixed laws
of nature should be/universally/thought to be the *will* of a superior being . . . one suspects that our will may/arise from/
as fixed laws of organization.—M. le Comte argues against all
contrivance—it is what my views tend to." Darwin's logic re-
luctantly leads him to conclude that, in this godless world of
cause and effect, man himself is determined by the "fixed laws
of nature," laws analogous to those that rule both organic and
inorganic creation: "Now free will of oyster, one can fancy to
be direct effect of organization. . . . If so free will is to mind,
what chance is to matter. / M. le Comte /." Darwin worries
anxiously over these deductions: "Put it so.—Probably some
error in argument, should be grateful if it were pointed out."
Such scientific determinism, muses Darwin, bears a strong resemblance to Calvinism, with one very significant difference:
"The above views would make a man a predestinarian of a new
kind, because he would tend to be an atheist."[1]
  Darwin's notes on "Mind, Man, and Materialism" were re-

cently published by Howard Gruber and Paul Barrett. Darwin's response to Comte provides a case in support of their thesis that the thinking in these early notebooks was to a large degree suppressed in Darwin's published work; not because Darwin doubted the truth of his conclusions, but because he simply wished to avoid the "headache" of an extremely controversial subject.[2]

Charles Darwin, of course, was only one of many Victorians who wrestled with the painful consequences of materialism. I turn to another case of mental anguish that is much closer to this particular Victorian circle: James Anthony Froude's controversial autobiographical novel, *The Nemesis of Faith* (1849). "The book after all had been but a cry of pain," Froude later apologized, after his youthful skepticism had given way to self-satisfied orthodoxy; "It might have been better to bear pain silently, but even with a bad toothache an occasional groan may be forgiven."[3] Aside from a rather chaotic and rambling plot, in which the hero of the novel, Markham Sutherland, an Anglican priest of Tractarian persuasion, loses his faith, has an affair with a married woman (whose child meets with a retributive drowning), attempts suicide, and is converted (ambiguously) to Catholicism—all in two hundred pages!—the novel is primarily an excuse for Froude's own musings on the subjects of faith and fate.

George Eliot read the *Nemesis* in the spring of 1849, and, in a letter to Sara Sophia Hennell, compared her response to Froude to that of Keats on first looking into Chapman's Homer.[4] She wrote an ecstatic review for Charles Bray's *Coventry Herald* in praise of "a spirit who is transfusing himself into our souls and so vitalizing them by his superior energy, that life, both outward and inward, presents itself to us in higher relief, in colours brightened and deepened. . . . The books which carry this magic in them are products of genius."[5] A warm correspondence between Froude and "the translator of Strauss" ensued, and Froude soon came to Coventry, to meet Marian Evans at Charles Bray's home. Tentative plans were even made for Froude to travel to Europe with George Eliot

and the Brays after Robert Evans's death; "Was there a faint
hope of a match between these two fallen angels?" speculates
Gordon Haight.[6]

Turning to the *Nemesis*, we find a powerful strain of scientific determinism in the darker musings of Markham Sutherland: "But, uniformly, given a particular condition of a man's
nature . . . his action is as necessarily determined . . . as a
bar of steel suspended between two magnets is determined towards the most powerful." Froude later returns with even
greater emphasis to his magnetic metaphor:

> I use magnetic illustrations, not because I think the mind mag-
> netic, but because magnetic comparisons are the nearest we have,
> and the laws are exactly parallel. Minds vary in sensitiveness and
> in self-power, as bodies do in susceptibility of attraction and re-
> pulsion. When, when shall we learn that they are governed by laws
> as inexorable as physical laws, and that a man can as easily refuse
> to obey what has power over him as a steel atom can resist the mag-
> net?

Like Darwin, Froude also seizes upon the theological aspects
of this necessitarianism. If man has no choice but to act as he
is determined, does this not obviate his moral responsibility?
"Sin, therefore, as commonly understood, is a chimera," he
concludes.[7]

Only two years later, Froude's youthful rebellion was spent.
Strong proof of this is provided by placing the *Nemesis of
Faith* side-by-side with his April 1851 essay in *Fraser's*, "Materialism: Miss Martineau and Mr. Atkinson," on the subject
of their *Letters on the Laws of Man's Nature and Development*
(hereafter cited as *Letters*). The landscape of the *Nemesis*, with
its colors "bright and deep," has given way to the nightmare
topography of Froude's vision of the *Letters*: "We have travelled along a grim, strange road, beset with ghastly figures;
and we are coming now towards the sullen land, where no sun
shines, and there is no sound of prayer, or any glad song of
Thanksgiving, where hope sickens and faith dies, and necessity, with its cold arms, folds us round, and freezes up our
veins." Here Froude, like Darwin, sees universal causality as

the direct road to atheism: "Effects following causes and law being as distinctly traceable in moral as in physical phenomena," according to Froude, leads to the deadly conclusion that "matter is all—matter and its functions. There is no God, no Father." But how do Atkinson and Martineau respond to this pestiferous materialism?: "They bid us come to them, orphans as we are, and shake off our terror and be happy in our new freedom."[8]

And indeed, it is only in Froude's eyes that Martineau's necessitarian landscape is a "sullen land, where no sun shines." In her *Autobiography* Harriet Martineau chronicles her gradual conversion to the doctrine of necessity, her "repose upon eternal and irreversible laws, working in every department of the universe, without any intervention from any random will, human or divine." And, in apparent defiance of all logic, Harriet Martineau *is* "happy in her new freedom": "With the last link of [her] chain snapped," she finds herself "a free rover on the broad, bright, breezy common of the universe."[9]

If Harriet Martineau calls into question Darwin's and Froude's prognosis for the health of the human will under a sentence of necessity, Charles Bray, author of *The Philosophy of Necessity* (1841), casts equal doubts upon the necessary conjunction of determinism and atheism: "I am no Agnostic; to me God is not an unknown God. . . . In the flower, in the insect, in the bird, I say here—this is God—His immediate work and presence." In a characteristic passage in his autobiography, *Phases of Opinion and Experience During a Long Life*, Bray stops in his garden to look at a poppy, with the pantheistic eye of the poet-scientist: "It was white, its fringed edges tipped with scarlet, the other part of the flower was beautifully and symmetrically striped. . . . I could not but think, with wonder, who made this, and who made it so beautiful to me? . . . Professor Tyndall tells us that it takes 477 millions of vibratory waves to produce the sensation of the colour we call red."[10] Bray concludes this discussion with the words of his friend George Eliot, speaking in *Adam Bede* of "an unfathomable ocean of love and beauty": "Our emotion in its keenest moment passes from expression into silence—our love at its highest flood rushes beyond its object and loses itself in the sense of Divine mystery."[11]

Darwin deals with the conflict between new scientific theories and conventional religion by ignoring it (at least in his published work). Froude retreats from youthful heresy into complacent middle-aged orthodoxy. But Charles Bray and Harriet Martineau take the *via media* characteristic of their circle, seeking reconciliation of polarities within a monistic cosmology. If George Combe and Robert Chambers are the scientists of this Victorian circle (albeit with a philosophical intent), Bray and Martineau are its theologians (their creed founded on scientific theory). They preach the gospel of necessity; based upon a positivistic methodology similar to Mill's and Comte's, and buttressed by an enthusiastic advocacy of phrenology. Their union of mesmerism with phrenology completes the synthesis of matter and spirit. Yet Darwin and Froude may seem more logically consistent in their anxious and doubtful conclusions than do Bray and Martineau in their sunny optimism.

In order to understand this cheerful necessitarian gospel, we will have to come to terms with two central paradoxes: (1) how can determinism be reconciled with the necessitarian's claim of freedom and (2) how can religious faith be made congruent with a scientifically determined cosmos? The painful torment that beset Darwin, Froude, and so many other Victorians was simply not present for the Victorians in this circle. I offer Bray and Martineau as two cases in point of the ways in which these Victorians were able to reconcile the ethical values inherited from a Christian tradition with the moral implications of a cosmos ruled by universal causation.

Before attempting to answer these questions, it will be useful to explore the common intellectual heritage of Unitarianism shared by Bray and Martineau, and to look briefly to Joseph Priestley, the eighteenth-century precursor and prototype of their philosophy of necessity.

Young Harriet Martineau has been called "the Unitarian

prophetess."[12] Before she abandoned herself to the philosophy of necessity and the repudiation of all orthodox religious creeds, Martineau was well-known for essays on subjects Unitarian for the *Monthly Repository*. Her beloved brother James—who broke with Harriet over his vituperative review of her *Letters*—was to remain one of the most prominent and prolific Unitarian clergymen of the nineteenth century. And the Unitarian background is important to other members of this circle as well. Charles Bray was rescued from a youthful Evangelical phase by a debate with a Unitarian minister; he later wed and wooed his wife Cara away from her family's strong Unitarianism. But her brother, Charles Christian Hennell, remained within the sect. In 1838 Hennell published his *Inquiry into the Origins of Christianity*, a critique of Biblical literalism that bore striking resemblance to the "higher criticism" of German scholars (with whom Hennell was at that time unacquainted). George Eliot's reading of Hennell's *Inquiry* has been well-documented as the event that precipitated her conversion from Evangelical piety to freethinking rationalism.[13]

The "new" Biblical criticism coming from Germany failed to startle the Unitarians, who had always believed in the application of reason to the study of the Scriptures; it was Unitarian divines who were largely responsible for the introduction of Biblical criticism from England to the continent. George Eliot, of course, went from Hennell to her translations of David Friedrich Strauss's *Das Leben Jesu* in 1846, and of Ludwig Feuerbach's *Essence of Christianity* in 1854.

Much attention has been paid to the Higher Criticism and its profound effect on the Victorian consciousness (and conscience). But here I wish to emphasize the other half of the Unitarian legacy to the Victorians: physiological psychology. These two interests are not, in fact, as disparate as they might at first seem. "Let us then study the *Scriptures, Ecclesiastical History*, and the *Theory of the Human Mind* in conjunction; being satisfied, that from the nature of things, they must, in time, throw a great and new light upon each other," Joseph

Priestley wrote in *The Doctrine of Philosophical Necessity Illustrated* (1777).[14] From its inception Unitarianism allied itself with the "theory of the human mind" as well as with Biblical studies. The conjunction of Biblical criticism and psychology provides another example of the monistic *Weltanschauung* characteristic of this frame of mind. The two fields share not content, but form: a common method.

In an 1831 essay on the German critics, "The State of Protestantism in Germany," Dr. R. H. Brabant, friend of the Brays and early mentor of George Eliot, defined Biblical rationalism in terms that make clear its affinities with the positivistic cosmos of Mill or Comte: "The fundamental principles of Rationalism we take to be these:—that human reason . . . is the sole arbiter as to what is to be received as truth . . . that facts recognized by sense or consciousness form the materials on which the reasoning faculty is to be exercised . . . that the phenomena of nature are so linked to each other, that the whole . . . constitutes a series invariably uniform."[15] Over thirty years later, George Eliot reviewed W. E. H. Lecky's *History of Rationalism* for the *Fortnightly Review*, and broadened her definition of the term rationalism beyond "the original application of the word to a particular phase of Biblical interpretation," to include scientific as well as religious pursuits; claiming that "The great conception of universal regular sequence, without partiality and without caprice—the conception of which is the most potent force at work in the modification of our faith . . . could only grow out of that patient watching of external fact, and that silencing of preconceived notions, which are urged upon the mind by the problems of physical science."[16]

Eliot's expanded definition has its roots in the eighteenth century. Its prototype is to be found in the philosophy of Joseph Priestley. Priestley (1733–1804) was not the literal founder of Unitarianism, but his intellectual respectability as a scientist lent the authority of leadership to his theological ventures. Although Priestley's influence was less important to nineteenth-century American circles of transcendentalist Unitarians, the theologian-scientist was an ideal inspiration to this particular group of scientifically-minded Victorian intellectuals. A chemist of international reputation, Priestley is probably best known for the discovery of oxygen, and for his experiments with electricity. He also gave a major impetus to association psychology by publishing an abridged version of David Hartley's *Observations on Man*, under the title *Hartley's Theory of the Human Mind on the Principle of the Association of Ideas* (1775) (a book that Harriet Martineau claimed to have "studied with a fervour and perseverance which made it perhaps the most important book in the world to [her] except the Bible"[17]).

But Priestley considered himself foremost a philosopher and a theologian. Of his works in these fields, those most relevant here are his *Disquisitions Relating to Matter and Spirit* and *The Doctrine of Philosophical Necessity Illustrated* (both 1777). Although it was a liaison that agnostic Leslie Shephen considered an "unnatural alliance," Priestley himself found his two careers entirely compatible.[18] "Hereafter, I hope that materialism . . . will be the favourite tenet of rational Christians," Priestley somewhat surprisingly prefaces his second edition of the *Disquisitions Relating to Matter and Spirit*. Priestley's scientific researches led him to conclude that "what we call *mind* . . . is not a substance distinct from the body, but the result of corporeal organization." It is easy to see how Priestley's Unitarian tradition would prepare the Victorians for phrenology: "The seat of the sentient Principle in Man, is the material substance of the Brain." Mind is subject to the same laws as matter; Priestley's scientific beliefs thus entail a philosophy of necessity: "The doctrine of necessity . . . is the immediate result of the doctrine of the materiality of man; for mechanism is the undoubted consequence of materialism," he asserts. Priestley employs the same magnetic metaphor to picture this necessity that Froude does: our reasoning with respect to the result of "our sensation from organization is exactly similar to our reasoning concerning the attraction of iron by magnetism."[19]

The Doctrine of Philosophical Necessity Illustrated was written as an "appendix" to *Matter and Spirit*: it is in this book that Priestley attempts to sort out some of the thornier ideological implications of the materialism of the previous work, in the form of arguments used later by Charles Bray and Harriet Martineau. Let me begin my discussion of Priestley's doctrine of necessity with the first paradox of this philosophy: its fundamental optimism. How could these necessitarians proclaim themselves "free rovers" on the "sullen landscape" of necessity? It is here that Priestley, as an eighteenth-century analogue, becomes particularly useful.

In order to understand the optimism of this philosophy of necessity, one must first understand its relationship to a very different form of necessitarianism, Calvinism. For the dark strand of the Calvinistic doctrine of predestination is woven into the background of all these dissenting Victorian thinkers, as it was for their Unitarian precursor Priestley. In her *Autobiography* Harriet Martineau goes to the trouble of pointing out that the first English Martineaus were expatriated Huguenots, Calvinists who passed from the "pseudo-Christianity" of Arianism to the truer faith of Unitarianism.[20] J. D. Y. Peel dubs Spencer, along with Bray, Combe, and Martineau, "neo-Calvinis[ts]."[21] Charles Bray's contemporaries considered him the exemplar of the "Calvinist branch of the science," and Bray himself acknowledges Jonathan Edwards's "Inquiry into the Freedom of the Will" as a major inspiration for *The Philosophy of Necessity*.[22] But "neo-Calvinism" is a misleading term unless one emphasizes the way in which these thinkers made careful distinctions between what they accepted and what they emphatically rejected of Calvinistic doctrines. George Eliot wrote in 1842: "Although I cannot rank among my principles of action a fear of vengeance eternal, gratitude for predestined salvation, or a revelation of future glories as a reward, I fully participate in the belief that the only heaven here or hereafter is to be found in conformity with the will of the Supreme."[23] Calvinism preached a fatalistic predestination: man was born already saved or damned. This might be a heartening doctrine for those who believed themselves among the former category of the elect, but the conscience-ridden who numbered themselves among the latter were less satisfied. Young George Combe was one of such poor souls: "The more I believed the more unhappy I became . . . the consequences were appalling! Some persons were elected to everlasting enjoyment in heaven; many more passed over by God's decree, before they were born, to everlasting torments in hell. I included myself at once in this category . . . So severely did these ideas oppress me, that I envied the cattle that had no souls, and ardently wished that I had been as fortunate as they."[24] One has only to open *The Constitution of Man* to recognize the distance George Combe travelled to arrive at his gospel of phrenology, and the immense liberation of its progressive optimism.

All these Victorian necessitarians retained a Calvinistic predisposition to determinism; but it was their particular modification of Calvinistic doctrines that accounted for the shared sense of relief and optimism that permeates their philosophies. In his *Doctrine of Philosophical Necessity*, Priestley takes care to devote a section to "The Calvinistic doctrine of PREDESTINATION compared to the philosophic doctrine of NECESSITY." Calvinism, Priestley argues, fails to promote virtue (witness George Combe's depressive inertia), because it claims that man can do nothing to alter his predestined fate ("I do not see what motive a Calvinist can have to give any attention to his moral conduct"). Priestley's necessity, on the other hand, emphasizes the power of man's reason, in this rational world of universal cause and effect, to understand the forces that determine his behavior: "In fact, the system of necessity makes every man the *maker of his own fortune.*"[25]

How can this be? The will, argues Priestley, is "a perfectly mechanical thing," it is "a particular case of the general doctrine of the association of ideas," whereby we will that which we associate with pleasure, reject that which we associate with pain. But such a mechanically predictable will can thus be modified by the understanding; by educating it, altering its motives: "The doctrine of the *necessary influence of motives* upon the mind of man makes him the proper subject of discipline, reward and punishment, praise and blame." This doctrine of necessity, unlike its fatalistic Calvinistic sibling, thus promotes an optimistic notion of human development and progress; furthermore, unlike its judgmental Calvinistic counterpart, it encourages a broadly-based sympathy: "absolute evil wholly disappears," since no man is innately damned, but only miseducated: "I cease to blame men for their vices," writes Priestley; "my system cannot help viewing them with a tenderness and compassion."[26]

This brief discussion of Priestley's philosophy of necessity, as distinguished from its Calvinistic precursor, helps to explain the essential optimism of this Victorian circle, freed from the gloomy burden of sin and damnation—"the thoroughgoing Calvinism that holds that the majority of mankind were created simply that the 'smoke of their torment' might serve as a condiment to give piquancy to the bliss of the elect," as George Eliot so colorfully put it![27] But my second paradox remains unanswered: how is such a system congruent with belief in God: Priestley offers no satisfactory solution here; one is inclined to agree, on this point, with Leslie Stephen's judgment that Priestley's is an unsuccessful "compromise between things incompatible." Priestley never disclaims the orthodox Christian God as First Cause of the universe, and this results in some rather serious inconsistencies in his argument: "The full persuasion that nothing can come to pass without the knowledge and express appointment of the greatest and best of beings, must tend to diffuse a joyful serenity over the mind, producing a conviction that . . . whatever is, is right."[28] This cannot but remind the reader of that optimistic eighteenth-century Deity that George Combe failed to unify with the implications of phrenology in *The Constitution of Man*. Priestley's "joyful serenity" here may be deceptive: is it not logically the flip-side of gloomy predestination? God's omnipotence seems in direct conflict with his notion of man's self-determination.

It remained for Charles Bray and Harriet Martineau to offer alternative solutions to the problem of God in a non-Calvinistic necessitarian universe. Both Martineau and Bray ultimately jettisoned Unitarianism as a means of reconciling religion and science.[29] Like Joseph Priestley, they sought to retain some form of religious belief within a scientific cosmos; but their solutions to the problem are far less orthodox than his. Bray's God becomes a non-Christian pantheistic "force"; Martineau goes one radical step beyond Bray, to a "force" that apparently eschews God altogether. But I would emphasize that both retain a strong sense of the spiritual, the intuitive. Like Priestley, they are fascinated with the interrelationship of matter and spirit, emphatically rejecting Froude's insinuation that "matter is all."

II. THE RATIONAL ROMANTIC—CHARLES BRAY: *THE PHILOSOPHY OF NECESSITY; OR, THE LAW OF CONSEQUENCES; AS APPLICABLE TO MENTAL, MORAL, AND SOCIAL SCIENCE* (1841)

On 29 August 1851 George Combe and his wife were met at the Coventry train station by Charles Bray. They traveled to Rosehill, where they were introduced by Bray to his wife Cara, sister-in-law Sara Sophia Hennell, and one "Miss Evans, the daughter of a farmer." At the outset of his friendship with Bray, Combe recognized a kindred spirt: "A ribbon manufacturer about 40; a Phrenologist and a convert to the natural Laws, with an . . . excellent coronal region, but great Comb[atitiveness] and Destruc[tiveness] and very deficient Concentrativeness. He is proprietor of the Coventry Herald, which he uses as the organ of the new philosophy and its applications."[30] As we have seen above, Combe was even more favorably impressed with Marian Evans. It is not remarkable that George Combe should have found George Eliot at Rosehill; for during the preceding decade, since meeting the Brays in 1841, "Mr. and Mrs. Bray and Miss Hennell, with their friends, were *her* world," as she told friend Mary Sibree.[31] The friendship continued long after George Eliot left the provinces for London; "a beautiful and consistent friendship, running like a thread through the woof of the coming thirty-eight years," according to George Eliot's husband and biographer John Walter Cross.[32]

In his autobiography, Bray nostalgically paints a lovely portrait of Rosehill in its freethinking prime:

> There was a free-and-easy mental atmosphere, harmonizing with the absence of all pretension and conventionality, which I believe gave a peculiar charm to this modest residence. "When the bear-skin is under the acacia," our friends used to write, "then we will come to you," and the spot is still associated with the flow of talk unrestrained, and the interchange of ideas, varied and peculiar according to the character and mood of the talkers and thinkers assembled there.[33]

Mary Sibree remembers telling George Eliot, "as we closed the garden door" at Rosehill, "that we seemed to be entering a Paradise." George Eliot concurred: "I do indeed feel that I shut the world out when I shut that door."[34]

After she settled in London in the early 1850s, George Eliot was still to return to that Edenic spot, to share the blessings of its seclusion and intellectual stimulation with the weary cosmopolites who now entered her life. During the time of her infatuation with and rumored engagement to Herbert Spencer, she intrigued with Bray to organize his invitations to these new friends to suit her liking: "He [Spencer] will prefer waiting for the pleasure of a visit to you until I am with you—if you will have him then. *Entre nous*, if Mr. Lewes should not accept your invitation now, pray don't ask him when I am with you."[35] Long after George Eliot's more desired companion had become George Henry Lewes, Herbert Spencer's friendship with Charles Bray continued autonomously over three decades, as Spencer paid solitary visits to Rosehill: "I hope you are likely to survive the heavy dose of theories you have had," Eliot joked to Cara after one such visit.[36]

The emotional bonds between George Eliot and Charles Bray were intense: "You are the dearest, oldest, stupidest, tiresomest, delightfullest, and never-to-be-forgottenest of friends to me," Eliot vowed in 1853; "As a daughter she was the most devoted I ever knew," Bray claimed to George Combe in 1854.[37] And the intellectual bonds were equally profound. "I may claim to have laid down the base of that philosophy which she afterwards retained," Bray asserted somewhat hubristically in his autobiography.[38] But his voice is unmistakable when George Eliot writes John Chapman in 1852: "I [believe] . . . that the thought which is to mould the Future has for its root a belief in necessity." "In the fundamental doctrine of your book," the *Philosophy of Necessity*, Eliot writes Bray in 1857, "that mind presents itself under the same condition of invariableness of antecedent and consequent as all other phenomena . . . I think you know that I agree."[39]

The deepest communion between Bray and Eliot espoused the common ground of emotion and intellect. Far more than rational necessity, the "invariableness of antecedent and consequent," the unity of head and heart in Charles Bray's philosophy provided a strong foundation for Eliot's compatibility with the sage of Rosehill. The first published letter from George Eliot to Charles Bray (dated 1848) suggests this fundamental affinity: "I heartily say amen to your dictum about the cheerfulness of 'large moral regions.' Where thought and love are active, thought the formative power, love the vitalizing, there can be no sadness. They are in themselves a more intense and extended participation of a divine Existence."[40] Thought is "formative," love "vitalizing"; intellect and emotion work in tandem. George Eliot moves easily from the language of phrenology—"large moral regions"—to that of faith—"a divine Existence." It also should be emphasized how remote Bray and Eliot are here from the stereotype of the atheistic freethinker. Although neither remains an orthodox Christian, faith in some very important form still clearly occupies a central position in their cosmos.

The essential statement of Charles Bray's philosophy in these early years can be found in *The Philosophy of Necessity; or, The Law of Consequences; as Applicable to Mental, Moral, and Social Science* (1841). I offer a reading of this book with two objectives in mind: first, to examine it in light of the fundamental paradoxes of necessitarianism that were established in the preceding section; and second, to show how Bray's philosophy fits squarely within the intellectual contexts defined in previous chapters of this study: the methodology of Mill and Comte, and the applied science of Combe and Chambers. Charles Bray, like so many of the Victorian intellectuals with whom this study deals, is a magpie thinker; he borrows unabashedly and quotes liberally from a host of sources. What is original and striking in the *Philosophy of Necessity* is not to be found in the parts, but in the whole: in Bray's juxtaposition of his sources. Chapter one began with the meeting of Utilitarianism and Romanticism in John Stuart Mill's essays on Bentham and Coleridge: his vision of polar opposites as allies, joined in a single progressive force. Written only a year after Mill's essay on Coleridge, the *Philosophy of Necessity* embodies a similar synthesis of two traditions, as Bray moves with ease from Locke and Bentham to Shelley and Carlyle.

In his introduction Bray acknowledges Bentham as a central source of inspiration. The utilitarian echoes throughout are unmistakable: "Pain and Pleasure [are] . . . the ultimate springs of all our actions"; "Virtue, to the Necessitarian, means that line of conduct which, *all* things considered, shall be productive of the greatest happiness to all."[41] But Bray makes the transition from utilitarianism to romanticism with remarkable ease: "The happiness of the individual must be subservient to that of the human race, and the human race is again only a part of the great whole of animated existence, and man's situation and position on this earth must have reference to the whole of God's plan for the happiness of all." He then proceeds to quote from that definitive romantic pantheist, Shelley, in "Queen Mab's" celebration of nature's unity:

> Those viewless beings,
> Whose mansion is the smallest particle
> Of the impassive atmosphere,
> Think, feel, and live, like man.

Bray sees no conflict between heart and head: "Such, though a poetical, is yet a logical deduction from the doctrine of necessity," he concludes.[42]

Of all his sources, Bray returns most frequently and at greatest length to fellow-Victorian Carlyle's *Sartor Resartus* (1833–34). In Carlyle, Bray finds the solution to Priestley's dilemma of God's role in a universe ruled by inexorable cause and effect. He is not a First Cause, but a pantheistic Force, says Bray, "the all-prevading influence which maintains the connexion between all antecedents and consequents."[43] Bray quotes Carlyle's rhapsodic musings in *Sartor*, which give perfect voice to this idealist faith: "This fair universe . . . is in every deed the star-domed City of God; . . . through every star, through every grass-blade, and most through every living soul, the glory of a present God still beams."[44] This mystical power is clearly not the Calvinistic Predestinator, nor is it an orthodox Christian God. Bray, the scientist and logician of necessity, admits to the unknowable; his God is an ineluctable force that unifies all: "And thus, in a mode mysterious and incomprehensible to Man, may the Creative Spirit of the Universe form a part of all Nature."[45] But Bray the pantheist also remains Bray the scientist. *The Philosophy of Necessity* contains the seeds of a philosophy that would mediate between the scientifically demonstrable and the transcendent. By *On Force*, in 1866, Bray finds in the concept of "force" a fully scientific embodiment of this pantheistic power.

For now, I wish to descend from these empyrean heights; to return to Charles Bray the Utilitarian empiricist; and to examine his philosophy of necessity as a product of the scientific cosmology shared by Mill and Comte, Combe and Chambers. Bray's philosophy of necessity is the logical corollary of universal causality.

Mill's *Logic* and *The Philosophy of Necessity* appeared within two years of one another, and the parallels between their views of necessity are striking. In chapter 2 of part 6, "On the Logic of the Social Sciences," John Stuart Mill turns to the subject "Of Liberty and Necessity," in a discussion he himself considered "the best chapter in the two volumes."[46] "*Are hu-*

man actions subject to the law of causality?" Mill opens his chapter; "the question, whether the law of causality applies in the same strict sense to human actions as to other phenomena is the celebrated question concerning the freedom of the will."[47] Similarly, Bray writes in his "Introduction": "I would show that the mind of man is not an exception to nature's other works; that like everything else it has received a determinate character; that all our knowledge of it is precisely the same as that of material things, and consists in the observation of *its order* of action, or the relation of cause and effect."[48]

Because human behavior conforms to the logic of cause and effect, man is scientifically predictable: "If we knew the person thoroughly, and knew all the inducements which are acting upon him, we could fortell his conduct with as much certainty as we can predict any physical event," claims Mill.[49] Again, compare Bray on the same point: "The character of man is the result of the organization he received at birth, and all the various circumstances acted upon it since, and these, if that were possible, being given, a mental philosopher would predict the line of conduct that will be invariably pursued by each individual; as readily as a chemist can predict the exact result of the mixture of any chemical substance." It is thus that there can be, as Mill claims, a "logic of the social sciences"; "The science of Morality is as certain as that of Physiology," asserts Bray.[50]

Like Priestley, Mill and Bray insist that necessitarianism does not doom man to a predestined fate. Mill makes a clear distinction between what he calls "fatalism" and "necessitarianism," a distinction very similar to that made by Priestley between Calvinism and Necessitarianism. Although our actions and characters "follow from our organization, our education, and our circumstances," nonetheless man "has, to a certain extent, power to alter his character," says Mill.[51] Necessity, argues Bray, does not "annihilate the *free agency* in man." Although man's behavior is determined by his "mental constitution" and his "circumstances," he can reasonably educate himself to understand, and thus potentially to alter, his behavior. It is thus the very logic of inexorable cause and effect that is the *key* to man's liberation: "If necessity did not regulate [the world of mind as of matter] . . . man's reasoning power, which depends for its exercise upon the uniformity of events in both, would be of no use," says Bray.[52] Similarly, Mill claims that moral reason comes from self-understanding: we are "able to modify our own character *if we wish*"; "A person feels morally free who feels that his habits or his temptations are not his masters."[53]

Once the positivist millennium arrives, scientifically enlightened men will be able to experience just such freedom. Significantly, Comte's *Cours de philosophie positive* preaches the same necessitarianism—and the same optimism—as Bray and Mill. Though Comte states emphatically that "true liberty is nothing else than a rational submission to the preponderance of the laws of nature," he also asserts that "man . . . can modify for his own good . . . the system of phenomena of which he forms a part . . . directed by an accurate knowledge of natural laws."[54] Unlike Mill, Bray had not encountered Comte as early as 1841. But in his autobiography, he acknowledges the essential compatibility of his philosophy of necessity and positivism, quoting positivist Dr. Bridges: "The first and last object of Comte's life was to instill that sense of steady firm conviction which scientific truth establishes in the regions of man's emotions and conduct." Bray replies: "It is this 'new thing' that I have been preaching for the last forty years, but I was not aware that I had so strong an ally in Positivism."[55]

Despite the striking similarity of their arguments, Bray and Mill wrote independently of one another. Both based their Victorian world view on a common tradition of British empiricism. "The importance of the principle of Association cannot be overestimated," Bray avows.[56] John Locke's *Essay Concerning Human Understanding* claimed, "The *liberty* Men have . . . [is] that they can *suspend* their desires, and stop them from determining their *will* to any action, till they have duly and fairly *examin'd* the good and evil of it."[57] Bray quotes a similar passage from Locke in *The Philosophy of Necessity*; he returns to Locke's *Essay* throughout the book.[58] John Locke was the "idol of the dissenters," and his work would have come to Bray through the Unitarian heritage; as it did to John Stuart Mill in the empiricist patrimony of Jeremy Bentham and his father James Mill.[59]

However, Bray moves beyond Locke and Mill in two significant ways: first, like Combe and Chambers, he goes beyond mere theory about a science of mind, to claim that in phrenology he has found the scientific embodiment of psychology. Second, the discoveries phrenology yields about the human mind take Bray beyond the boundaries of empiricism. Or rather, they *expand* the boundaries of traditional empiricism. For Bray does not leave behind the principles of association psychology, but combines them with phrenology to yield a new intuitionism, with significant implications for the fledgling science of evolutionary biology. This newborn hybrid of the empirical and the intuitive is consistent with the intellectual temperament of a man who quotes Shelley and Carlyle side-by-side with Locke and Bentham. It points the way to the more lucidly and explicitly stated organicism of George Henry Lewes and the evolutionary psychology of Herbert Spencer. I will spend the remainder of my discussion of Charles Bray exploring the evidence for the above assertions.

Although Locke laid the foundations for a scientific psychology in the *Essay on Human Understanding*, he had stopped short of what he called "physical considerations."[60] The science of the day, he argued, was not yet capable of such activities. A century and a half later, Bray believed that he could fill in the Lockean *lacunae*, establish the "first principles" of a science of psychology on the basis of a "clear chart of the mental faculties," "by a method strictly inductive": "Such a chart, the necessity for which Locke so clearly expressed his conviction . . . seems to have been furnished by the new philosophy of Phrenology."[61] As we have seen, Bray was an early disciple of George Combe, and a sizable portion of *The Philosophy of Necessity* is devoted to a straight exposition of the tenets of phrenology. Bray acknowledges that he takes his phrenological charts directly from *The Constitution of Man*; when discussing the physical, organic, and moral laws (in a section allusively titled "Man Considered in Relation to External Objects"), he is able to abbreviate his discussion: "The whole of this subject has been so clearly illustrated in Mr. Combe's well-known work . . . that it is unnecessary to pursue it here to any length."[62]

Taken in conjunction with the philosophy of necessity, phrenology provides the bridge from Bray's empiricism to his intuitionism. John Stuart Mill stated in *Auguste Comte* that "the phrenological study of Mind thus supposes as its necessary preparation the whole of the Association psychology."[63] We have already seen that Bray continues to assert the importance of associationism in *The Philosophy of Necessity*. But significantly, Bray writes in his autobiography that he initially thought phrenology and association psychology to be less than compatible: "Now I had at that time a most supreme contempt for Phrenology. . . . I thought I knew how our Feelings had been gradually formed by Association, and that they did not therefore exist as primitive instincts as the Phrenologists asserted."[64] The fundamental optimism of this necessitarianism—the belief that man can modify his desires, alter his character—depends upon the principles of associationism: man changes himself by forming new associations, new patterns of cause and effect. Yet Bray is outspokenly a phrenologist in *The Philosophy of Necessity*. How did he reconcile the old philosophy with the new science?

I believe that Bray found a satisfying method of reconciling the two within phrenology itself; a way in which he could claim both that feelings are "gradually formed by association" *and* that they "exist as primitive instincts." This method contained within it the germ of an evolutionary biology, which would come to full fruition in the thought of Herbert Spencer. It is not only an ingenious stratagem to reconcile antitheses, but a major contribution to the history of ideas in the nineteenth century. On the simplest level, phrenology would seem unequivocally to substantiate the notion of innate mental characteristics ("primitive instincts"): if each man is born with a certain brain, is not his character thus predetermined at birth? Accordingly, George Henry Lewes writes in the *Biographical History* that "Gall may be said to have definitively settled the dispute between the partisans of innate ideas and the partisans of Sensationalism, by establishing the connate tendencies both affective and intellectual, which belong to the organic structure of man."[65] Yet this position, logically pursued, would lead to a sort of secular Calvinistic predestination (as Darwin, for example, realized), entailing the fatalism that these necessitarians so clearly rejected.

Their solution to this dilemma is an ingenious one: association can modify brain structure; this new brain structure descends to the next generation, which is thus born with "innate" tendencies that are, nonetheless, acquired by "experience." "Associations do not always originate with the individual," writes Bray, "but . . . the state of the brain, on which they depend, is transmissable to offspring."[66] Innate mental capacities are thus formed by ancestral "experience," and this experience is passed on from parent to child. On one level Bray departs radically from the empiricism of Locke and his followers: " 'Nihil est in intellectum quod non prius fuerit in sensu' is not true," he states; "the Phrenologists have discovered the connexion between the primitive faculties of the mind and certain parts of the brain. . . . The indications that such faculties give us . . . must be received as first truths, upon which all reasoning is founded." But he nonetheless is able to remain true to the fundamental utilitarian principles of association psychology by claiming that these innate "first truths" are products of sense experience: "All moral rules are derived from utility, but the pleasures and pains . . . on which they are based are transmitted to offspring and thus become intuitions."[67]

Thus Charles Bray bridges the romantic and the rational, the intuitive and the empirical: "Kant's *categories* are his mode of arriving by Reflection or consciousness at the list of Intellectual Faculties or modes of thought which Gall and his followers have arrived at by observation," he writes in *On Force*.[68] It

was Herbert Spencer who was to make explicit the extraordinary evolutionary implications of this new psychology, implications that should be tantalizingly apparent in what I have
said above. But I would argue that what has been considered
Spencer's most original contribution to scientific psychology,
the concept of racial heredity as the source of innate ideas that
Spencer formulated in *The Principles of Psychology* in 1855,
was already present, less systematically, in earlier phrenological theory.

Phrenology provided Charles Bray with both a solution to
the dilemma of determinism and a scientific basis upon which
to reconcile empiricism with intuition. But Bray himself was
ultimately less interested in scientific theory than he was in
spiritual truths. In good Victorian fashion, Bray would evolve
beyond phrenology to the even more radical tenets of mesmerism and "force."

III. MIND OVER MATTER: "FORCE" AND THE MESMERIC MANIA

Like Robert Chambers, Charles Bray turned emphatically to
the metaphysical in the latter portion of his career. The process
culminated in 1866 with the publication of his book *On Force,
Its Mental and Moral Correlates; and On That Which is Supposed to Underlie All Phenomena; with Speculations on Spiritualism, and Other Abnormal Conditions of Mind.* Bray's
concept of force is a logical next step from his philosophy of
necessity, an epitome of the monistic impulse that animates all
of these Victorians.

If Bray's *Philosophy of Necessity* contains many parallels to
Joseph Priestley's *Doctrine of Philosophical Necessity, On
Force* can be read as the successor to Priestley's *Disquisitions
on Matter and Spirit.* But with a revealing difference: Priestley
begins with *Matter and Spirit,* whose "principal object is to
prove the uniform composition of man, or that what we call
mind . . . is not a substance distinct from the body"; he follows this with what he calls an "appendix" volume on philosophical necessity: "The doctrine of necessity . . . is the im-

mediate result of the doctrine of the materiality of man."[69] Here again, the familiar idea: if mind is matter, it is thus subject to the necessity of physical laws. But Charles Bray reverses Priestley's order, following his study of necessity with *On Force*. Herein lies the clue to his radical divergence from this eighteenth-century predecessor. Bray begins his career as an advocate of phrenology; like Priestley, he emphasizes the materiality of mind—and the attendant philosophy of necessity. But in *On Force*, Bray completes a circle: "Thus physical force creates the mind and the mind creates the world."[70] Though the thesis of *On Force* may at first appear similar to Priestley's claim that spirit is really matter, in fact, Bray reverses Priestley, to argue that all matter is ultimately spirit.

Before demonstrating this claim, let me begin by insisting that Bray's interests were not simply from the lunatic fringe, notwithstanding George Henry Lewes's scathing condemnation of his later work as unworthy of serious attention. In fact, some highly respectable Victorian scientists were fascinated with the concept of force. For example, Bray writes that he was inspired by W. R. Grove's *Correlation of the Physical Forces* (1846). Grove was "the first to give complete and systematic expression to the new views"; but by 1865 his work could be collected in an omnibus on *The Correlation and Conservation of Forces: A Series of Expositions*, containing works on the subject by such outstanding scientific names as Helmholtz, Mayer, Faraday, Liebig, and Carpenter.[71] At least two of our Victorians other than Bray were familiar with Grove's work. An 1855 edition of the *Correlation* in George Henry Lewes's library is covered with his marginalia and markings.[72] In her Journal for 3 May 1870, George Eliot writes: "I began Grove on the 'Correlation of the Physical Forces'—needing to read it again—with new interest, after the lapse of years."[73]

The controversial aspect of Bray's work lies in his extension of the concept of force from physics to metaphysics. In his *Correlation* Grove announced that he had "purposely avoided" claiming that the concept of force "might be applied to the organic as well as the inorganic world."[74] It is just this larger correlation that Bray will claim: "I could not see why correlation should stop at the physical forces, and why it should not be extended to mental force."[75] Bray, however, was not alone in this notion; a leading physiological psychologist had undertaken a similar path. Scientist W. B. Carpenter (who was, interestingly, the son of a Unitarian minister) wrote in 1865:

> In a memoir of my own, "On the Mutual Relations of the Vital and Physical Forces" [1850] . . . I aimed to show that the general doctrine of the "Correlation of the Physical Forces" proposed by Mr. Grove, was equally applicable to those vital forces which must be assumed as the moving powers in the production of purely physiological phenomena. . . . This memoir attracted but little attention at the time, being regarded, I believe, as too speculative; but I have since had abundant evidence that the minds of thoughtful Physiologists as well as Physicists, are moving in the same direction.[76]

For Bray, as for Grove and Carpenter, the concept of force originates in the physical sciences: "Light, Heat, Electricity, Galvanism, Chemical Affinity, Attraction and Repulsion."[77] Since like Carpenter, Bray continues to believe in a science of mind, he can logically extend this concept from physical science to mental science. Thus, Bray opens *On Force* with the claim that "Life and Mind" are forces analogous to, or rather, identical with, electricity or chemical affinity: "There is but One simple, primordial, absolute Force."

"Matter and Spirit the same in Essence," proclaims Bray in Priestleyan tones. But one would be gravely mistaken if he concluded from this that Bray was a materialist. "Force and mind . . . are . . . really identical, and the material order probably exists, as the Idealists say, only as mental." Bray offers what seems a startling pronouncement, coming from a physiological psychologist: "The two apparently *diverse* classes of phenomena may be only one, and . . . the material order may exist only as mental." In *On Force* Bray is even more conversant with what might loosely be called German idealist philosophies than he was in *The Philosophy of Necessity.* "Force," he writes, is "the true doctrine of 'Absolute Identity,'

taught in another form by Schelling, Hegel and Cousin." He goes on to quote Fichte and Spinoza: "There is but one infinite Substance, and that is God." He even draws on the Hindu and Buddhist philosophies. In *On Force* Bray reiterates the pantheism of *The Philosophy of Necessity*: "All we see is but the vesture of God, and what we call laws of Nature are attributes of Deity."[78]

But again, it should be emphasized that Bray in no way considers this belief incompatible with a scientific world view: "Science, then, proves the Unity of Force."[79] In fact, the very appeal of the concept of force for Bray is its origin in the realm of the physical sciences. Electricity offered the prototype of force (note Priestley's fame as an electrical experimenter); electrical force was both invisible and measurable, spiritual and yet material. One cannot, finally—despite his assertion that "mind is all"—simply type Bray as an idealist or a metaphysician. The concept of force incarnates a dynamic unification of the polarities of matter and spirit, physiological science and the pantheistic oversoul. "A new class of beings or entities was thus made known, which seem to exist between the opposite confines of matter and spirit, and to partake in a degree of the nature of both," wrote J. C. Prichard in 1829, in his *Review of the Doctrine of the Vital Principle*.[80] Like the Comtean hierarchy of the sciences, or the development hypothesis, force is one more formulation of a monistic cosmology.

Appropriately, Samuel Taylor Coleridge was an early believer in force, writing in his "Essays on Method" that "the masses act by a force, which cannot be conceived to result from the component parts. . . . In the phenomena of magnetism, electricity, galvanism, and in chemistry generally, the mind is led . . . to regard the working powers as conducted, transmitted, or accumulated by the sensible bodies, and not as inherent." He continues: "This Fact has, at all times, been the stronghold alike of the materialists and the spiritualists, equally solvable by the two contrary hypotheses, and fairly solved by neither." Coleridge, like Bray, asserts that both hypotheses must cooperate for the full truth to emerge: "Religion therefore is the ultimate aim of philosophy, in consequence of which philosophy itself becomes the supplement of the sciences . . . as supplying the copula, which modified in each in the comprehension of its parts to one whole . . . as integral parts of one system."[81] My reader will remember that Coleridge's *Theory of Life* provided a major inspiration for *On Force*, via its explication in James Hinton's essay on "Physiological Riddles" in the *Cornhill* in 1860.

"Why should not *gravity* afford the conditions requisite for an organic relation of the masses of which the universe consists?" queries Hinton. And does not this force of gravity, he continues, constitute "a true analogue to the vital force?" Force, like the development hypothesis, predicates the vital unity of man and the natural world. Hinton rhapsodizes:

> To feel the subtle links that tie together the diverse forms of Nature's energy, and recognize, in the sportive youth or vigorous maturity of bird or beast, tokens of the same powers that make firm the earth beneath their tread, give fluence to the waves, and cunningest chemistry to the all-embracing, all-purifying air, opens to the lover of the animated tribes a new delight. . . . Each thrilling wave of life flows warm and fresh, from fountains which the sunbeams feed, which roll through every fibre of the solid globe, and spring up glowing from the central fires.[82]

Where the *Vestiges* avowed the unity of the created cosmos, from the nebular hypothesis to the mind of man, the pantheistic priests of force embraced an even grander monistic faith: "This wondrous dynamic chain [of force] binds into living unity the realms of matter and mind, through the measureless amplitudes of space and time."[83]

Where, one might gasp, does one go from here? Let me shift from the macrocosm to the microcosm, to the specific manifestation of force that most interested this Victorian circle: "Brain force, the result of cerebration, also exists in excess in some nervous constitutions; it then forms a sphere or atmosphere around individuals by which one brain is brought into direct communication with others and mind becomes a unity. Individual will-power can act through this medium beyond the range of individual body. In this way may be explained

. . . the Phenomena of Mesmerism, and the Curative Power of individuals."[84] This statement comes from Charles Bray's autobiography, part of his summary of *On Force*. Henry George Atkinson's and Harriet Martineau's *Letters on the Laws of Man's Nature and Development* is predicated on the same theory: "What is mind but an evolved condition or form of the powers of nature, like light, heat, magnetism?—a form of the phenomena of the fundamental power which is acting throughout nature, and may, perhaps, be said to constitute nature."[85] The laws of mental force might be fully analogous to the laws of gravitation, but they had yet to find a satisfying scientific exposition: "We have discovered the law of gravitation, and we now want a Newton in the department of mind," exhorts Bray in *On Force*; "mesmerism, clairvoyance, and the 'modern spiritual manifestations,' . . . are now pressing for explanation and reduction to law, and when that is accomplished . . . the power of mind will be as greatly and rapidly increased as physical power has been by recent discoveries in steam and electricity."[86]

Franz Anton Mesmer first propagated his theories of "animal magnetism" in pre-Revolutionary France. In his study of "'The Mesmeric Mania': the Early Victorians and Animal Magnetism," Fred Kaplan summarizes Mesmer's twenty-seven key propositions from the *Mémoire sur La Découverte Du Magnetism Animal* (1779):

> 1. Mechanical laws working in an alternate ebb and flow control "a mutual influence between the Heavenly bodies, the Earth, and Animate Bodies which exist as a universally distributed and continuous fluid . . . of an incomparably rarefied nature."
> 2. Since all "the properties of matter and the organic body depend upon this operation" whose influence or force may be communicated to animate and inanimate bodies, it is possible to create a new theory about the nature of influence and power relationships between people, and between people and the objects in their environment.[87]

In "'The Mesmeric Mania,'" Kaplan divides Victorian respondents to mesmerism into three camps: its spiritual defenders, its scientific defenders, and its opponents. Characteristically, the advocates of mesmerism in this Victorian circle belong in both of the first two categories. In his study of *Dickens and Mesmerism*, Kaplan astutely observes that mesmerism was a child of the Enlightenment that flourished in revolutionary times, a genealogy that produced a peculiar hybrid: a romantic heritage of "intuition, spontaneity, man as God, the role of mystery and magic in the cosmos" in conjunction with the eighteenth-century values of "order, social norms, centralized reform, progress and science."[88] And so, in mesmerism, "Coleridge" and "Bentham" meet again. Mesmerism was ideally suited to a Victorian temperament seeking the bridge between spirit and science.

Charles Bray dates his introduction to mesmerism from 1841, the same year he met George Eliot.[89] By 1866 he remained a strong believer: "My own opinion is that there is an emanation from all brains, the result of both conscious and unconscious cerebration, forming, not spirits, but a mental or spiritual atmosphere, by means of which peculiar constitutions— mediums and others, are put *en rapport* with other brains or minds, and become conscious of whatever is going on there."[90] In 1844, shortly after her journey to London with Bray for a phrenological reading, young Marian Evans ("M. A.") was mesmerized at a dinner party she attended with the Brays: "He nearly succeeded in mesmerising M. A. to the degree that she could not open her eyes, and begged him most piteously to do it for her, which he did immediately by passes," wrote Bray's wife, Cara.[91]

The vocabulary of mesmerism, like that of phrenology, colors George Eliot's metaphors during the 1840s: "It is like a diffusion or expansion of one's own life to be assured that its vibrations are repeated in another, and words are the media of those vibrations"; the atmosphere of Geneva has "the effect of mesmerism or chloroform."[92] In her first published fiction, "The Notebook of an Eccentric," in Charles Bray's *Coventry Herald* (1846–47), Eliot's hero suffers from "alleged states of mesmeric lucidity, in which the patient obtains an unenviable cognizance of irregularities, happily imperceptible to us in the

ordinary state of our consciousness." Eliot describes her early
hero in the terms of electrobiology: "Any who were capable of
a more discriminating estimate and refined analysis of his
character, must have had a foreboding that it contained elements which would too probably operate as non-conductors,
interposed between his highly-charged mind and the nega-
tively electrified souls around him."[93]

As with phrenology George Eliot became more rigorously
critical but no less interested in mesmerism once she left the
provinces for the *Westminster* and George Henry Lewes.
"Thank you very much for the facts about Dr. Gregory's patient," she writes to George Combe in 1852; "we get impatient
of phenomena which do not link on to our previous knowledge. . . . This and the great mass of loose statement and credulity which surround the whole subject of mesmerism repel
many minds from it. . . . But indications of claire-voyance
witnessed by a competent observer are of thrilling interest and
give me a restless desire to get more extensive and satisfactory
evidence."[94] Eliot had little patience with faddish spiritualistic
mediums: "Better be occupied exclusively with the intestinal
worms of tortoises than with that!" (i.e., better be a pure materialist) she scornfully announced.[95] Lewes's skepticism
would have guaranteed Eliot's intellectual rigor on the subject.
He was eager to expose "A Mesmeric Quack" in the *Saturday
Review* in 1856: "Throughout this pretentious volume, we
have seen no acquaintance with physiology—hence the supreme confidence of its dogmatism," he wrote in review of
William Neilson's *Mesmerism in its Relation to Health and
Disease.*[96]

Mesmer himself was no charlatan, and many of his earliest
advocates in Victorian England were reputable medical prac-
titioners (at least until they began to advocate mesmerism). But
as the vogue for mesmerism grew during the 1840s, mesmerism
became a fad as well as a science. In the midst of what contemporaries called the "mesmeric mania of 1851," an anonymous
essayist in the *Westminster* turned to the subject of "Electro-
Biology" (the name scientists often gave to mesmerism or ani-

mal magnetism), and painted an amusing portrait of Victorian society entranced with its new plaything:

> In a fashionable assembly, experiments on the mental functions take the place of quadrilles. Ladies of sensitive and "susceptible" organization, gratify a drawingroom with the exhibition of "involuntary emotions," instead of a fantasia on the piano-forte. Students at Universities excite them in each other till they find themselves incapacitated for attendance upon their classes; and boys at school forsake marbles to play tickles with the nervous system of their companions; for which the most serious consequences have sometimes ensued.[97]

However, mesmerism, like phrenology, was subject to serious scientific investigation as well as party games. In his "Science" column for the *Westminster Review* in January 1854, T. H. Huxley bemoaned the "New Demonology" of mesmerism and its related occult sciences: "What . . . is our educated Englishman to do?" Huxley recommended as an antidote to this "Witch's *Sabbat*" a thorough study of "the chapters on the Physiology of the Mind in Dr. Carpenter's excellent 'Human Physiology.'" Yet Carpenter himself had proposed "the correlation of the physical and vital forces" in 1850. Not coincidentally, Dr. Carpenter took a strong scientific interest in "Electro-biology and Mesmerism," publishing an essay by that title in the *Quarterly Review* in 1853. There, he attempts to being the phenomena of mesmerism into accord with scientific truth, by examining mesmerism as a biological phenomenon in light of such theories as unconscious cerebral function.[99] George Eliot and George Henry Lewes responded with enthusiasm to such a genuinely scientific approach: "You should read the article in the Quarterly on Electro-Biology," Eliot writes to Bray in October 1853; "It is by Dr. Carpenter—a 'naked neddy' in your esteem, but still the first physiologist in England."[100]

It should be noted that scientific mesmerists were often likely to be phrenologists as well. After 1838 phrenology wed animal magnetism, and its offspring was the new science of phrenomagnetism, or phrenomesmerism.[101] In 1843 George Combe added a chapter on "mesmeric phrenology" to his textbook,

The System of Phrenology; and two years earlier, Charles Bray had noted his mesmeric interests amidst the phrenological philosophy of *The Philosophy of Necessity*.[102] "Every mesmerizer should understand phrenology and phreno-magnetism," write Atkinson and Martineau in their *Letters on the Laws of Man's Nature and Development*.[103]

Why was this so? On the crudest popular level, mesmerism was used to substantiate the claims of phrenology, as subjects in a mesmeric trance enacted the appropriate behavior in correspondence to the touch on a given "organ" of their brain. In a broader sense, it is easy to see the compatibility of these two ostensibly materialist ideologies, both of which claimed that psychology was a physical science. But finally, and most important, mesmerism provided a temperamentally necessary complement to phrenology. Mesmerism is "the mind of phrenology," write Atkinson and Martineau.[104] They might more appropriately have called it the heart of phrenology. Mesmerism provided a spiritual complement to phrenology that transcended the materiality of the brain, yet still claimed to remain scientifically quantifiable.

Contemporary critics of mesmerism were quick to note the apparent paradox of this spiritual materialism. W. R. Grove himself wrote skeptically on mesmerism for *Blackwood's* in 1845, and called it a "transcendental philosophy."[105] Asking "What Is Mesmerism?" in the same journal six years later, John Eagles drew attention to what he called a "wonderful inconsistency in some advocates of mesmerism, who . . . deny that there is any such thing as spirit at all, showing at the same time phenomena that cannot belong to matter."[106] But such "wonderful inconsistency" is the stuff of this Victorian frame of mind. Within that context it becomes a fully logical and necessary synthesis of polar antitheses.

IV. MATERIALISM AND SPIRITUALISM—HARRIET MARTINEAU
AND HENRY GEORGE ATKINSON: *LETTERS ON THE LAWS OF
MAN'S NATURE AND DEVELOPMENT (1851)*

The *Letters on the Laws of Man's Nature and Development* differs from the other texts selected for this study. It adds no new elements to the Victorian frame of mind shared by this circle. Martineau is perhaps the least intellectually gifted thinker among them; her *Letters* often seem close to the lunatic fringe, light-years away from the logical rigors of John Stuart Mill, or even the respectable Victorian system-making of Herbert Spencer. But if I had to select, from among the kindred minds that this study depicts, a prototypical expression of their Victorian world-view, it would be Martineau's. The *Letters on the Laws of Man's Nature and Development* has been relegated to dusty obscurity, unread and seemingly unreadable in the twentieth century. But a survey of Victorian periodicals reveals that it aroused remarkable furor upon its publication, and merited considerable attention from highly-respected journals and critics. Why?

The context of the preceding chapters of my study should make this forgotten Victorian essay on man more accessible, and help to account for the amazing amount of controversy it engendered in its own time. The *Letters* contains a synthesis of every interrelated Victorian ideology I have discussed: universal causality, positivism, phrenology, the development hypothesis, the philosophy of necessity, force. It epitomizes the Victorian monist's conception of the universe, the union of head and heart, empiricism and intuition. The issues this book raises were central to the Victorian age. *Letters on the Laws of Man's Nature and Development* is thus a fascinating case study of the way in which lesser Victorian minds seized upon seminal ideas of the period. It provides a fine example of the symbiotic interrelationships among the Victorian ideologies shared by this circle of thinkers.

Like her book, Harriet Martineau's fame in her own day was far more considerable than her subsequent reputation. Until recently, if she was remembered at all, it was often as Carlyle's "too happy and too noisy distinguished female," a probable model for Dickens's Mrs. Jellaby and Mrs. Pardiggle; an appallingly energetic spinster with an ear-trumpet, who was capable of producing, in one two-and-a-half year period alone, three series of tales on political economy, taxation, and the poor laws—a total of some thirty-four volumes!—for earnest Victorian readers. Even at age three, lisping out "Never ky for tyfles!" and "Dooty fust and pleasure afterwards!"—the child was the mother of the woman.[107]

Martineau, as I have already noted, began her productive career as the "Unitarian prophetess." But by the late 1830s, this famous woman of letters experienced something of a mid-life crisis. On 16 March 1840, at the peak of her fame, she was stricken with a mysterious ailment, a malaise as much spiritual as it was physical: "Here closed the anxious period during which my reputation, and my industry, and my social intercourses were at their height of prosperity; but which was so charged with troubles that when I lay down on my couch of pain in my Tynemouth lodging, for a confinement of nearly six years, I felt myself comparatively happy in my release from responsibility, anxiety and suspense." It might justly be said that Harriet Martineau took to her bed a doubting Unitarian, and rose up a believing atheist: "A large portion of the transition from religious inconsistency and irrationality to freethinking strength and liberty was gone over during that period."[108] Here is yet another Victorian paradox: Martineau found a necessary emotional fulfillment in the passionate rationality of mesmerism and the philosophy of necessity that she could not find in the too-reasonable dogma of Unitarian faith.

The agent of Martineau's salvation, her miraculous cure by the powers of mesmerism, was young Henry George Atkinson, an intellectual gadfly and amateur mesmerist of considerable seductive charms (apparently of a Platonic nature) for older women.[109] Though the voluminous letters Atkinson left behind (and Martineau herself sent him over 1000) have condemned him to posterity as "a bore of the first quality," many of Atkinson's contemporaries were charmed: "The noblest man I have ever known," pronounced Dr. Samuel Brown; "Powerful and sagacious," concurred Margaret Fuller.[110] Closer to this Victorian circle, Atkinson claimed a long friendship with Charles Bray: "For more than twenty years I corresponded with Mr. H. G. Atkinson. . . . He was very fond of writing, I suppose, as I generally received two or three letters a month," Bray comments.[111] Lest we think that Bray did not take this deluge of correspondence seriously, I point out that he quotes extensively from these letters in his autobiography, and prints a great many of them in full in a lengthy appendix devoted entirely to that purpose in *On Force.*

"The firm of Atkinson and Martineau" (as Eliot dubbed them) came to call on George Eliot in March 1852, a year after the publication of the *Letters*: "I can't help liking him," Eliot confessed of Atkinson on June 5; again, two months later: "pleasant and intelligent and one can't help liking him." George Eliot claims Atkinson an "agreeable addition" to her visit at Martineau's Ambleside home in October 1852; "I am quite straight with good, clear-eyed Mr. Atkinson," she avows in July 1853.[112]

But Unitarian brother Reverend James Martineau was less favorably impressed: "Harriet's exceptional submission to an inferior was mortifying to me. It seemed a kind of fascination—part of the contemporaneous disturbance of judgment which . . . was conspicuous in her reports of mesmeric phenomena."[113] For Atkinson had raised Harriet Martineau from her Unitarian bed of pain by the powers of mesmerism. Preliminary reports in a series of "Letters on Mesmerism" from Martineau to the *Athenaeum* in November and December of 1844 prepared the way for the public outrage that would greet the more extensive *Letters on the Laws of Man's Nature and Development* in 1851. "The explicit announcement, by the most influential woman-writer of her day, that she had abandoned the whole religious system in which she had been educated . . . was a portentous thing in English life," writes J. M. Robertson in the *History of Freethought in the Nineteenth Century.*[114]

Harriet Martineau abandoned Unitarianism to make way for a new faith. She wrote ecstatically to the *Athenaeum*: "If I had been a very pious and very ignorant catholic, I could not have escaped the persuasion that I had seen heavenly visions.

Every glorified object before my open eyes would have been a revelation; and my Mesmerist, with the white halo round her head . . . would have been a saint or angel." But Martineau's emotional response deifies Reason, not God: "Such a state of repose, of calm, translucent intellectuality, I had never conceived of." Or to put it another way: Martineau was converted to Reason by the powers of Intuition: "It is a deep philosophic truth . . . that simple faith is as necessary to the perception of truth as sound reason."[115]

Many of Martineau's previous admirers were aghast; the editor of the *Athenaeum* himself offered "A Few Words by Way of Comment on Miss Martineau's Statement" on 28 December 1844, repudiating what he called "the prevailing humbug of the hour," lest any of his readers think his journal supported all that it printed.[116] But other Victorians were intrigued: Martineau writes that Robert Chambers, for example, came to call on her at Tynemouth to investigate her mesmeric recovery.[117] And just four months after the infamous letters were published in the *Athenaeum*, the Brays and George Eliot first met the new convert at a dinner party: "M. A. [Marian] and I both felt that we admire Miss M[artineau] much more for having seen her. C[harles] was disappointed with her small ordinary-looking woman's head. . . . Her conversation is delightful. . . . She talked much with me about her brother James . . . and of course very much about mesmerism," Cara Bray wrote to Sara Sophia Hennell.[118] George Eliot described the same party to Martha Jackson: "She is a charming person—quite one of those great people whom one does not venerate the less for having seen. Full of mesmerism and its marvels, you may suppose."[119]

There is no record of any further acquaintance between Martineau and George Eliot for the next six years. Significantly, the "considerable intimacy" that John Walter Cross claims between the two women did not begin until Martineau again came to Eliot's attention, as the author of the notorious *Letters on the Laws of Man's Nature and Development*.[120] As fledgling assistant to John Chapman, editor of the *Westminster Review*,

Eliot naturally took an interest in his other publishing ventures: "Miss Martineau's book is come out, but there was not
so great a sale the first day as was anticipated," she writes to
the Brays on 28 January 1851.[121] Conservative Henry Crab Robinson reported in his journal of March 1851 that Eliot "spoke
of Harriet Martineau's and Atkinson's letters as studiously offensive. It seems as if this book is absolutely atheistic!"[122] But
that August the more freethinking George Combe was to begin
his friendship with George Eliot on the note of her "instinctive
soundness of judgment" on the phrenology of the *Letters*.[123]
And Eliot recognized the favorable audience the book would
receive at Rosehill, asking Chapman to send Charles Bray a
copy in October 1851 and recommending it for his review in
the *Coventry Herald*.[124]

The following spring George Eliot's friendship with Harriet
Martineau blossomed, and if Eliot did have reservations about
the *Letters*, she must also have been in fundamental sympathy
with Martineau's cause, at a time when so many of the mesmeric advocate's old friends were closing their doors. The admiration was mutual. Martineau entrusted Eliot with her fund
for Comte's publication. Eliot writes: "She is a *trump*—the only
English woman that possesses thoroughly the art of writing."[125]

The next fall George Eliot made an extended visit to the
north to spend time with both the Combes at Edinburgh and
Martineau at Ambleside. Martineau's "simple, energetic life"
proved a "tonic" to the urban fatigue of the *Westminster*'s assistant editor. She described her arrival at the Lake Country
retreat in glowing terms: "The coach brought me to Miss Martineau's gate at ½ past six yesterday evening and she was there
with a beaming face to welcome me. . . . Miss M. is quite
charming in her own home—quite handsome from her ani-
mation and intelligence. She came behind me, put her hands
round me and kissed me in the prettiest way this evening."[126]

This fond sisterhood ceased abruptly when Eliot eloped to
Germany with Lewes in 1854. Harriet Martineau, like many of
Eliot's acquaintances, was overwhelmed with moral indigna-
tion, and not above some rather vicious rumor-mongering at

Eliot's expense.[127] Clearly, Martineau's heterodoxy did not extend beyond the intellectual realm; nor was she willing to repay Eliot's tolerance in kind. Nonetheless, George Eliot writes to John Chapman in 1856 with what she realizes as an "odd request" (in light of their publicly broken friendship) that upon Martineau's death—which Harriet herself was incorrectly advertising as imminent at that time—"I should like to write an article upon her. I need hardly say that mine would be an admiring appreciation of her."[128]

There were many, after 1851, whose response to Harriet Martineau was a far cry from admiring appreciation. Martineau's heretical intellectual crimes were as shocking to proper Victorians as George Eliot's sexual transgressions would prove to be. Martineau was prepared for the worst when she published the jointly-authored *Letters*: "I anticipated excommunication from the world of literature, if not from society." However divergent their *mores*, one can see clearly the basis for George Eliot's admiration of this fellow strong-minded woman: "This book is, I believe, the greatest effort of courage, I ever made," Martineau wrote in her *Autobiography*.[129] This was not hyperbole.

George Henry Lewes opened his "Literature" column in the *Leader* of 22 February 1851 with the announcement of his intention to review this controversial book in the next issue: "Perhaps of all the new books we hear seriously discussed, just now, the *Letters* . . . is the most prominent. People seem uneasy—when they are not alarmed—at it; and this is explicable." Lewes admitted that he himself was made uneasy by the book's "atheism," but applauded Martineau's bold expression of her convictions: "What has reputation to do with truth?" "We hope next week to treat it with the gravity it deserves," he concludes, before going on to his review of Herbert Spencer's *Social Statics* in that same issue.[130] I wish to reserve my discussion of Lewes's subsequent review until the next chapter, for the light I believe it sheds on Lewes himself six months prior to his first meeting with George Eliot. But let me touch here upon other contemporary response, to substantiate the serious and uneasy manner in which the *Letters* was read.

Although the conflict between Judeo-Christian orthodoxy and the new science is incipient in Combe or Bray, Harriet Martineau was the first member of this Victorian circle brazenly and unequivocally to assert that God was dead: "Uninformed and misdirected, we personify, humanize, materialize, the object of this sense [of infinite and abstract power]."[131] "After the publication of the 'Atkinson letters,' " Martineau writes somewhat acerbically, "anonymous notes came in elegant clerical handwriting, informing me that prayers would be offered up throughout the kingdom, for my rescue from my awful condition."[132] Martineau's friend Charlotte Bronte's response was typical: "It is the first exposition of avowed atheism and materialism I have ever read; the first unequivocal declaration of disbelief in the existence of a God . . . I have ever seen. . . . The strangest thing is, that we are called on to rejoice over this helpless blank . . . to welcome this unutterable desolation as a state of pleasant freedom."[133] Reviewers in the popular press could be considerably more hostile. John Eagles fumed in *Blackwood's*:

> Miss Martineau's atheistical publication has passed through my hands. It professes to be a joint work by herself and a Mr. Atkinson, one of the clique of infidel phrenological mesmerizers; but it is manifestly the doing of Miss Martineau herself. . . . The female atheist ("and here the female atheist talks you dead") must have manufactured and cooked most of his philosophy. . . . A work more thoroughly degrading to character, whether moral or intellectual, has never come from the press.[134]

Even the *Westminster Review* had difficulty in living up to its usual freethinking standards, as W. R. Hickson, in a lengthy essay entitled "Life and Immortality," struggled painfully at the upper limits of his liberal sensibility: "Mr. Atkinson belongs to a class of writers of whom we wish to speak with respect, from the moral courage they evince in giving expression to an opinion which they know exposes them to obloquy. We differ with them, but would rather be supposed to hold the same views, than join in an outcry against any form of ultra skepticism."[135]

Charles Bray's enthusiastic response to the *Letters* is striking, because it differs markedly from others, in its emphasis on the psychological rather than the theological aspects of the book: "I consider this work the most valuable contribution towards Psychology based on Physiology which we have had since Gall and Spurzheim's works on Cerebral Physiology, or Phrenology," he writes in *On Force* (going on to quote liberally from the *Letters* throughout that book).[136] Bray found in Martineau an ardent fellow-convert to phrenology; indeed, she was among the first of the phrenological faithful. As early as 1832, she records talks with the Combes about phrenology and education. She had phrenological casts of her head taken in 1833 and 1853, and bequeathed her skull and brain "to the ablest phrenologist I know of."[137] In her *Autobiography* Martineau recounts at amusing length the comedy of errors she experienced during an anonymous head-reading by two eminent professionals: one concluded that her problem was "constant failure through timidity"; the other "pronounced my genius to be for millinery"! But Martineau, like other phrenological intellectuals, drew a careful distinction between popular practice and scientific theory: "The proceedings of the fortune-telling oracles, are no more like those of true and philosophical students of the brain than the shows of itinerant chemical lecturers . . . are like the achievements of a Davy or a Faraday."[138]

Interestingly (and somewhat inconsistently, due to their obvious interrelationship), reviewers of the *Letters* took less umbrage at the book's physiological psychology than they did at its religious heterodoxy. The anonymous author of a lengthy review article in the *Westminster*, after condemning the "absolute predestination" of the authors' philosophy of necessity, went on to praise its chapters on the brain: "Since the discoveries of Gall, physiologists have for the most part abused and misrepresented phrenology; but they have been compelled to

admit its truth, at least so far as the broad principle that different parts of the brain have different functions to fulfill."[139]
Even such an unsympathetic reader as James Anthony Froude
praised the discussion of phreno-mesmerism as "the really important part of the book."[140]

As with other Victorians in this circle, phrenology was but
one thread in a matrix of interrelated beliefs. The book begins
with Martineau's claim that she is a true Baconian in her application of scientific method to psychology: "My wonder is,—
not that there are few so-called Mental philosophers who use
or even advocate any experimental method of inquiry into the
science of mind; but that there seem to me to be none."[141] The
tenets of Mill's universal causality are quite at home in Atkinson and Martineau. "The whole aim of science is a search
into . . . those general laws which link the phenomenon together in the eternal and universal chain of existence and the
uniform rule," Atkinson wrote to Charles Bray.[142] A passage
from the *Logic* is presented between quotations from Bacon
and Newton: "I do not believe that there is now one object or
event in all our experience of nature . . . which has not . . .
been ascertained by direct observation to follow laws of its
own."[143] These general laws are operative in all branches of
knowledge. Independently of Comte, Atkinson and Martineau
argue for the interconnectedness of the sciences and their hier-
archical structure: "Chemistry, Geology, Astronomy, Optics
&c., are now freed from superstition, and have become true sciences. It remains for philosophers to place Physiology and
Mental and Moral Philosophy in the same position as positive
science reached by induction."[144] The grounds for Martineau's
later rapturous discovery of the *Cours* are readily apparent in
her *Letters*.

A direct link can be traced between universal causality,
phrenological tenets, and the seeds of an evolutionary biology:

> Man has his place in natural history . . . his nature does not dif-
> fer essentially from that of the lower animals . . . he is but a
> fuller development and varied condition of the same fundamental
> nature or cause. . . . Mind is the consequence or product of the

material man, its existence depending on the action of the brain. Mental Philosophy is, therefore, the *physiology of the brain*, as Gall termed it. Spurzheim called it Phrenology.[145]

Man's place in the natural world makes him part of a continually evolving cosmos: "Nature never rests; but all is action, change and growth." The phrenologist does not limit himself to pure physiology; mind is shaped by the external world. Both environment and heredity determine the development of the individual:

> The true physiologist studies the laws of matter, and the whole process of development, disentangling himself from all spiritual and metaphysical dogma, and will take into consideration all the circumstances which influence the man from childhood to the grave. He will observe the conditions of the parents before the child is born, or even conceived; and back through many generations, noting these conditions which more particularly descend, and are impressed on the constitution. . . . After the child is born, he will watch the treatment of the infant, and the gradual development of its instincts and powers. . . . He will note how the child is trained to good or evil how its passions are stimulated and directed.[146]

What are the moral implications of this disentanglement from spiritual and metaphysical dogma, the psychologist as natural historian? Initially, Atkinson's and Martineau's liberated view of moral man seems to substantiate their critics' worst fears: "As a part of Nature, as a creature of necessity, as governed by law, Man is . . . neither good nor evil . . . but simply nature, and what is possible to nature, and could not be otherwise."[147] They have two solutions to this potentially enervating fatalism: one borrows from a heritage of eighteenth-century rationalism; the other is distinctly nineteenth century. First, this pair offer the familiar argument that it is paradoxically because of universal causality in the realm of mind that man can improve his fatalistic lot. He has the intellectual power to reason his way to an altered future: "Without determining laws there could be no hope, and no regenerating principle; and all teaching, preaching, and training would be useless."[148]

But Atkinson and Martineau were more than mere necessitarians; they appeared to many to be full-fledged materialists. In an essay on Joseph Priestley, T. H. Huxley drew a witty distinction between the epithet "necessitarian" and the far graver calumny, "materialist":

> A man may be a necessarian without incurring graver reproach than that in being called a gloomy fanatic, necessarianism, though very shocking, having a note of Calvinistic orthodoxy; but, if a man is a materialist; or, if good authorities say he is . . . respectable folks look upon him as an unsafe neighbour of a cashbox, as an actual or potential sensualist, the more virtuous in outward seeming, the more certainly loaded with secret "grave personal sins."[149]

James Anthony Froude unequivocally entitled his condemnatory essay "Materialism: Miss Martineau and Mr. Atkinson." Other reviewers concurred in a literal-minded application of the concept. The *Westminster* reviewer writes: "Here we have two clever, well-informed people, persuading themselves that they experience extraordinary raptures mingled with the most exquisite philosophic calm, from believing that unconscious matter is the cause of conscious thought, that the truest human affection is nothing worthier than the love of a spoonful of nitric acid for a copper penny. . . . From such views both the intellect and the heart of man recoil with well-founded disgust."[150] Even Charles Bray, recounting his friendship with Atkinson, takes care to differentiate himself (as a mere "necessarian") from the more dreaded denomination: "We had some fundamental agreements, as he was a Phrenologist and Mesmerist, and so was I, but I leaned towards Idealism, and he decidedly towards Materialism."[151]

A careful reading of the *Letters*, however, reveals that Atkinson and Martineau themselves emphatically deny these charges. "Men's minds are so beset with 'gross materialism,' with their concrete and mechanical notions, that they shrink from the obscure, imponderable agents, and the study of vital action, and the real powers of nature."[152] Mesmerism, not rationalism, is ultimately the key to Atkinson's and Martineau's optimism, the primary source of their cheerful liberation from the darker moral implications of materialism.

To give them their due, even the unsympathetic critics recognized in Atkinson and Martineau something beyond the reductionistic tenets of atheistic "materialism." "In spite of all that we have said," confesses Froude, "there is a tone in Mr. Atkinson's thoughts far above those of most of us who live in slavery to daily experience. The world is awful to him—truth is sacred."[153] W. R. Hickson quotes a lengthy passage of Atkinson's autobiographical reminiscence from the *Letters*, in which Atkinson sits "on the marble rocks of Devonshire," looking out upon the landscape and imagining his own inevitable transformation into the earth: "Nature is one, and all things varieties of the same material."[154] Yet Hickson recognizes that this "material" is in some very important way *not* equivalent to "materialism": "These reflections . . . carry us far beyond the bounded views implied in the proposition with which he sets out, of mind being a product of the brain. We now learn, that the brain is but one of the forms or manifestations of an infinite being,—a being,—the essence of all substance,—working throughout nature by general laws."[155]

Truth is to be found neither (or rather, not entirely) in idealist imaginings nor in materialist experiments: "Mind was fashioned into fanciful forms by the metaphysicians, while the physiologists were, on the other hand, slicing up the brain as they would a turnip"[156] Atkinson and Martineau do deny that the spiritual is opposed to or separable from the material. But if there is no spirit apart from matter, there is, equally, no matter apart from spirit. Like Charles Bray, Atkinson and Martineau found in the combination of phrenology with mesmerism what they considered the perfect synthesis: a science that is also a religion; an empirical explanation for the realm of intuitive truths; the union of positivist law with phenomena beyond the ordinary powers of the senses.

The scientific inadequacies of this solution must not blind

us to its ideological significance for a Victorian frame of mind. "Christ, the prophets, the oracles, all exhibit features of the same great fact,—the existence of faculties in Man beyond sense, experience, and reason," assert Atkinson and Martineau. And they mean "faculties" in the most literal phrenological sense: "Beneath the central organ of Comparison, lying under Benevolence, is what has been termed by a somnambule the Eye of the Mind. This seems to be power of judgment:—we might call it the Intuitive faculty; for it is this which is chiefly concerned in *clairvoyance*." *Clairvoyance* is that state of mystical insight reached in a mesmeric trance: "All time seems to be as one duration; space seems as nothing; all passions and desires become hushed; truth becomes an insight, or *through sight*; and life a law." The mesmerist transcends traditional definitions of empiricism: "Rejecting the dogmas of metaphysicians, and disbelieving that Ideas are the relics of Sensations"; yet his insight comes through the "energy of the senses" in the form of a "higher sense,—of divination." Only in the mesmeric state, believes Harriet Martineau, can man experience a direct apprehension of that monistic, cosmic force that is hidden from the eye of sense: "Nothing in the experience of my life can at all compare with that of seeing the melting away of forms, aspects and arrangements under which we ordinarily view nature, and its fusion into the system of forces which is presented to the intellect in the magnetic state."[157] It is not necessary to belabor the point that what Martineau is describing seems to be a religious experience. I will simply reiterate that mesmerism, for Atkinson and Martineau, was intended to be a fully scientific phenomenon. Not only is intuition, or instinct, a phrenological organ, it is also the product of evolutionary biology. Atkinson queries Bray: "What we call inspiration, or intuition, or genius . . . are all to be reduced to a general and uniform law. It is clear that many of the lower animals . . . are so guided, as we may be, by instinct. . . . is it hard to suppose that more highly-developed man should under all circumstances be wholly free from such so-called instinct?"[158]

This visionary "fusion" experienced during the mesmeric trance becomes a perfect metaphor for that monistic conception of the universe after which all of these Victorians strive: "Thus we draw the circle of facts closer and closer to the centre, which is Unity," conclude Atkinson and Martineau. This pair become fully representative not only in their striving for that visionary moment of Unity—or even in their achievement of that moment—but also in their refusal to take that achievement as an end in itself. They continue: "While we dilate the sight in the sense of the unity of Nature, and the relations of the sciences, we must not forget to contract the sight to every particular and circumstance; that nothing may be omitted, and Nature may be searched for truth."[159] Man must look outward as well as inward, to the particular as well as to the general; the key to the cosmos lies in the smallest scientific detail as well as in the visionary religious synthesis.

In mesmerism Bray and Martineau both found satisfying personal solutions to their need for a faith consistent with a scientific world view. Although mesmerism had much to offer as a new religion, it was unfortunately less successful in correctly accounting for scientific detail. It was in another guise altogether that this circle would most accurately find the one in the many: the development hypothesis. We have seen how the groundwork for an evolutionary cosmology was laid by Robert Chambers. George Henry Lewes and Herbert Spencer would give it a substantive incarnation, with particular significance for the history of psychology.

1. Charles Darwin, *Darwin on Man*, transcribed and annotated by Paul H. Barrett, ed. Howard E. Gruber (New York, 1974), pp. 280, 278, 279. Edward Manier writes that "it is likely that Darwin had information about Comte's views beyond that he obtained from Brewster's 1838 review" (*The Young Darwin and His Cultural Circle* [Boston, 1978], p. 40).

2. See Howard Gruber, "A Psychological Study of Scientific Creativity," in Darwin, *Darwin on Man*, pp. 3-257. "From all these documents we can conclude that Darwin first worked out a thoroughgoing materialist approach to the evolution of mind and brain, man included. . . . In writing the *Origin*, however, he withdrew to

a more cautious position, making only the briefest allusions to higher mental processes" (p. 31). "In the M and N notebooks we see Darwin's growing awareness that his evolutionary theorizing opened the way for a thoroughgoing materialism, with all its painful consequences" (p. 180).

In a recent essay, Robert J. Richards argues that Darwin did not publish the ideas in these early notebooks, not because he "feared suspicions of materialism," but rather because he had "several conceptual obstacles . . . to overcome if his theory of evolution by natural selection were to be made scientifically acceptable" ("Instinct and Intelligence in British Natural Theology: Some Contributions to Darwin's Theory of Evolution of Behavior," *Journal of the History of Biology* 14 [1981]:229).

3. James Anthony Froude, quoted in Waldo Hilary Dunn, *James Anthony Froude: A Biography* (Oxford, 1961), 1:148.

4. George Eliot to Sara Sophia Hennell, *George Eliot Letters*, 1:280.

5. George Eliot, review of *The Nemesis of Faith, Coventry Herald*, 16 March 1849, quoted in Haight, *George Eliot: A Biography*, p. 68.

6. Bray, *Phases of Opinion*, pp. 77, 75; Haight, *George Eliot: A Biography*, p. 69. Froude was one of nine (including Dickens, Thackeray, Tennyson, Ruskin, and Mrs. Carlyle) to whom the new novelist George Eliot sent copies of *Scenes of Clerical Life* (*George Eliot Letters*, 2:418); and likewise, *Adam Bede* (*George Eliot Letters*, 3:6). Froude contributed frequently to the *Westminster* under Eliot's editorship. Their admiration was mutual: *Adam Bede* "gave no pleasure, it gave a palpitation of the heart," writes Froude; "That was not pleasure; but it was passionate interest" (quoted in Haight, *George Eliot: A Biography*, p. 275).

7. James Anthony Froude, *The Nemesis of Faith*, 2d ed. (London, 1849), pp. 91, 134, 92.

8. James Anthony Froude, "Materialism: Miss Martineau and Mr. Atkinson," *Fraser's* 43 (1851):430. Froude's biographer writes: "He had thrown off hindering speculations . . . and had chosen a positive faith. . . . Henceforth his progress was straightforward and rapid. Within nine years he had established himself as a distinguished historian" (Dunn, *Froude*, 1:141).

9. Martineau, *Autobiography*, 1:111, 116.

10. Bray, *Phases of Opinion*, pp. 199, 197–98.

11. George Eliot, *Adam Bede*, quoted in Bray, *Phases of Opinion*, p. 199.

12. Edward Francis Mineka, *The Dissidence of Dissent* (Chapel Hill, 1944), p. 235.

13. In his *History of English Rationalism*, Benn emphasizes "the action of Unitarianism as a rationalistic ferment" (1:397); the "Unitarian spirit is more than a transition point, it is a leaven" (2:62–63). See Willey's *Nineteenth Century Studies*, pp. 207–20 for the best discussion of Eliot's conversion from Evangelicalism to rationalism.

14. Joseph Priestley, *The Doctrine of Philosophical Necessity Illustrated* (London, 1777), p. xvi. Benn writes: "Under the guidance of Priestley Unitarianism became associated with determinism in morals and with empiricism in psychology" (*History of Rationalism*, 2:67).

15. R. H. Brabant and Thomas Moore, "The State of Protestantism in Germany," *Edinburgh Review* 54 (1831):247. Moore wrote to Brabant: "Your excellent exposition on Rationalism . . . is the best part" of the essay (quoted in W. M. W. Call, "George Eliot, Her Life and Writings," *Westminster Review* 116 [1881]:160 n).

16. George Eliot, "Influence of Rationalism," *Fortnightly Review* 1 (1865), in Pinney, p. 413.

17. Martineau, *Autobiography*, 1:104. Martineau paid fictional tribute to Priestley: "In 'Briery Creek' I indulged my lifelong sentiment, of admiration and love of Dr. Priestley, by making him, under a thin disguise, the hero of my tale" (*Autobiography*, 1:254).

18. Leslie Stephen, *History of English Thought in the Eighteenth Century* (1876; rpt. New York, 1962), 1:55, 365.

19. Joseph Priestley, *Disquisitions Relating to Matter and Spirit*, 2d ed., Improved and Enlarged (London, 1782), pp. xxiii, iv, 44, v, 151-52.

20. Martineau, *Autobiography*, 1:36-37.

21. Peel, *Herbert Spencer*, p. 109.

22. James Simpson, quoted in deGuistino, *Conquest of Mind*, p. 87; Bray, *Philosophy of Necessity*, p. vi.

23. George Eliot to Mrs. Abijah Hill Pears, *George Eliot Letters*, 1:125.

24. George Combe, autobiographical fragment, in Gibbon, *Life*, 1:39.

25. Priestley, *Philosophy of Necessity*, pp. 149-65, 154, 99.

26. Priestley, *Philosophy of Necessity*, pp. 36, 86, 110, 112.

27. George Eliot, "Literature," *Leader*, 13 May 1854, p. 447 (see Haight, *George Eliot Letters*, 2:150 n for Eliot's authorship).

28. Priestley, *Philosophy of Necessity*, p. 109.

29. In her *Autobiography* Martineau criticizes the intellectually dishonest compromises of Unitarianism: "a mere clinging, from association and habit, to the old privilege of faith in a divine revelation, under an actual forfeiture of all its essential conditions" (1:40). This position was shared by the Coventry circle. Bray's sister-in-law, Sara Sophia Hennell, writes: "However agreeable the panacea that Unitarianism affords, and even temporarily beneficial, as a reactionary solace, a cordial tonic to restore the healthy cheerfulness after Calvinist gloom, the doctrine furnishes no satisfactory resting-place for a consistently thoughtful mind" ("Essay on the Sceptical Tendency of Butler's 'Analogy' " [London, 1859], p. 13).

30. George Combe Journal, *George Eliot Letters*, 8:27-28.

31. Mary Sibree, quoted in John Walter Cross, *Life of George Eliot* (1885; rpt. London, 1908), 1:118.

32. Cross, *Life of George Eliot*, 1:84-85.

33. Bray, *Phases of Opinion*, p. 70.

34. Eliot, quoted in Cross, *Life of George Eliot*, 1:118.

35. George Eliot to Charles Bray, *George Eliot Letters*, 2:37.

36. George Eliot to Mrs. Charles Bray, *George Eliot Letters*, 2:119. Spencer visited Rosehill from 16-22 October 1853. He also notes visits in 1852 (*Autobiography*, 2:471), 1853 (1:504), and 1856 (2:567). In 1886 he invited Cara Bray and Sara Sophia Hennell to join him at upper Norwood (2:483). See also, Haight, *George Eliot Letters*, 2:256 n.

37. George Eliot to Charles Bray, *George Eliot Letters*, 2:82; Charles Bray to George Combe, *George Eliot Letters*, 8:128.

38. Bray, *Phases of Opinion*, p. 73.

39. George Eliot to John Chapman, *George Eliot Letters*, 2:48-49; George Eliot to Charles Bray, *George Eliot Letters*, 2:403.

40. George Eliot to Charles Bray, *George Eliot Letters*, 1:265-66.

41. Bray, *Philosophy of Necessity*, 1:vi; 1:255; 1:206.

42. Shelley, "Queen Mab," quoted in Bray, *Philosophy of Necessity*, 1:238-39.

43. Bray, *Philosophy of Necessity*, 1:113.

44. Thomas Carlyle, *Sartor Resartus*, quoted in Bray, *Philosophy of Necessity*, 1:114. In his autobiography Bray compares his own youthful religious conflicts to Carlyle's (*Phases of Opinion*, p. 16). He made a phrenological reading of his mentor based on a photograph (pp. 26-27), and quotes Carlyle at several points (see pp. 157, 191, 199).

45. Bray, *Philosophy of Necessity*, 1:114.

46. Mill, *Earlier Letters*, in *Collected Works*, 13:569. George Levine's excellent essay, "Determinism and Responsibility in the Works of George Eliot" (*PMLA* 77 [268-279]) compares Eliot's fictional application of determinism and free-will with Mill's treatment of the subject in this chapter of the *Logic*. I note that by the time Eliot read Mill, she was already familiar with Bray's very similar position.

47. Mill, *Logic*, in *Collected Works*, 8:836.

48. Bray, *Philosophy of Necessity*, 1:6.

49. Mill, *Logic*, in *Collected Works*, 8:837.

50. Bray, *Philosophy of Necessity*, 1:175; 1:276.

51. Mill, *Logic*, in *Collected Works*, 8:840. By the second edition of the *Philosophy of Necessity* (1863), Bray had read the *Logic* and had altered his discussion to suggest strong echoes of Mill, differentiating between "necessity" and "fatalism": "The fatalist believes that everything is written in the book of fate. . . . On the other hand, the necessarian believes that for every effect there is a cause" (*Philosophy of Necessity*, 2d ed., p. 419).

52. Bray, *Philosophy of Necessity*, 1:171.

53. Mill, *Logic*, 8:841.

54. Comte, *Cours*, in Lenzer, pp. 214, 137.

55. Bray, *Phases of Opinion*, p. 93.

56. Bray, *Philosophy of Necessity*, 1:151.

57. Locke, *Essay Concerning Human Understanding*, p. 26.

58. Bray quotes Locke: "In this lies the liberty that a man has. He has the power to suspend the execution of this or that desire" (*Philosophy of Necessity*, 1:171); see also 1:95-96, 97, 99, 100, 104, 171, 215 for references to Locke. See Locke's *Essay*, pp. 237 ff., "Liberty and Necessity," for a pertinent discussion of necessitarianism. Joseph Priestley was also strongly influenced by Locke, and it is often difficult to separate Priestley's influence on Bray from Locke's. For example: Locke writes, "Voluntary then is not opposed to Necessary; but to Involuntary" (*Essay*, p. 239); Priestley, "Voluntary is not opposed to *necessary*, but only to *involuntary*, and that nothing can be opposed to necessary, but contingent" (*Philosophical Necessity*, p. 15); Bray, "True necessity is not opposed to that which is voluntary, but to that which is contingent" (*Philosophy of Necessity*, 1:170). Priestley does not acknowledge Locke as his source; nor does Bray mention either Locke or Priestley.

59. Mineka, *Dissidence of Dissent*, p. 13. Mill writes in his *Autobiography* that he read Locke's *Essay* around 1822, "and wrote out an account of it, consisting of a complete abstract of every chapter, with such remarks as occurred to me: which was read by, or (I think) to, my father, and discussed throughout" (p. 43).

60. Locke, *Essay*, p. 43.

61. Bray, *Philosophy of Necessity*, 1:97.

62. Bray, *Philosophy of Necessity*, 1:69; 1:266.

63. Mill, *Auguste Comte*, p. 66.

64. Bray, *Phases of Opinion*, p. 21.

65. Lewes, *Biographical History*, p. 754.

66. Bray, *Philosophy of Necessity*, 1:152.

67. Bray, *Philosophy of Necessity*, 1:104-5; 2d ed., p. 87.

68. Bray, *On Force*, p. 33.

69. Priestley, *Matter and Spirit*, pp. iv, v.

70. Bray, *Phases of Opinion*, p. 98 (summarizing his arguments in *On Force*).

71. Edward L. Youmans, "Introduction," *The Correlation and Conservation of Forces: A Series of Expositions* (New York, 1865), p. xxix.

72. William Baker, *The George Eliot-George Henry Lewes Library*, p. 82.

73. George Eliot, *George Eliot's 'Middlemarch' Notebooks*, ed. John Clark Pratt and Victor A. Neufeldt (Berkeley, 1979), p. 128.

74. W. R. Grove, *The Correlation of Physical Forces*, in *The Correlation and Conservation of Forces*, in Youmans, p. 172.

75. Bray, *Phases of Opinion*, p. 97.

76. W. B. Carpenter, *On the Correlation of the Physical and Vital Forces*, in Youmans, p. 406: see Hearnshaw, *Short History of British Psychology*, p. 20.

77. Bray, *Phases of Opinion*, p. 256.

78. Bray, *On Force*, pp. 3, 73; *Phases of Opinion*, pp. 257, 254; *On Force*, p. 49; *Philosophy of Necessity*, quoted in *On Force*, p. 66.

79. Bray, *On Force*, p. 51.

80. J. C. Prichard, *Review of the Doctrine of the Vital Principle*, quoted in June Goodfield-Toulmin, "Some Aspects of English Physiology: 1780–1840," *Journal of the History of Biology* 2 (1969):295.

81. Samuel Taylor Coleridge, "Essays on the Principles of Method," Section the Second, Essay 5, in *The Friend*, ed. Barbara E. Rooke (Princeton, 1969), 1:462.

82. Hinton, "Physiological Riddles," pp. 429, 428. See Bray, *Phases of Opinion*, p. 98.

83. Youmans, "Introduction," *Correlation*, p. xli.

84. Bray, *Phases of Opinion*, pp. 102-3.

85. Martineau and Atkinson, *Letters*, p. 257.

86. Bray, *On Force*, pp. 141-42.

87. Franz Anton Mesmer, *Mémoire*, summarized in Kaplan, "'The Mesmeric Mania,'" p. 692.

88. Fred Kaplan, *Dickens and Mesmerism* (Princeton, 1975), p. 232.

89. Bray, *Phases of Opinion*, p. 107.

90. Bray, *On Force*, p. 103.

91. Mrs. Charles Bray to Mrs. Charles Christian Hennell, *George Eliot Letters*, 1:180.

92. George Eliot to John Sibree, Jr., *George Eliot Letters*, 1:225 (note the future novelist's shift to *language* as the medium of communication); George Eliot to Mr. and Mrs. Charles Bray, *George Eliot Letters*, 1:302.

93. George Eliot, "Notebook of an Eccentric," *Coventry Herald* (1846–47), in Pinney, p. 15. This "unenviable" hero is the prototype for the miserable *clairvoyant* Latimer, in the later story "The Lifted Veil" (1859).

94. George Eliot to George Combe, *George Eliot Letters*, 8:45.

95. George Eliot to Sara Sophia Hennell, *George Eliot Letters*, 2:267.

96. George Henry Lewes, "A Mesmeric Quack," *Saturday Review*, 2 February 1856, p. 263.

97. "Electro-Biology," *Westminster Review* 55 (1851):321. "The Mesmeric Mania of 1851" is the title of a pamphlet by J. H. Bennett (see Hearnshaw, *Short History*, p. 15).

98. T. H. Huxley, "Science," *Westminster Review* 61 (1854):266.

99. W. B. Carpenter, "Electro-Biology and Mesmerism," *Quarterly Review* 93 (1853):501–57. See especially pages 510, 532, 535.

100. George Eliot to Charles Bray, *George Eliot Letters*, 2:121; see also George Eliot to Sara Sophia Hennell, *George Eliot Letters*, 2:126.

101. See Kaplan, "Mesmeric Mania," 697. In "The Lifted Veil" Eliot depicts the characteristic juxtaposition of phrenology, education, and electrobiology in her hero, Latimer: " 'The deficiency is there, sir,—there; and here;' he added, touching the upper sides of my head,—'here is the excess. That must be brought out, sir, and this must be laid to sleep.' . . . natural history, science, and the modern languages were the appliances by which the defects in my organization were to be remedied. . . . I was to be plentifully crammed with the mechanical powers; the elementary bodies, and the phenomena of electricity and magnetism" (1859; rpt. *Complete Works*, St. James Edition [London, 1908] 1:372–73.

102. Bray, *Philosophy of Necessity*, 1:142.

103. Martineau and Atkinson, *Letters*, p. 65. See Terry M. Parssinen, "Mesmeric Performers," *Victorian Studies* 21 (1977–78):87–104. Phrenology was "an essential prelude to mesmerism" (91).

104. Martineau and Atkinson, *Letters*, p. 34.

105. W. R. Grove, "Mesmerism," *Blackwood's* 57 (1845):219.

106. John Eagles, "What Is Mesmerism?" *Blackwood's* 70 (1851):72.

107. Thomas Carlyle, quoted in Vera Wheatley, *Life and Work of Harriet Martineau* (London, 1957), p. 202. See Wheatley, *Life and Work*, p. 337, on Dickens and Martineau. Martineau quotes her own baby-talk in *Autobiography*, 1:12.

R. W. Webb's *Harriet Martineau: A Victorian Radical* (New York, 1960) places Martineau within the rich intellectual background of early Victorian England (including the Unitarian tradition and the influence of Priestley and Hartley). Though Webb quickly dismisses the "fourth or fifth-rate philosophizing" of the *Letters* (p. 21), calling it "one of the strangest books to carry the name of a reputable writer" (p. 293), he recognizes its centrality for Martineau's intellectual development: "Anti-clericalism, scientific method, materialism, necessitarianism, radicalism, education, humanity, and martyrdom—every major concern of Harriet Martineau's life was caught up in this new crusade" (p. 253). Valerie Kossew Pichanick's more recent *Harriet Martineau* (Ann Arbor, 1980) dismisses the *Letters* as "not intrinsically important. It does not deserve a special place in the hierarchy of Victorian literature of philosophy. It is long-winded, often illogical, and sometimes even arrant nonsense" (p. 187).

108. Martineau, *Autobiography*, 1:146, 182. Was Martineau's illness psychosomatic? She did, in fact, have an ovarian cyst, which finally killed her (see Webb, p. 194; Pichanick, p. 13).

109. Webb speculates that Atkinson was homosexual, in light of frequent mysterious trips to the continent and the absence of any visible romantic attachments (*Harriet Martineau*, p. 20).

110. Wheatley, *Life and Work*, p. 296; Brown and Fuller, quoted in Wheatley, *Life and Work*, pp. 261, 262.

111. Bray, *Phases of Opinion*, p. 78.

112. George Eliot to Mrs. Charles Bray, *George Eliot Letters*, 2:16; George Eliot to Sara Sophia Hennell, *George Eliot Letters*, 2:33; George Eliot to Sara Sophia Hennell, *George Eliot Letters*, 2:54; George Eliot to Mrs. Charles Bray, *George Eliot Letters*, 2:62; George Eliot to Bessie Rayner Parkes, *George Eliot Letters*, 2:109.

113. James Martineau, quoted in James Drummond, *Life and Letters of James Martineau* (New York, 1902), p. 223.

114. Robertson, *History of Free Thought*, 1:235.

115. Harriet Martineau, Letters on Mesmerism, to the *Athenaeum*, 23 November 1844, p. 1,072; 14 December 1844, p. 1,145. The letters appeared on 23 November 1844, pp. 1,070-72, 30 November 1844, pp. 1,093-94, 7 December 1844, pp. 1,117-18, 14 December 1844, pp. 1,144-46, and 21 December 1844, pp. 1,173-74.

116. "A Few Words by Way of Comment on Miss Martineau's Statement," *Athenaeum*, 28 December 1844, p. 1,199.

117. Martineau, *Autobiography*, 1:140. There was a considerable audience for Martineau's preachings: her *Athenaeum* letters were printed in six issues, through three editions, and then reprinted as a pamphlet, which sold out in three days (Webb, *Martineau*, p. 230).

118. Mrs. Charles Bray to Sara Sophia Hennell, *George Eliot Letters*, 1:188 (April 1845).

119. George Eliot to Martha Jackson, *George Eliot Letters*, 1:189.

120. Cross, *Life of George Eliot*, 1:196.

121. George Eliot to Mr. and Mrs. Charles Bray, *George Eliot Letters*, 1:343-44.

122. Henry Crabb Robinson, quoted in *George Eliot Letters*, 1:346 n. This may have been Robinson's own opinion; he found the *Letters* extremely "disagreeable," and announced his intention to "break with [Martineau] entirely" (*Henry Crabb Robinson on Books and Their Writers*, ed. Edith Morely [London, 1938], 2:707-8).

123. George Combe Journal, *George Eliot Letters*, 8:28.

124. George Eliot to Charles Bray, *George Eliot Letters*, 1:364.

125. George Eliot to Mr. and Mrs. Charles Bray and Sara Sophia Hennell, *George Eliot Letters*, 2:32.

126. George Eliot to Bessie Rayner Parkes, *George Eliot Letters*, 2:65; George Eliot to Mr. and Mrs. Charles Bray, *George Eliot Letters*, 2:62. See also 8:64 for more praise of Martineau in a letter to George Combe.

127. False rumors of a letter from Eliot to Martineau (postmarked Weimar) circulated, and Eliot indulged in a rare moment of vituperative recrimination in a letter to John Chapman: "Amongst her good qualities we certainly cannot reckon zeal for other people's reputation. She is sure to caricature any information for the amusement of the next person to whom she turns her ear trumpet" (George Eliot to John Chapman, *George Eliot Letters*, 2:180). But yet a year later, Eliot "think[s] of her with deep respect and admiration" (2:230).

128. George Eliot to John Chapman, *George Eliot Letters*, 2:258.

129. Martineau, *Autobiography*, 2:343.

130. George Henry Lewes, "Literature," *Leader*, 22 February 1851, p. 178.

131. Martineau and Atkinson, *Letters*, p. 79. The book takes the form of letters between the pair; but it is safe to attribute the ideas therein to both authors (see *Autobiography*, 2:336–37). Alfred Benn singles out Martineau and Eliot from their less controversial male counterparts: "More fearless consistency" was displayed by the women of their circle than by the men (*History of Rationalism*, 2:67).

132. Martineau, *Autobiography*, 2:444.

133. Charlotte Brontë, quoted in Elizabeth Gaskell, *Life of Charlotte Brontë* (1857; rpt. Harmondsworth, Middlesex, England, 1975), p. 441.

134. Eagles, "What Is Mesmerism?", 76 n. Brother James Martineau's venomous attack was the unkindest cut of all. Once James's ardent disciple, Harriet's radical conversion aroused both his sexual and his intellectual jealousies: "We remember nothing in history more melancholy than that Harriet Martineau should be prostrated at the feet of such a master; should lay down at his bidding her early faith in moral obligation, in the living God, in the immortal sanctities" ("Mesmeric Atheism," *Prospective Review* 7 [1851]:234). George Eliot, later to suffer an equally painful break with her brother, Isaac, clearly found more in common with Harriet than with James. In 1852 she writes to Chapman in disparagement of James Martineau and his " 'School of thought' " as potential contributors to the *Westminster* (*George Eliot Letters*, 2:48–49).

135. W. R. Hickson, "Life and Immortality," *Westminster Review* 56 (1851):208.

136. Bray, *On Force*, p. 71 n; see pp. 84–85 n, 87, 124, 126, 135.

137. Martineau, *Autobiography*, 1:415, 391. Webb writes that Atkinson failed to claim this most unusual legacy (*Harriet Martineau*, p. 20)!

138. Martineau, *Autobiography*, 1:394–96.

139. Review of *Letters on the Laws*, *Westminster Review* 55 (1851):84–85.

140. Froude, "Materialism," p. 426.

141. Martineau and Atkinson, *Letters*, pp. 3, 5–6.

142. Henry George Atkinson to Charles Bray, in *On Force*, p. 164.

143. Mill, *Logic*, quoted in Martineau and Atkinson, *Letters*, p. 311.

144. Martineau and Atkinson, *Letters*, pp. 117–18.

145. Martineau and Atkinson, *Letters*, p. 16. They quote Chambers's "Sequel" in the *Letters* (appendix, pp. 308, 309).

146. Martineau and Atkinson, *Letters*, pp. 132, 202.

147. Martineau and Atkinson, *Letters*, p. 232.

148. Martineau and Atkinson, *Letters*, p. 100.

149. T. H. Huxley, "Joseph Priestley," in *Science and Culture* (New York, 1890), pp. 121–22. Huxley's essay first appeared in *Macmillan's* in 1874.

150. Review of *Letters*, *Westminster*, 89.

151. Bray, *Phases of Opinion*, p. 78.

152. Martineau and Atkinson, *Letters*, p. 268.

153. Froude, "Materialism," p. 432.

154. Atkinson, quoted in Hickson, "Life and Immortality," p. 207.

155. Hickson, "Life and Immortality," p. 207.

156. Martineau and Atkinson, *Letters*, p. 127. See, similarly, Martineau, *Autobiography*, 2:330–32.

157. Martineau and Atkinson, *Letters*, pp. 216, 76, 177, 91, 110, 122.

158. Henry George Atkinson to Charles Bray, in *On Force*, p. 159.

159. Martineau and Atkinson, *Letters*, p. 255.

CHAPTER FOUR

Synthetic Philosophy: George Henry Lewes and Herbert Spencer

Those who have handled sciences have been either men of experiment or men of dogmas. The men of experiment are like the ant: they only collect and use; the reasoners resemble spiders, who make cobwebs out of their own substance. But the bee takes a middle course; it gathers its material from the flowers of the garden and of the field, but transforms and digests it by a power of its own. Not unlike this is the true business of philosophy; for it neither relies solely or chiefly on the powers of the mind, nor does it take the matter which it gathers up from natural history and mechanical experiments and lay it up in the memory whole, as it finds it; but lays it up in the understanding altered and digested.—Francis Bacon, Novum Organum

I. THE HEART AND THE BRAIN—GEORGE HENRY LEWES: "SPINOZA'S LIFE AND WORKS" (1843)

It has been said of George Henry Lewes that he "represented perhaps the more effervescent, more eccentric, and yet also the more truly philosophical aspects of the mid-Victorian mind."[1] A single chapter cannot do full justice to the breadth of Lewes's thought: he was a literary critic, a novelist, a playwright, an editor, a physiologist, a psychologist, a philosopher, an historian of ideas; a true Victorian polymath. What little attention has been paid to Lewes by previous scholars has tended to center on his relationship with George Eliot, or on his role as literary critic and man of letters. But Lewes viewed himself preeminently as a philosopher of science. My focus here will be on Lewes's earlier philosophical work, particularly in the field of psychology; those aspects of his intellectual biography that link him most closely with this Victorian circle.

Lewes called his final and most ambitious project, *Problems of Life and Mind* (5 vol., 1874–79), his "key to all Psychologies."[2] Therein, he attempted to resolve "the long debates respecting the true position of Psychology among the sciences," within a continuum of ideas from the 1840s and 1850s, freely acknowledging his debts to Comte, Mill, and Spencer as the thinkers with whom he was "most in agreement."[3] As we have seen, Lewes was an early disciple of Mill and Comte; but Herbert Spencer was his friend and intellectual equal. This chapter will establish some of the early sources of Lewes's and Spencer's ideas, and chronicle the path of their mutual intellectual development during the decade of the 1850s, their lively and reciprocal interplay of ideas. As with so many in this circle, it is often difficult to determine the exact origin of an idea. Spencer's greater philosophical fame has tended to obscure Lewes's own important contributions to nineteenth-century intellectual history—and to Herbert Spencer's intellectual history.

Lewes's debts to Mill and Comte notwithstanding, Johann Wolfgang von Goethe was his most-admired mentor. In his

1852 essay on "Goethe as a Man of Science" (the germ of Lewes's classic biography of Goethe), Lewes quotes Goethe speaking of a life "passed in creating and observing, in synthesis and analysis: the systole and diastole of human thought were to me like a second breathing process—never separated, ever pulsating."[4] The dual strands of philosophy and biology, synthesis and analysis, general and particular, span the decades of Lewes's intellectual development. Twenty-four years later, in an essay entitled "Materialism and Spiritualism," which summarizes his work-in-progress on *Problems of Life and Mind*, Lewes would remember Goethe's words: "Analysis and synthesis are the systole and diastole of science."[5] It was Lewes's lifelong ambition to effect the perfect fusion of part and whole, that individuation in which each part is uniquely particular and yet fully subsumed within a greater unity. Like Herbert Spencer, Lewes would find the key that would unlock the apparent paradox of the many in the one, the one in the many, in evolutionary biology.

But in his search for this delicate balance, it has been Lewes's fate to be both oversimplified and misinterpreted. For example, Rosemary Ashton has difficulty reconciling Lewes's early enthusiasm for Hegel's aesthetics with his later embrace of Comte's positivism. She resorts to a simple dichotomy: "From 1843 on, Lewes ranged himself on the side of analysis, not synthesis in criticism, just as he stood for empiricism rather than *a priorism* in philosophy."[6] Similarly, Robert M. Young is incorrect in his interpretation of Spencer's debt to Lewes: "Just as the reading of Lyell's refutation of Lamarck turned Spencer *towards* belief in inheritance of acquired characteristics, the reading of Lewes's positivist polemics seemed to have turned him towards metaphysics."[7] In fact, Lewes was not an idealist turned empiricist; nor was he a positivistic polemicist who drove his friend to metaphysics.

To be fair, Lewes himself is partially responsible for the confusion: in the *Biographical History of Philosophy*, he argued emphatically for the death of metaphysics at the hand of positivistic natural science. But it should be clear from my discussion of Comte in chapter 1 that positivism is not simply to be allied with science in opposition to metaphysics. It occupies a middle ground between the two. Other critics have more correctly perceived the similar mediating tendencies in Lewes's work, but have incorrectly located their philosophical counterparts. In his essay on "The Empirical Metaphysics of George Henry Lewes," Jack Kaminsky divides nineteenth-century English philosophy into the "opposing tendencies" of "empirical positivism" (Mill and Spencer) and its "philosophic reaction" (exemplified in "Carlyle's transcendentalism, Newman's Catholicism, and Green's idealism"). Kaminsky correctly argues that Lewes sought to "heal the bifurcation in philosophy, [urging] that the study of metaphysical problems might be pursued with an empirical rather than a transcendental method." But Mill and Spencer themselves share many fundamental similarities with Lewes. Kaminsky considers Lewes "one renegade positivist," crying alone in a wilderness of skeptics and Roman catholics, biologists and German idealists. In reality Lewes was far from solitary in his pursuit of a middle ground. Kaminsky ruefully concludes that "the full import of Lewes's views on metaphysics was completely lost to nineteenth-century philosophers."[8] Although it may be true that his ideas were not influential within the academy, the interconnections between Lewes and an important circle of Victorian minds were rich and pervasive.

One might expect that George Henry Lewes would have given a favorable review to Atkinson's and Martineau's *Letters on the Laws of Man's Nature and Development* in his three "Literature" columns in the *Leader* devoted to that subject in February and March 1851. Although Lewes did claim the *Letters* worthy of "serious discussion" and acknowledge them the "result of honest, independent thinking," he was otherwise highly critical. One immediate source of Lewes's disapprobation is suggested by his intolerance of phrenological faddism, mesmeric quacks, and pseudo-scientific notions of force—and indeed, "the mesmeric and clairvoyant revelations" of the pair do "excite [his] ridicule." But unexpectedly, Lewes is more critical of what could loosely be termed the theological aspects of the book than he is of its dubious scientific underpinnings: "We are among those who must unequivocally dissent from the opinions it ushers in": "the open avowal of Atheism and denial of Immortality." Lewes here sides with Froude and those critics who were offended by what they considered a dangerous materialism: "Reason is daylight; by it we see all that can be seen in daylight; but there *are* realities the perception of which daylight destroys, and among these are the stars."[9] These are hardly the words one might expect from a clear-eyed empiricist.

George Henry Lewes and Harriet Martineau have more in common than Lewes grants (as chapter 3 demonstrates). Although he misreads Martineau as a simple atheist, this misreading is highly illuminating of Lewes himself: *"The soul is larger than logic,"* he argues; "there is . . . a logic of emotions, and a logic of instincts as well as a logic of ideas." George Henry Lewes, amateur scientist and positivist, five years after condemning metaphysics in the *Biographical History* and on the eve of his study of Comte, speaks in strikingly idealist terms: "We are not Kantists, but detect in his system the indistinct expression of that consciousness of a transcendental faculty we feel within ourselves."[10]

Although Lewes was never an orthodox religious believer, this transcendental streak was strong in him from the start. In his 1876 essay on "Spiritualism and Materialism," Lewes indulges in a rare moment of autobiographical reminiscence:

> There was one brief period when I was very near a conversion. The idea of a noumenal Mind, as something distinct from mental phenomena—a something diffused through the Organism giving unity to Consciousness, very different from the unity of a machine, flashed upon me one morning with a sudden and novel force, quite unlike the shadowy vagueness with which it had heretofore been conceived. For some minutes I was motionless in a rapt state of thrilled surprise. I seemed standing at the entrance of a new path, leading to new issues with a vast horizon. The convictions of a life seemed tottering. A tremulous eagerness, suffused with the keen light of discovery, yet mingled with cross-lights and hesita-

tions, stirred me; and from that moment I have understood something of sudden conversions. There was, as I afterwards remembered, no feeling of distress at this prospect of parting with old beliefs. Indeed it is doubtful whether sudden conversions are accomplished by pain, the excitement is too great, the new ideas too absorbing. The rapture of truth overcomes the false shame of having been in error. The one desire is for more light.[11]

Lewes's self-portrait here has much in common with Martineau's own rhapsodic account of her conversion to mesmerism, with its strong overtones of religious experience mingled with scientific conviction. Characteristically, Lewes asks for the "light" of intellectual illumination in the midst of this most emotional moment.

A brief scientific essay, "The Heart and the Brain," which Lewes wrote for the *Fortnightly Review* in 1865, provides a theoretical analogue to his personal account of the interworkings of heart and brain. It is important to remember that for Lewes, as for Atkinson and Martineau, "transcendental faculties" were also biological phenomena. Much of "The Heart and the Brain" is, quite literally, a biological discussion of those two organs. "Heart and Brain are the two lords of Life," Lewes opens. But he immediately suggests that this statement may also be read figuratively: "In the metaphors of ordinary speech and in the stricter language of science, we use these terms to indicate two central powers, from which all motives radiate, to which all influences converge."[12]

The phrenologists had claimed that the brain was the organ of the mind, and were branded godless materialists. Lewes seems at first to disagree with phrenology, condemning as unscientific "the modern doctrine respecting the brain . . . as the exclusive organ of sensation." Lewes has come full circle within physiological psychology, "to appreciate the truth . . . in the ancient doctrine respecting the heart as the great emotional organ." But instead of repudiating the materialism of the phrenologists, Lewes actually enlarges their claims. The heart is physiologically the "great emotional center": "As the central organ of the circulation [it] is so indissolubly connected with every manifestation of Sensibility, and is so delicately susceptible to all emotional agitations." Heart does not replace brain as center; both are simply parts of a greater whole, "the vital activities of the whole organism."[13] Read figuratively (as Lewes invites), the "two lords of life," each equal in power yet interdependent, are the emotions and the intellect. Lewes insists that metaphor and fact, poetry and science, mirror one another. The transcendent logic of emotions has its correspondent physiology.

In this context I turn back to the 1840s, when Lewes was introduced to the study of philosophy by the work of Benedict Spinoza, a seventeenth-century Dutch philosopher who mechanized human passions in the form of geometrical propositions, and argued for the unification of mind and matter as manifestations of a single substance. In the philosophy of Spinoza, Lewes was to find both a solution and a dilemma: the prototype of his ideal philosophic temperament, and what he saw as the greatest obstacle to any philosophical endeavor.

Whether by fortunate coincidence or careful design, George Henry Lewes was asked to contribute to the "S" volume of the *Penny Cyclopaedia* in 1842; his task: to define the terms "Subject, Subjective," "Substance," and "Spinoza." His trip to Germany in 1838 had fueled Lewes's early fascination with German idealist philosophies; but even in these short entries, among his earliest published writing, we can see the characteristic bias of Lewes's mind. Lewes's definition of "subject" is inseparable from its polar antithesis: "The very subject itself (the mind) can become an object by being psychologically considered."[14] In his definition of "substance," Lewes similarly insists on a two-sided vision, the equivalence of subject and object: "The stronghold of Idealism is consciousness. In Consciousness there is nothing but transformations of itself—no substance, no external world is given. . . . But consciousness is equally the stronghold of Realism; for we are as conscious that what we call substance, or the world, is not ourselves, and does not depend on us, and is a distinct existence."[15]

Spinoza is identified with both subject and substance,

closely linked with the idealist school: "All the German philosophers, from Kant downwards, owns [sic] him as its master."[16] Lewes confessed elsewhere that he considered Spinoza's
"the grandest and most religious of philosophies."[17] The continuity of Lewes's interest in Spinoza is evident in his return to
the philosopher in 1843 and again in 1866. In an autobiographical moment in the 1866 *Fortnightly Review* essay,
Lewes travels to a small tavern in Red Lion Square in the mid-
1830s, "where the vexed questions of philosophy were discussed with earnestness, if not insight," by young George,
not yet twenty, and a mixed group of speculatively-minded
friends. Supreme among them was a German Jew, a watch-
maker named Cohn: "He remains in my memory as a type of
philosophic dignity"; "I venerated his great calm intellect. He
was the only man I did not contradict in the impatience of argument," Lewes recalls. It was Cohn who tutored the group
weekly in Spinoza. Lewes's intense feelings for Spinoza were
inextricably mixed with those for his mentor, Cohn: "I habit-
ually think of him in connexion with Spinoza, almost as much
on account of his personal characteristics, as because to him I
owe my first acquaintance with the Hebrew thinker. My admiration for him was of that enthusiastic temper which in
youth we feel for our intellectual leaders."[18] Lewes's essay on
"Spinoza's Life and Works" in the *Westminster Review* (1843)
came at a time when Spinoza was not translated into English,
and was generally acknowledged as a ground-breaking attempt
to bring this difficult philosopher to the attention of the English reading public.[19] I consider this essay the cornerstone of
Lewes's early thought; it epitomizes both his characteristic
frame of mind and his central intellectual dilemma at the time,
to be resolved through his friendship with Herbert Spencer in
the early 1850s.

Lewes's attraction to Spinoza is fraught with a most interesting tension: Lewes venerates Spinoza as a religious philosopher, and writes essays on the man at both ends of his career.
Yet Lewes's early insistence in the *Biographical History* on the
objective, psychological view, in contradistinction to the sub-

jective, philosophical one, his assertion that consciousness is not all—this seems in conflict with Spinoza, by Lewes's own definition the forefather of Kantian idealism. Ashton argued that Lewes's early flirtation with German romanticism and *a priori* idealism gave way to the later empiricism of the *Biographical History*. And indeed that book does seem to support a reading of Lewes as an *a posteriori* empiricist. Lewes's fundamental disagreement with Spinoza in 1843 becomes the germ of his central argument throughout the 800-page history. The "fundamental error of Spinozism," Lewes writes, will be rectified by the objectivity of the new positivist psychology:

> It is our firm conviction that no believer in Ontology, as a *possible* science, can escape the all-embracing dialectic of Spinoza. To him who believes that the human mind can know *noumena*, as well as *phenomena*—who accepts the verdict of the mind as not merely the *relative* truth, but also the *perfect, absolute* truth—we see nothing, humanly speaking, but Spinozism as a philosophical refuge. . . . If you do not believe that your knowledge is *absolute*, and not simply *relative*, you have no sort of ground for belief in the possibility of ontology.

Lewes takes the latter position. In the *Biographical History*, the error of the ontologist becomes for scientific psychologist Lewes the fundamental error of *all* philosophers: the notion that the mind can intuitively, clearly and distinctly, know Truth, that Ideas exist independent of experience. "Spinozism or Skepticism?" Lewes demands; "choose between them, for you have no other choice."[21] But if Lewes was not a Spinozist, was he a Skeptic? I will look to both Lewes's 1843 essay and Spinoza's *Ethics*, and suggest two possible solutions to this dilemma: first, in the dialectic that Lewes sets up in that essay between the idealist, subjective Spinoza and the man Lewes considers his realist, objective polar antithesis, Francis Bacon; second, and more intriguing, in the philosophy of Spinoza itself, which in many ways attempts to reconcile antitheses in ways directly relevant to this Victorian circle.

"Spinoza's Life and Works" provides ample documentation of Lewes's continued attraction to the great philosopher since his student days in Red Lion Square. But Lewes's essay adopts a peculiar stratagem, given its ostensibly admiring stance towards Spinoza. Once Lewes has outlined Spinoza's life, he shifts unexpectedly to Francis Bacon, as a counterpoint to Spinoza: "From Bacon [comes] the whole school of scientific men, the materialists, Scotch physiologists, and political economists," in contradistinction to the "Cartesian" school, in which Lewes includes Spinoza, Kant, and Hegel. After Lewes's denunciation of the fundamental error of Spinozism, Bacon arises as the hero of a new, empirical psychology, which claims to escape the subjective boundaries of the reflective consciousness: "We might have gone on baffled, yet persisting, seeking the unknowable, and building palaces on air . . . had not Bacon arisen to point out that the method men were pursuing was not the path of transit to the truth, but led only to a land of chimeras." Bacon heralds the new spirit of Positive Science, and it is this nineteenth-century Baconianism, in opposition to the "arachnae philosophers of Germany," that Lewes praises throughout the *Biographical History of Philosophy.*[22]

Yet to suggest that he simply abandoned Spinoza at this point belies the intensity of Lewes's fascination with the Dutch philosopher. Lewes not only returned to the subject of Spinoza in 1866, he also encouraged the earliest efforts to translate Spinoza into English. In January 1843 George Eliot had borrowed Spinoza's works from R. H. Brabant (who had been introduced to Spinoza by no less than Samuel Taylor Coleridge himself, in 1815-16[23]), and began a translation for her friend Charles Bray—probably the *Tractatus*, but also possibly "De Deo," the opening of the *Ethics.*[24] In February 1847 Eliot returned Brabant's copy of the philosopher's Latin works and borrowed publisher John Chapman's.[25] Cara Bray wrote to Sara Sophia Hennell in the spring of 1849 of Eliot's "great desire to undertake Spinoza." It was to her translation of the *Tractatus* that Eliot turned while nursing her father through his final illness: "It is such a rest to her mind," Cara wrote.[26] But in the grief and aimlessness of those months following Robert Evans's death in May 1849, Eliot and Spinoza were "divorced"; though she agreed grudgingly to uphold her bargain with Chapman for a translation of the *Tractatus Theologico-Politicus*, to be published in conjunction with an American translation of the *Ethics*: "If you are anxious to publish the translation in question I could, after a few months, finish the Tractatus Theologico-Politicus to keep it company—but I confess to you, that I think you would do better to abstain from printing a translation." Grief may have dampened Eliot's energies, but her discouragement with the translation also took a more complex form: "What is wanted in English is not a translation of Spinoza's works, but a true estimate of his life and system. After one has rendered his Latin faithfully into English, one feels that there is another yet more difficult process of translation for the reader to effect, and that the only mode of making Spinoza accessible to a larger number is to study his books, then shut them and give his analysis."[27]

Spinoza was surely not the least of that community of intellectual interests that Eliot and Lewes found when they met and fell in love between 1851 and 1854; when they eloped to Germany in 1854, Eliot began a translation of the *Ethics* while Lewes labored on his *Life of Goethe*, and they returned to England to see both books through publication.[28] In October 1855 an announcement in Lewes's *Goethe* proclaimed that "Spinoza will ere long appear in English, edited by the writer of these lines," as a joint product of George Eliot and George Henry Lewes. Such was not to be: Lewes's agreement with publisher Bohn for his edition of Eliot's translation ended in acrimonious financial squabbles between Lewes and Bohn during the early weeks of June 1856.[29]

George Eliot's interest in the *Tractatus* was clearly of a piece with her translation of the German rationalist critics Strauss and Feuerbach. Spinoza is "Vater der Speculation unserer Zeit; er ist auch Vater der biblischen Kritik," Strauss himself wrote.[30] It was Lewes who turned Eliot to work on the *Ethics*, a book more directly relevant to my discussion here. For in the *Ethics* itself, we find many clear reasons for Spinoza's strong appeal to the frame of mind shared by this Victorian circle.

A brief outline of the basic argument of the *Ethics* is useful at this point.[31] Descartes introduced dualism into Western philosophy: mind and body are partners, in a reciprocal, causal relationship (and Spinoza was a Cartesian, albeit a critical one, for half of his philosophic life). But Spinoza perplexingly defies either category, monist or dualist. His theory of the relation between mind and body is a dualism of sorts: mind and body coexist amicably; yet unlike Descartes, Spinoza posits no causal relationship between them. There is a material event for every body event, but body does not *cause* mind, nor mind, body; nor do they interact, as in Descartes. Mind and body are two aspects of the identical *substance*, which informs the entire universe: "Substance thinking and substance extended are one and the same substance."[32] This substance, Spinoza calls God. This God bears a superficial resemblance to the Judeo-Christian God: He is eternal, infinite, omnipotent. But just as Spinoza resists the dualism of mind and body, he denies the duality of God and His creation, the world. Spinoza's God did not make the world; the world *is* God, one substance, immutable. God's infinity necessitates his unity with the cosmos.

Furthermore, His perfection results in a deterministic universe; everything functions according to universal and necessary laws: "Nothing in the universe is contingent, but all things are conditioned to exist and operate in a particular manner by the necessity of the divine nature." If things could be other than they are, then God would not be perfect: "God's will cannot be different from God's perfection." Spinoza rejects any notion of divine teleology, argument from design, God's "purposes" in the world: "Nature has no particular goal in view . . . final causes are mere human figments."[33]

Spinoza's method in the *Ethics* follows closely upon his metaphysics. The entire treatise is written in the form of a series of geometrical propositions: "These effects follow as necessarily from the said emotion, as it follows the nature of the triangle, that the three angles are equal to two right angles." Minds are subject to the same laws as bodies: "The laws of nature have regard to nature's general order, whereof man is but a part. I mention this, in passing, lest any should think that I have wished to set forth the faults and irrational deeds of men rather than the nature and properties of things. For . . . I regard human emotions and their properties as on the same footing with other natural phenomena."[34]

Herein the link between Spinoza's metaphysics and his ethics: the mind, consciousness, can be studied in the same manner as the body, since it is part of the same substance, subject to the same necessary laws. It would seem that the logical result of this would be a pure form of psychological determinism. How can it make sense to talk of ethics, if all mental behavior is necessitated by invariable laws? Yet just as Spinoza wishes to argue for the coexistence of mind and body, his philosophy encompasses freedom as well as necessity.

In the *Ethics* Spinoza presents a three-tiered theory of knowledge. The first level at which man arrives is that of confused ideas. Man "knows" in a purely mechanical, passive, fragmentary way. He is at the mercy of both external events or sensory impressions and his own unregulated emotions: "We are in many ways driven about by external causes, and . . . like waves of the sea driven by contrary winds we toss to and fro unwitting of the issue of our fate." This Spinoza calls "bondage." At the second level, man arrives at adequate ideas, exercising his powers of reasoning in order to understand the causal relationships among things. In the first stage, he sees only particulars; now he is capable of generalizations. This is as far as most of us, unendowed with the philosopher's intellect, can get. Understanding brings man a kind of moral liberty: "The more we endeavour to be guided by reason, the less do we depend on hope; we endeavour to free ourselves from fear, and, so far as we can, to dominate fortune, directing our actions by the sure counsel of wisdom."

But there is a third, highest stage: "scientia intuitiva," intuitive knowledge. It is a mystical state, where man arrives at the true "love of God." But what is God in Spinoza's universe?—simply the Unity of all that is particular, individual:

"The more we understand particular things, the more do we understand God." At this third stage of knowledge man fully understands each particular thing in the order of its general relation to the cosmos; he apprehends the full harmony of the universe in a simultaneous transcendentalism and descendentalism. In this state man does not rise above human passions, but rather incorporates them with a visionary reason; intellect and emotion are at one. "This love or blessedness is in the Bible called Glory, and not undeservedly. For whether this love be referred to God or to the mind, it may rightly be called acquiescence of spirit."[35] Little wonder that Spinoza would attract the philosopher who sought to "reduce all knowledge into harmony," and that his earliest champion in England was Samuel Taylor Coleridge.

The above summary, although it hardly does justice to the complexities of a profound and difficult philosophy, should serve to illuminate some of the sources of Spinoza's powerful attraction for the Victorian intellectual. Spinoza clearly makes way for a scientific psychology, in accordance with the laws of nature. The psychology of Hartley and Priestley has been called "a kind of bargain-basement Spinozism."[36] I draw attention to the little-known and fascinating fact that the first published translator of Spinoza into English was Dr. Robert Willis, a practicing phrenologist![37] Spinoza's single "substance," and the pantheism that is its product, suggest many parallels with Charles Bray's and Harriet Martineau's "force," which similarly partakes of the nature of both mind and body. The necessitarian implications of Spinoza's universal causation and his faith in the qualified liberty that reason can effect resonate clearly with the discussion of necessitarianism in chapter 3. And Spinoza's "scientia intuitiva" is remarkably similar to the systole and diastole of analysis and synthesis with which this chapter began, that desire to see the many in the one, the one in the many, which is the common ground of all these Victorian thinkers.

Leslie Stephen, writing on Spinoza in 1880, summarizes the preceding decades of English response when he suggests that

Spinoza "has been defended as he has been attacked from the most opposite points of view. The materialist and the idealist; the dogmatist and the sceptic; the mystic and the man of science have each found in him something congenial, and with equal ease something antagonistic."[38] Spinoza's appeal to the mystic who was *also* a man of science would be powerful; his balance of necessitarianism and ethical idealism, rationalist and visionary, intellect and emotion, irresistible to a Victorian sensibility.

And yet we must not forget "the fundamental error of Spinozism" that so troubled Lewes and necessitated the Baconian corrective. This error becomes all the more consequent in light of the otherwise powerful seductions of Spinoza's philosophy. It obviously troubled Lewes to the extent that it sparked an 800-page disquisition on what Lewes considered the failures of the ontological method: "If you do not believe that your knowledge is *absolute*, and not *relative*, you have no sort of ground for belief in the possibility of ontology." But it is in error to conclude from this statement that George Henry Lewes was a relativist skeptic. It would be truer to say that Lewes in fact yearned for absolute knowledge; but was unable to accept the Absolute when it was grounded—as it was for Spinoza and the arachnae philosophers of Germany—purely on the subjective basis of individual consciousness. What Herbert Spencer was to give George Henry Lewes in *The Principles of Psychology* was a key to all mythologies, a ground for the Absolute that was based upon sense experience; the grand Spinozistic synthesis of mind and body, rewritten in Baconian terms to fit a Victorian frame of mind.

II. THE FOUNDATIONS OF A FRIENDSHIP—HERBERT SPENCER: *SOCIAL STATICS* (1851)

In his journal for January 1859, George Henry Lewes looked back upon the momentous beginning of his lifelong friendship with Herbert Spencer in the spring of 1850:

I owe him a debt of gratitude. My acquaintance with him was the brightest ray in a very dreary *wasted* period of my life. I had given up all ambition whatever, lived from hand to mouth, and thought the evil of each day sufficient. The stimulus of his intellect, especially during our long walks, roused my energy once more, and revived my dormant love of science. His intense theorizing tendency was contagious, and it was only the stimulus of a *theory* which could then have induced me to work.—I owe Spencer another, and a deeper debt. It was through him that I learned to know Marian—to know her was to love her—and since then my life has been a new birth.[39]

The late 1840s had been lean years both personally and intellectually for Lewes, as his wife Agnes entered into a liaison with his best friend and coeditor of the *Leader*, Thornton Hunt, and Lewes turned from philosophical and scientific subjects to piecework literary criticism and two rather dreadful novels, *Ranthorpe* (1847) and *Rose, Blanche, and Violet* (1848)[40] But the stimulus that Spencer offered Lewes was far more than simply a contagious penchant for theorizing. Lewes found in Herbert Spencer the germ of "a *theory*" that was to flourish in the rich soil of their mutual discourse on contemporary scientific ideas from 1850-55, bursting forth in full bloom in Spencer's *Principles of Psychology*; a resolution to the intellectual stalemate of the 1840s reflected in Lewes's ambivalence towards Spinoza.

Herbert Spencer's first book, *Social Statics*, originated in a series of twelve letters to *The Nonconformist* in 1842. In the spring of 1850, when he was near to finishing the study, Spencer met Lewes: "In the course of our walk home from a *soirée*, a conversation between us produced mutual interest." The acquaintance that began on that walk was renewed a year later as a result of Lewes's review of *Social Statics* in *The Leader* in March and April 1851: "When *Social Statics* came out he spoke highly of it, both privately and in public . . . and naturally when we met again, a further step was taken towards intimacy. As we had many tastes and opinions in common, the intimacy grew rapidly."[41] The manner in which Lewes announced his upcoming review of *Social Statics* in the *Leader* suggests in no uncertain terms the intensity of his intellectual excitement over this "profound and suggestive work": "We remember no work on ethics since that of SPINOZA to be compared to it in the simplicity of its premises, and the logical rigor with which a complete system of scientific ethics is evolved from them. This is high praise; but we give it deliberately."[42]

But before pursuing *Social Statics* in more detail, to see just what Lewes found in this Victorian Spinoza that so excited him, I should like to turn first to the "deeper debt" of mutual acquaintance with young Marian Evans, who arrived fresh from the provinces as the new assistant editor of the *Westminster Review* on 29 September 1851. Among the Friday guests at 142 Strand, George Eliot writes Charles Bray on October 4 of that year, was "a Mr. Herbert Spencer who has just brought out a large work on 'Social Statics,' which Lewes pronounces the best book he has seen on the subject. You must see the book if possible."[43] The previous August Eliot had been introduced to Spencer while on a London visit to the Crystal Palace with the Brays, and the friendship flourished when they met again soon after Eliot's permanent move to London. By April 1852 Spencer was writing to friend Edward Lott: "the most admirable woman, *mentally*, I ever met."[44]

"We have agreed that we are not in love with each other," George Eliot avows that same month. It is but a "deliciously calm *new* friendship," a "delightful *camaraderie*" only, she explains, despite the fact that the world incorrectly "sets [them] down" as engaged, she protests to Charles Bray on 14 June 1852.[45] But three passionate love-letters, written during July 1852 and only recently published after their long incarceration in the British Museum, tell quite a different story, as George Eliot confesses her devotion to Spencer—"those who have known me best have always said that if I ever loved any one thoroughly my whole life must turn upon that feeling, and I find they said truly"—is spurned as a lover—"No credit to me for my virtues as a refrigerant"—but reconciles herself to an offer of friendship—"Let us, if you will, forget the past, except in so far as it may have brought us to trust in and feel for each other. . . . I can promise you such companionship as there is in me, untroubled by painful emotions."[46]

And the intellectual intimacy did continue unabated; in mid-August Spencer was back with George Eliot at Broadstairs, discussing Mill's *Logic* and his plans for the *Principles of Psychology*. "In physique there was, perhaps, a trace of that masculinity characterizing her intellect," Spencer wrote in his *Autobiography*; but what Spencer considered a sexual liability, he found an intellectual asset: "Her philosophical powers were remarkable. I have known but few men with whom I could discuss a question in philosophy with more satisfaction. Capacity for abstract thinking is rarely found along with capacity for concrete representation, even in men; among women, such a union of the two as existed in her has, I should think, never been paralleled."[47]

Any sympathy we might feel for George Eliot should quickly be tempered by the fact that the witty and loving George Henry Lewes stood ready to replace Spencer in Eliot's affections. Unlike Spencer, Lewes considered Eliot's intellect worthy of love as well as admiration; and he recognized the sensitive human heart beneath that "masculine" brain (and face). The following summer it was he who was now vacationing at Broadstairs with the *Westminster*'s female editor, on considerably more romantic terms. By autumn Spencer was aware of the situation, and rather ungraciously relieved to pass her on to his friend.

Romance had little adverse effect on friendship for the three. Eliot had met both men in the previous autumn, several months after Lewes's favorable review of *Social Statics*.[48] The two quickly expanded their new-found friendship to include her. From the start it was an intellectual *ménage à trois*, as Spencer and Lewes frequently stopped by Marian Evans's lodgings at John Chapman's, just around the corner from the *Leader*'s offices. During 1853–55 Eliot zealously read proof of Lewes's *Comte*, read the manuscript of his *Life of Goethe*, took dictation of his *Leader* essays, and filled in with an occasional column herself.[49] She unquestionably shared in the general intellectual *camaraderie* between Lewes and Spencer during these years. The close friendship among the trio continued into the 1870s, as Spencer often took advantage of his standing invitation to the Priory: "Our talk, if not very often enlivened by witticisms, always contained a mixture of the gay with the grave: good stories and a little *badinage* breaking our discussions, which were generally quite harmonious; for there were but few points on which we disagreed."[50] On her part George Eliot was always slightly amused by Spencer's furious system-making: "I went to Kew yesterday on a scientific expedition with Herbert Spencer, who has all sorts of theories about plants—I should have said a *proof*-hunting expedition. Of course, if the flowers didn't correspond to the theories, we said, 'tant pis pour les fleurs!' "—this to Sara Sophia Hennell in June 1852, at the peak of her romantic infatuation with Spencer.[51] Yet her final words on the subject of Herbert Spencer, twenty-eight years later (just two and a half weeks before her death) were admiring: "He has so much teaching which the world needs."[52]

It will be my task in the remainder of this chapter to suggest what it was in Spencer's teaching that George Eliot and George Henry Lewes considered to be so necessary. To that end I turn to *Social Statics*, to see what Lewes and Eliot would have found there for the foundation of the intellectual intimacy with Spencer that sprang up so quickly and so intensely for both of them.

J. D. Y. Peel succinctly summarizes the diminished reputation of Herbert Spencer: "Posterity is cruellest to those who sum up for their contemporaries in an all-embracing synthesis the accumulated knowledge of their age."[53] Many twentieth-century scholars, appalled by the sheer volume of Spencer's repetitious and abstract tomes, have been content to suggest vaguely that he is a quintessentially Victorian thinker, and then to turn with relief to the more readable prose of Mill or Carlyle or Ruskin. But Spencer was an immensely popular and influential writer in his own time. "Spencer's paradoxi-

cal . . . combination of evangelical spirit and rationalist substance was peculiarly congenial to the mid-Victorians," Peel
writes; his "achievement was virtually the answer to the plea
which Coleridge had made years before: 'Socinianism moonlight; Methodism a stove. O for some sun to unite heat and
light!' "[54] In *Social Statics* George Henry Lewes found a Spinozistic "sun" to unite the heat of passion with the light of
reason.

"I have been reading Bentham's works," Spencer notes in
1843, "and mean to attack his principles shortly, if I can get
any review to publish what will appear to most of them so
presumptuous."[55] Presumption was the by-word of Herbert
Spencer's philosophizing. Spencer's immodest disagreement
with Bentham provided the germ of *Social Statics*. The first
section of the book's lengthy introductory chapter is entitled
"The Doctrine of Expediency," and Spencer unequivocally asserts from the outset that such a doctrine is "futile."[56] The he-
donistic calculus of "the greatest happiness of the greatest
number" is inadequate on two interrelated counts: it fails to
take into consideration the individual, and it overlooks the
heart. "The standard of happiness is infinitely variable,"
Spencer objects; "To educe from the infinitely-ramified com-
plications of universal humanity, a true philosophy of national life, and to found thereon a code of rules for the obtain-
ment of 'greatest happiness,' is a task far beyond the ability of
any finite mind."[57] Furthermore, these utilitarian philosophers believe that such moral calculations are matter for pure,
logical reason. From the outset Spencer lets the reader know
that his philosophy is to be of another sort: "Should exception
be taken to the manifestations of feeling now and then met
with, as out of place in a treatise having so scientific a title; it
is replied that, in their present phase of progress, men are but
little swayed, by purely intellectual considerations." "Faith
not sight must be our guide," he continues.[58]

The reader will recall the Utilitarian underpinnings of
Charles Bray's *Philosophy of Necessity*. George Eliot recognized the tension between Bray's and Spencer's ideas when she

provided Bray with a copy of *Social Statics* in March 1852: "I did not send you 'Social Statics' because I thought you would admire the book—far from it—but because you expressed a wish to have it."[59] When she writes Bray on his *Philosophy of Necessity* in 1857, her objections to the book at that time follow lines similar to Spencer's attack on Utilitarianism in *Social Statics*:

> In the fundamental doctrine of your book . . . you know that I agree . . . but I think it is very likely that I should be unable to agree with much that you say in relation to the religious ideas and the moral tendencies. . . . you appear to consider the disregard of individuals a lofty frame of mind. My own experience and development deepen every day my conviction that our moral progress may be measured by the degree in which we sympathize with individual suffering and individual joy.[60]

The Utilitarians were closely allied with the association psychology of the eighteenth century, as James Mill and Jeremy Bentham, writing in the tradition of Gay and Hartley, argued that moral feelings were the result of experience, association, and reasoning. Herbert Spencer's counter to their philosophy comes from a contrary dogma, emphasizing the innate foundations of the human mind, which he loosely terms the "Shaftesbury School." The second half of his introduction, in juxtaposition to "The Doctrine of Expediency," is entitled "the Doctrine of the Moral Sense." Spencer was, of course, one of a long line of political moralists, including thinkers like Joseph Priestley and William Godwin, who had grounded their prescriptions in a divinely-implanted moral sense. This innate moral sense, unlike the calculations of the Utilitarians, speaks directly to "the religious ideas and the moral tendencies" that Eliot claimed as so essential in her letter to Bray.

George Henry Lewes's essay on "Hereditary Influence" (1856) clearly bears the imprint of *Social Statics*. Lewes provides a definition of the term "moral sense," clarifies his appeal to emotions over intellect, and places himself emphatically on the side of the angels (and Herbert Spencer):

> One school of thinkers has energetically denied that we are born with any Moral Sense; another school has energetically affirmed that we are born with it. And of the two we think the latter are nearest the truth. It is certain that we are so organized as to be powerfully affected by actions which appeal to this "Moral sense," in a very different way from mere appeals to the intellect—the demonstration of abstract right or wrong; were it otherwise, the keenest intellects would also be the kindest and the justest.

Furthermore, continues Lewes, this moral sense is innate, not acquired: "This aptitude . . . varies not according to . . . intellect but according to . . . native tendencies in that direction."[61]

However, Herbert Spencer adds a distinctively Victorian twist to this eighteenth-century doctrine: for Spencer, the moral sense is not simply a philosophical abstraction, it is a phrenological organ.[62] Spencer's argument in *Social Statics* is based on a philosophy in harmony with the phrenological view of man. Let me return to George Eliot's 1857 letter to Charles Bray, to emphasize that if there were grounds of disparity between Bray and Spencer, there was also important agreement on what Eliot called "fundamental doctrines": "that mind presents itself under the same condition of invariableness of antecedent and consequent."[63] Both Bray and Spencer found in phrenology a would-be science of mind in accordance with the doctrine of universal causality, and believed that a scientific morality should be the product of a scientific phychology. "As with the physical, so with the ethical," writes Spencer in *Social Statics*; "A belief . . . is beginning to spread among men, that there is an indissoluble bond between cause and consequence, an inexorable destiny, a 'law that altereth not.'" What Spencer calls "beneficent necessity" rules in mind as well as matter, according to the principles of universal causation: mental laws "are like the laws of the universe—safe, inflexible, ever active, and having no exceptions."[64] Spencer's lifework was dedicated to this notion of a fully scientific morality. So Herbert Spencer, like Charles

Bray, must make space for moral growth within the "inexorable destiny" of cause and effect.

The concept of a divinely-implanted moral sense is clearly one answer to this dilemma; but it makes an uneasy ideological bedfellow with inflexible universal law, however attractive it may seem as an antidote to Utilitarianism. And in fact Spencer is also critical of the Shaftesbury school for reasons antithetical to his attack on the Benthamites: "Confounding the functions of feeling and reason, they required a sentiment to do that, which should have been left to the intellect. . . . They were not right in assuming . . . instinct to be capable of intuitively solving every ethical problem submitted to it. To suppose this, was to suppose that moral sense could supply the place of logic."[65] Ultimately, the similarities between Bray and Spencer override their differences, as Spencer, like Bray, attempts to mediate between a science of mind and a system of ethics. If the Utilitarians eliminate emotion, the moral sense school attempts to do without reason. Spencer wants both: "Whilst the decisions of this moral sense . . . are inaccurate and often contradictory, it may still be capable of generating a true *fundamental intuition*, which can be logically unfolded into a *scientific morality*."[66] First articulated in *Social Statics*, this goal will be fully realized in *The Principles of Psychology*. There, Spencer argues for what he believes to be a truly scientific basis for intuitive truths, as the product of an evolutionary psychology.

In essence *Social Statics* is nothing less than Spencer's attempt to synthesize two opposing schools of social theory: Shaftesbury's moral sense with Bentham's greatest happiness for the greatest number. At this stage in his career, Spencer frames the problem in terms of political economy; once his friendship with Lewes begins, the same questions will be reformulated in the language of developmental biology. The fundamental issues remain the same, however; issues that should be familiar from Charles Bray and Harriet Martineau: how can we reconcile the uniqueness of the individual with the inexorable logic of scientific causality? How can we accommodate within a single perspective the subjective, introspective vision with the objective, empirical view? The synthetic whole with the analytic part?

In *Social Statics* Herbert Spencer finds his answer in a single, quintessentially Victorian word: "progress." "Progress, therefore, is not an accident but a necessity."[67] For Spencer progress is the necessity that engenders the ultimate freedom; or rather, that renders freedom and necessity in perfect harmony. *Social Statics* is a misleading title, because "social statics" will be reached only once society has progressed to the ideal state, the millennium (not unlike Comte's positivistic nirvana). "Social dynamics" is the real subject of Spencer's book.[68]

"All evil results from the non-adaptation of constitution to conditions. This is true of every thing that lives," writes Spencer. But according to Spencer's law of Progress, "constitution" will gradually adapt itself to "conditions"; man's "latent capabilities" will blossom under "favorable circumstances."[69] Once this progressive adaptation has perfected itself, Spencer believes, there will no longer be any tension between constitution and conditions. The individual will be harmoniously at one with his environment; the part will be perfectly assimilated into the whole.

It is here that Samuel Taylor Coleridge's law of individuation, as discussed in the "Prelude" of this study, enters Spencer's system:

> Paradoxical though the assertion looks, the progress is at once toward complete separateness and complete union. . . . Civilization is evolving a state of things . . . in which two apparently conflicting requirements are reconciled. To achieve the creative purpose—the greatest sum of happiness, . . . the extremest mutual dependence [is necessary]: while on the other hand, each individual must have the opportunity to do whatever his desires prompt.

In other words, concludes Spencer, human progress is toward *both* "greater mutual dependence" and "greater individuation." Spencer believes that "this ultimate identity of personal and social interests" (the perfect adaptation of constitution to conditions) will effect the reconciliation of utility and the moral sense. In this ideal society, the "greatest sum of happiness" for the whole will thus be in full accord with the progressively-perfected "innate desires" of each individual part:

> Thus the production of the greatest happiness, though inapplicable as an immediate guide for men, is nevertheless the true end of morality, regarded from the Divine point of view; and as such, forms part of the present system. The moral-sense principle, also, whilst misapplied by its propounders, is still based on fact; and, as was shown, harmonizes when rightly interpreted, with what seemed conflicting beliefs, and unites them to produce a complete whole.[70]

Social Statics is fundamentally a work of social science and political economy. But significantly, as early as 1851, Spencer frames his Utopian social vision in biological metaphor: "A physiological view of social actions was taken, the aggregation of citizens forming a nation was compared with the aggregation of cells forming a living body; the progress from a whole made up of like parts which have little mutual dependence, to a whole made up of unlike parts which are mutually dependent to a high degree, was shown to be a progress common to individual organisms and social organisms."[71] In this future state of social statics, society will be an harmonious living organism, just as the human body is an organic whole "compounded of innumerable microscopic organisms," each of which nonetheless possesses "a kind of independent vitality."[72] The concept of evolution lurks just behind Spencer's "progress." Spencer is already intrigued by "social" development as a model for "individual" development.

I have had little to say about George Henry Lewes's review of *Social Statics*. Much of it consists of large chunks of direct quotation from Spencer. But Lewes singles out for particular praise Spencer's Law of Progress, the progressive adaptation of organization to circumstances. One passage is of particular importance: "The universal law of physical modification is the law of mental modification also."[73] Of course, this argument follows logically upon Spencer's belief, nurtured in phrenology, that mind is subject to the same laws as body. But here, in this simple statement, can be found the germ of Herbert Spencer's great contribution to nineteenth-century intellectual history: an evolutionary psychology.

It is in this notion of "mental modification" that we find the inception of what would ultimately constitute a far profounder reconciliation of two philosphical traditions than the mediating social theory of *Social Statics*. In his first book, Spencer attempts to reconcile two conflicting schools of social philosophy; in *The Principles of Psychology*, he moves a step further, to reconcile the divergent assumptions about the nature of the human mind that underpin these two schools. John Stuart Mill considered Spencer an "anti-Utilitarian." In a letter to psychologist Alexander Bain, Spencer denied the title; in fact, he both drew upon Utilitarian principles for his evolutionary psychology and modified them significantly: "I believe that the experiences of utility, organized and consolidated through all past generations of the human race, have been producing corresponding nervous modifications, which, by continued transmission and accumulation, have become in us certain faculties of moral intuition—certain emotions responding to right and wrong conduct—which have no apparent basis in the individual experiences of utility."[74] This passage speaks of Spencer's achievement in *The Principles of Psychology* (of which I will have more to say below), the reconciliation of intuition and experience through a theory of racial heredity. But it also draws attention to the origins of that reconciliation in the synthetic approach to Bentham and Shaftesbury, "experiences of utility" and "moral intuition," begun in *Social Statics*.

Herbert Spencer was George Henry Lewes's Victorian Spinoza for many reasons: the sheer audacity of an all-embracing system; the highly abstract, reasoned deification of passionate emotion; the belief in a scientific psychology that would treat mind and body as one substance. But for Lewes, Spinoza finally remains a transcendental philosopher, the ground of his

philosophy fenced within the subjective realm of consciousness. As the Victorian Spinoza, Spencer would combine
"German" philosophy with "Baconian" science by way of evolutionary biology, providing a ground for the Absolute that
transcended the limitations of the individual mind.

III. STATICS AND DYNAMICS—TRANSCENDENTAL ANATOMY AND
THE DEVELOPMENT HYPOTHESIS—SPENCER AND LEWES: ESSAYS,
1851-1857.

All discovery must be the discovery either of a fact *or of a* relation. . . . *The discovery of a fact* may *be a consequence of
pre-eminent faculties in the discoverer, but it is not necessarily
so. The discovery of a relation, on the contrary, is strictly and
exclusively the consequence of pre-eminent faculties, or* power
of origination.—*George Eliot to George Combe, 22 April 1852*

As Herbert Spencer recalled, the subject of his first conversation with George Henry Lewes in the spring of 1850 was not
social statics, but the development hypothesis.[75] Thereafter, it
was not backward to social theories inherited from the eighteenth century, but forward, to the exciting scientific developments of their own times, to which the new friends turned during the "long Sunday-rambles," beginning in the summer of
1851, which gradually grew into more wide-ranging excursions about the English countryside. One four-day journey up
the valley of the Thames was especially significant: "It was to
the impulse he received from the conversations during these
four days that Lewes more particularly ascribed that awakened
interest in scientific theories," writes Spencer. "And in me,"
he continues, "observation on the forms of leaves set going a
train of thought which ended in my writing an essay on 'The
Laws of Organic Form'; an extended exposition of which occupies some space in *The Principles of Biology*" (1864).[76]

In that essay, published in the *British and Foreign Medico-
Chirugical Review* in 1859, Spencer reminisces about the same
ramble, mentioning Lewes by name as his companion. He remembers picking a buttercup, gazing upon its form, and

reflecting on the effects of soil and climate on structure. Spencer's interest is equally divided between the questions of environmental influence and the inherent structural principles within the plant itself. "The conditions are manifestly the antecedent, and the form the consequent," he concludes; "it may be fairly presumed that like relationship holds throughout the animal kingdom." Spencer is also impressed with the "universal harmony" of morphological forms, "the unity which pervades the organic creation."[77]

These were the same terms to which Spencer and Lewes would return again and again in their essays of the early 1850s: the unity of composition and the multiplicity of adaptation; in man, the animal kingdom, organic creation, and, in a grand progressive synthesis, the cosmos itself. Within the next year after that theory-hunting expedition, both Lewes and Spencer made public their adherence to the controversial "development hypothesis": Lewes first, the autumn after those summer rambles, in "Lyell and Owen on Development" (*Leader*, 18 October 1851); Spencer in the same journal in March 1852, on "The Development Hypothesis."

In his essay Lewes articulates his disagreement with particular scientific details in Lyell, Owen, and Robert Chambers. Yet he also argues for the larger ideological correctness of evolutionary theory: "The differences are reconcilable between all forms of the development hypothesis directly we substitute for it the more abstract and comprehensive formula of the law of Progressive Adaptation."[78] Although Spencer acknowledges that the theory of evolution is not yet "adequately supported by the facts" (many of which Darwin would provide), he also asserts unequivocally that "any existing species immediately begins to undergo certain changes of structure fitting it for new conditions." These changes follow the same pattern of progressive development that Spencer traced in *Social Statics*: "Complex organic forms have arisen by successive modifications out of simple ones."[79]

It is often remarked that during the decade before Charles Darwin's *Origin of Species*, evolution was "in the air." Chapter 2 demonstrated that Chambers's *Vestiges of Creation* was an important source of Lewes's and Spencer's early notions about evolution. Both men were also well-acquainted with the many other scientific guises in which precursors of Darwin appeared during the nineteenth century in the work of men such as Lyell, Owen, Lamarck. But it is important to remember that for both Lewes and Spencer, the faith preceded the facts. I have chosen Chambers as my prototypical Victorian evolutionist, precisely because he was, as Lewes said, the most "metaphysical" of these scientific theorists. For Lewes and Spencer began with certain beliefs about the order of things; when they read contemporary scientists, they sought the facts to fit those beliefs (*"tant pis pour les fleurs"*).[80]

In the discussion of Lewes's and Spencer's evolutionary beliefs that follows, I make no claim to do full justice to the complex matrix of contemporary scientific developments that influenced these two Victorian thinkers. Rather, I will isolate the concepts I believe were central to their evolutionary cosmologies as they developed in the early 1850s, and suggest some of the sources for these concepts. They are: the unity of composition (from Goethe and St. Hilaire); the organism and the medium (from Comte); and the development from homogeneity to heterogeneity (from von Baer). The interrelation of these three concepts (and they were inseparable for Lewes and Spencer) reveals the thesis / antithesis / synthesis structure so characteristic of these Victorians: the static morphology of the unity of composition; the dynamic evolution of the developmental process; and what Lewes calls "the Staticodynamical view," in which the inherent "transcendent" structure of the individual organism is counterbalanced against the ever-changing forces of the medium as a whole.[81]

Unity of Composition

Lewes's choice of Goethe as the subject for a full-length biography (the first ever written on the German) was motivated by a subject who was scientific and philosophical, as well as literary. Lewes clearly saw Goethe as a model for his own yearning to fuse science and humanism. Appropriately, Goethe was deeply involved in the rediscovery of Spinoza by the German romantics, praising Spinoza as one "who had wrought so powerfully on me, and who was destined to affect so deeply, my entire mode of thinking."[82] Goethe, like Herbert Spencer, was another genius in the Spinozist mold, the man of passionate emotions and far-reaching abstractions. In his *Life of Goethe*, Lewes singles out Goethe's ability to "[unite] the mastery of Will and Intellect to the profoundest sensibility of Emotion."[83] In an extended passage from that book, Lewes compares Goethe's "poetical Pantheism" to Spinoza's, with evolutionary overtones: "In it the whole universe was conceived as divine . . . as the living manifestation of divine energy . . . St. Paul tells us that God lives in everything and everything in God. Science tells us that the world is always *becoming* . . . the primal energies of Life are . . . issuing forth under new forms, through metamorphoses higher and higher."[84]

When Herbert Spencer writes in his *Autobiography* that "the inability of a man of science to take the poetic view simply shows his mental limitation; as the mental limitation of a poet is shown by his inability to take the scientific view. The broader mind can take both. Those who allege this antagonism forget that Goethe, predominantly a poet, was also a scientific inquirer," he unmistakably takes his cue from Lewes.[85] Goethe is not just a scientist who is also a poet; he is a poetical scientist. Head and heart, reason and imagination are fully integrated in him. As such Goethe epitomizes the intellectual temperament of both Lewes and Spencer themselves: "Do not mistake him for a metaphysician. He was a positive thinker on the *a priori* Method."[86]

Lewes's interest in Goethe germinated in the essay "Goethe as a Man of Science," published in the *Westminster* under Eliot's editorship in 1852, which reappeared as chapter 9, book 5 in the *Life*, retitled "The Poet as a Man of Science." The seeds of Lewes's interest in Goethe were scientific, not literary.

Lewes was the first to discuss seriously Goethe's work as a scientist on the metamorphosis of plants, the vertebral structure of the skull, and the discovery of the intermaxillary bone common to both man and animals. Lewes begins his essay by categorizing scientists as "analytical" or "synthetical" (those favorite Spencerian terms), as epitomized by Cuvier and St. Hilaire: "The former starts from Individuals in order to arrive at a Whole. . . . The latter carries within himself the image of this Whole, and lives in the persuasion that little by little the Individuals will be deduced from it."[87] He goes on to trace the similarities between the work of St. Hilaire and Goethe, arguing that Goethe, like St. Hilaire, is a "synthetical" scientist.

Lewes credits St. Hilaire with the grand concept of "Unity of composition," a notion not only of service to zoological studies, but of philosophical significance as well.[88] He would return to this same idea at length in an essay on the "Life and Doctrine of Geoffrey St. Hilaire," again in the *Westminster*, in 1854: "What is his Doctrine? . . . That throughout the infinite variety of organic forms there runs one principle of composition: that there is one type underlying all diversities. This is . . . the greatest idea contributed by zoology to philosophy." St. Hilaire's "anatomy was philosophic, or transcendent, because *transcending* the vision of the eye, it had the vision of the mind"; it is "this addition of Reason to Observation which characterizes philosophic anatomy."[89] Herbert Spencer announced in his own essay on "Transcendental Physiology" in 1857 that he too was a "transcendental anatomist" who sought "general principles of structure common to vast and varied groups of organisms—the unity of plan discernible throughout multitudinous species."[90]

But Goethe was not merely "synthetical." He was also "eminently a positive thinker . . . the attitude of his mind, the organic tendency of his nature, was eminently scientific."[91] Revealingly, Lewes compares Goethe with Bacon as one "penetrated by the spirit of positive philosophy." In systole

and diastole, Goethe descends from the philosophical generalization to the scientific fact, "and thus brings the whole diversity of forms within the unity of Life."[92] Lewes notes that
Goethe himself was an early believer in the development hypothesis. Like Spencer, Goethe looks not just at static structure, but also to progressive development. In the *Life* Lewes
quotes Goethe on the "law of Individuation," in language that
bears an unmistakable similarity to Spencer's in *Social Statics*:
"The more imperfect a being is, the more do its individual
parts resemble each other, and the more do these parts resemble
the whole. The more perfect the being, the more dissimilar are
the parts. . . . The more the parts resemble each other, the
less subordination is there of one to the other. Subordination
of parts indicates high grade of organization."[93]

Lewes believes that Unity of Composition is a profound truth.
Unity of Composition is the necessary starting point for an evolutionary biology; but taken by itself, it places too much emphasis on the static inherent order of the individual organism.
It is not adequate to explain the changing nature of the universe. "It is only by connecting this theory with another, viewing it as the Statical Law of which the Development is the Dy-
namical Law, that, in our opinion, it can be accepted," Lewes
concludes.[94] Lewes and Spencer found the key to progressive
adaptation in the dynamic interrelationship of organism and
medium.

Organism and Medium

Writing on "The Natural History of German Life" in 1856,
George Eliot made clear that she had thoroughly assimilated
Herbert Spencer's movement from a biological to a social
model in *Social Statics*: "The external conditions which society has inherited from the past are but the manifestation of inherited internal conditions in the human beings who compose
it; the internal conditions and the external are related to each
other as the organism and the medium; and development can

take place only by the gradual constantaneous development of both."[95]

When Lewes investigated "Mr. Darwin's Hypothesis" in 1868, he credited French scientist Jean-Baptiste Lamarck (1744-1829) with the "law of Adaptation" that Charles Darwin enlarged into "natural selection," praising "the singular importance of Lamarck's hypothesis in calling attention to modifiability of structure through modifications of adaptation." Although Lamarck erred in placing too much emphasis on the medium at the expense of the organism, he provided a necessary corrective to the static viewpoint of transcendental anatomy. "Naturalists before his time had been wont to consider the Organism apart from the Medium in which it existed; [Lamarck] clearly saw that vital phenomena depended on the relation of the two."[96]

Auguste Comte's emphasis on the relationship of organism and medium developed the same idea.[97] Lewes found the most explicit statement of the concept in Comte's definition of life in the *Cours de philosophie positive*: "The idea of Life supposes the mutual relation of two indispensible elements—an organism and a suitable medium or environment."[98] Lewes returns to the concept repeatedly throughout his book on Comte: "So far from organic bodies being independent of external circumstances they become more and more dependent on them as their organization becomes higher, so that organism and a medium are the two correlative ideas of life."[99]

This same notion of mutual interdependence lies directly behind Herbert Spencer's famous definition of life in *The Principles of Psychology*: "the continuous adjustment of internal relations to external relations."[100] Lewes's own emphasis on the relationship between organism and medium as the cornerstone of his evolutionary philosophy never wavered. His final book, *Problems of Life and Mind*, echoes the ideas of twenty-five years earlier: *"Every vital phenomena is the product of two factors, the Organism and the Medium"*; "Life may be defined as the mode of existence of an organism in relation to its medium."[101]

Homogeneity and Heterogeneity.

But taken by themselves, Unity of Composition and the interdependence of Organism and Medium do not necessitate a belief in progressive evolutionary development. The final seeds of Lewes's and Spencer's evolutionary theory were planted when Spencer reviewed W. B. Carpenter's *Principles of Physiology* in the autumn of 1851. In reading Carpenter writes Spencer, "I became acquainted with von Baer's statement that the development of every organism is a change from homogeneity to heterogeneity. The substance of the thought was not new to me, though its form was." The substance of von Baer's theory is anticipated in *Social Statics* as "an unshaped belief in the development of living things; including, in a vague way, social development."[102] Spencer's sociological notions of "individuation," in which each part becomes progressively more individualized and complex, yet simultaneously more interdependent with the whole, are given explicit scientific foundation by the German zoologist and embryologist Karl Ernst von Baer (1792-1876). Carpenter writes in the summary of von Baer that Spencer read: "The lower we descend in the scale of being, whether in Animal or in Vegetable series, the nearer approach do we make to that *homogeneousness* which is the typical attribute of organic bodies, wherein every particle has all the characters of individuality . . . as we ascend in the scale of being, we find the fabric—whether of the Plant or the Animal—becoming more and more heterogeneous."[103]

Reviewing Carpenter's book in 1855, T. H. Huxley claimed that von Baer's laws "are to Biology what Kepler's great generalizations were to Astronomy."[104] Spencer's application of von Baer gave the proof to Huxley's analogy. His researches in embryology led von Baer to conclude that development proceeds from the general to the more highly specialized. Not surprisingly, Herbert Spencer titled the 1857 essay that took von Baer's "homogeneity" and "heterogeneity" as its passwords "Progress: Its Law and Cause." Just as Spencer moved analogously from sociology to biology in *Social Statics*, so he made the even greater leap, in "Progress," from von Baer's embryology to a full-blown Victorian cosmology:

> The series of changes gone through during the development of a seed into a tree, or an ovum into an animal, constitute an advance from homogeneity of structure to heterogeneity of structure. . . . This is the history of all organisms whatever. . . . Now, we propose in the first place to show, that this law of organic progress is the law of all progress. Whether it be in the development of the Earth, in the development of Life upon its surface, in the development of Society, of Government, of Manufactures, of Commerce, of Language, Literature, Science, Art, this same evolution of the simple into the complex through successive differentiations, holds throughout.[105]

Spencer's intellectual kinship with Robert Chambers is most apparent in this essay. Chambers gathers the universe into "one majestic Whole," from the nebular hypothesis and the formation of the solar system to the mind of man, under the universal law of development.[106] In "Progress: Its Law and Cause," Spencer follows the same structural model as the *Vestiges*, tracing the "law of progress" (the development from homogeneity to heterogeneity) through the solar system, the formation of the earth, plants and animals, man, society, language, religion, and art.

George Henry Lewes and George Eliot were also much taken with von Baer. In June 1853 Lewes devoted an essay in the *Leader* to "Von Baer on the Development Hypothesis," stressing "the law of *organic modification* in adaptation to circumstances."[107] Lewes also quotes the German scientist in his *Life of Goethe* in 1855: "The history of Development is the true torchbearer in every inquiry into organic bodies." Lewes continues in his own words, in terms that make clear that the notion of a broader, nonbiological application of von Baer's biological principles did not originate with Herbert Spencer in 1857: "In Geology, in Physiology, in History, and in Art, we are now all bent on tracing the phases of development. To understand the *grown* we try to follow the *growth*."[108] In that same year, Lewes notes that he and George Eliot are reading Carpenter's *Principles of Physiology* again—along with Gall's *Anatomie et physiologie du cerveau.*[109]

Of George Eliot's interest in von Baer, we have only a small but intriguing clue, to be found in the first of those three passionate love letters to Spencer in July 1852. The lovesick intellectual depicts herself filled with "a loathing for books," regressing on the scale of mental evolution: "You see I am sinking fast towards 'homogeneity,' and my brain will soon be a mere pulp unless you come to arrest the downward process."[110] Gordon Haight footnotes Spencer's essay on the "Development Hypothesis" of 20 March 1852 as the source of Eliot's "homogeneity"; but in fact "homogeneity" and "heterogeneity" do not make their first entrance in print until Spencer's essay on "The Philosophy of Style," in October 1852—and are not explicitly related to Spencer's evolutionary beliefs until "Progress," in 1857.[111] Spencer discovered von Baer's law while reading Carpenter in the autumn of 1851, and George Eliot offers a small but unmistakable clue that she was present at the creation. Eliot, like Herbert Spencer, was nurtured in the progressive cosmology of the phrenological world view; like Lewes, she met Spencer with an intellectual disposition ready to resonate with his. This was the woman who had opened her first essay for the *Westminster Review* in January 1851 "with a profound belief in the progressive character of human development."[112]

After 1859 Eliot, Lewes, and Spencer all accepted Darwin's evolutionary thesis—although each did so with qualifications. In the late 1860s, a congenial scientific correspondence between Charles Darwin and George Henry Lewes ensued, recently published in volume 8 of *The George Eliot Letters.* Lewes produced a series of lengthy essays on "Mr. Darwin's Hypothesis" in the *Fortnightly* in 1868 with the evolutionist's blessing: "The articles strike me as *quite* excellent, and I hope they will be republished; but I fear they will be too deep for many readers," Darwin writes Lewes.[113]

Although much that he says about Darwin in 1868 is beyond

the scope of this study, it is appropriate to note here that Lewes did not see Darwin's ideas as radically different from evolutionary predecessors like St. Hilaire, Lamarck, and Robinet. Lewes did argue that Darwin's unique contribution, natural selection, though only another hypothesis, is "the best hypothesis at present." He credits Darwin with a more explicit formulation of the "law of adaptation" than his predecessors, but he also finds reflected in Mr. Darwin's hypothesis much that should seem familiar to the reader of Herbert Spencer in the 1850s: "The evolution of Life is the evolution of the special from the general, the complex from the simple. An organism rises in power as it ramifies into variety. From a homogeneous organic mass a complex structure is evolved," writes Lewes— summarizing Darwin in very Spencerian language. Within Darwin's theory of natural selection, Lewes found a persuasive reformulation of his own dual emphasis on the dynamic interrelationship of "conditions" and "form," medium and organism: "Minds unconvinced [by previous theories] . . . were at once subdued by the principles of Natural Selection, involving as it did, on the one hand, the incontestible 'Struggle for Existence,' and on the other, the known laws of Adaptation and Hereditary Transmission."[114] But in the final analysis, the affinities between Herbert Spencer and Robert Chambers's *Vestiges* are much closer than any with Charles Darwin's *Origin*. Spencer is a cosmologist rather than a practicing scientist. He is interested in evolution as a universal process that could be applied not just to individual organisms, but to the solar system, social structures, and everything in between.

Spencer's second book, *The Principles of Psychology* (1855), takes the general evolutionary notions that first appeared in the social theory of *Social Statics*, and combines them with the scientific concepts of the early 1850s shared by Lewes and Spencer. The product: a model of the human mind that grows out of the distinctive intellectual matrix of this Victorian circle. For Herbert Spencer in the 1850s, the most productive application of the universal law of "progress" was to be found in the field of human psychology. This was to be

Spencer's most original contribution to the history of ideas. It was Herbert Spencer, not Charles Darwin, who first conceptualized an adaptive, evolutionary psychology.[115]

IV. LIFE AND MIND—HERBERT SPENCER: *THE PRINCIPLES OF PSY-CHOLOGY* (1855)

Both George Eliot and George Henry Lewes were closely involved with the creation of *The Principles of Psychology*. Spencer's "general interest in mental phenomena" had been increased by reading Lewes's *Biographical History of Philosophy* in the autumn of 1851. He dated the inception of the *Principles* from a letter to his father in March 1852 when he began his reading (starting with Mill's *Logic*, lent him by Eliot) for his "Introduction to Psychology."[116] The reader will remember that March 1852 dates the beginning of the most intense period of Eliot's and Spencer's relationship. Although the romance soon cooled, their continuing intellectual intimacy is evident in George Eliot's ecstatic letter to Sara Sophia Hennell in July 1854: "Herbert Spencer . . . will stand in the Biographical Dictionaries of 1954 as 'Spencer, Herbert, an original and profound philosophical writer, especially known by his great work XXX which gave a new impulse to psychology and has mainly contributed to the present advanced position of that science, compared with that which it had attained in the middle of the last century.' "[117]

After *The Principles of Psychology* was published in 1855, Eliot lent copies to her friends, and, reported George Henry Lewes, "*nailed* to the book by his interest in it."[118] Lewes, who had learned the art of adaptive survival of the fittest in the literary marketplace, wrote two quite different reviews of the book, one for the more conservative *Saturday Review*—"As the Saturday Review is not to be heterodox, he was necessarily gêné," explains Eliot[119]—the other, a series of three essays for the less orthodox *Leader*. Both are fascinating: the first for what it reveals of the impact of *The Principles of Psychology* on the general Victorian reader; the second for the clarity with which it represents Spencer's theories as the culmination of Lewes's search for the Victorian Spinoza.

The Principles of Psychology is grounded on the application of the physiological method to the study of the human mind: "He makes Psychology one of the great divisions of Biology," Lewes writes in the *Leader*.[120] The same readers who had been shocked by Combe, Chambers, and Martineau would respond in like manner to the *Principles*, as Lewes well knew when he wrote his "gêné" essay for the *Saturday Review*: "This is an exposition of psychical phenomena which will find little favor except with those who advocate materialism." Spencer's "denial of free-will" and "identification of mind with life" will be particularly controversial, observes Lewes; the *Principles* "cannot hope for much acceptance from the English public."[121] He was correct: "It does not appear to us scientific in character. . . . We are opposed to Mr. Spencer's fundamental principles," wrote the *British Quarterly Review*.[122] In the Unitarian *National Review*, R. H. Hutton entitles his essay "Atheism": "We find philosophers like Mr. Spencer, instead of *examining* the moral realities of human life, actually dissipating or distorting them, in the hope of *deducing* them from physiological assumptions."[123] Such objections should by now sound familiar.

But when Lewes turns to his first essay in the *Leader*, "Herbert Spencer's Psychology," the tactful mask of the common reader cast aside, the intensity of his intellectual excitement is unrestrained. Lewes designates Herbert Spencer as the third and culminating figure in a crucial process of scientific discovery, which begins with St. Hilaire's zoology and continues with Schwann's cell theory. Just as "Schwann set aside the old methods," writes Lewes, "and proved the Unity of Composition which really underlies all the variety of forms, so Herbert Spencer sets aside" the old philosophical psychology: "We may pause by the way to notice the stages of the history of this doctrine of Unity, which succeed each other according to the law of development, i.e. from general to particular. First comes Geoffrey St. Hilaire, who proclaims the Unity of Composition in the animal *forms*; then Schwann, who proves the Unity in the animal *tissues*; and finally, Herbert Spencer, who proves that Unity in the animal intelligence."[124]

Forms, tissues, intelligence—from the most homogeneous and general to the most particular, complex, and specialized forms of life; all are a part of that great Whole, that single Substance that constitutes the monist's universe. "The Law rules the whole, one process is seen amid the endless variety," writes Lewes. He reminds the reader of his 1851 review of *Social Statics*, and feels compelled to reiterate, even more emphatically, the analogy he drew there: "In reviewing Herbert Spencer's former work, we compared him with Spinoza: a comparison which seemed strange and even hyperbolical to those who knew nothing of the old Hebrew logician; but this *Principles of Psychology* is so like Spinoza in the mental qualities it exhibits, and frequently in the very doctrine it professes, that no one acquainted with the two can fail to perceive their kindred."[125]

In Spencer's *Principles of Psychology*, the positivist millennium has, in theory, arrived. Spencer has rescued British psychology from the airy insubstantialities of "arachnae" metaphysics. In editions of his *Biographical History* after 1855, Lewes added footnotes to that effect.[126] And thirty years after that first history of philosophy, he returns to the same subject in *Problems of Life and Mind*. Locke, Hobbes, Berkeley, and Hume "have produced essays, not systems. There has been no noteworthy attempt to give a conception of the World, of Man, and of Society, wrought out with systematic harmonizing of principles. . . . Mr. Herbert Spencer is now for the first time deliberately making the attempt to found a Philosophy."[127] This is a philosophy on the positive plan. At the heart of the *Principles* lies Spencer's most original contribution: he takes the biological principles he shared with Lewes during the early 1850s—the unity of composition, the organism and the medium, progressive adaptation from homogeneity to heterogeneity—and applies them to mental development: within the individual, but, with more far-reaching implications, to the human race as a whole.

George Henry Lewes entitled his third review essay of Spencer's *Principles*, "Life and Mind," twenty years before his own *magnum opus* by that title. In order to appreciate Spencer's theories of mind, we must first state his definition of life. This subject has been discussed at some length in my prelude, in the context of Spencer's borrowings from Samuel Taylor Coleridge. Taken in conjunction with von Baer's development from homogeneity to heterogeneity, Spencer's "individuation" becomes an evolutionary process. This process is effected by the dynamic and adaptive interaction of organism and medium. Thus Spencer arrives at his "broadest and most complete definition of life": *"The continuous adjustment of internal relations to external relations."*[128]

This definition may strike the twentieth-century reader as less than earth-shaking. But we must place Spencer's definition against the psychology of Locke, Hume, Berkeley, and prior to Darwin's biology, to perceive its genuinely radical impact. In his own *Principles of Psychology*, William James paid homage to Spencer:

> At a certain stage in the development of every science a degree of vagueness is what best consists with fertility. On the whole, few recent formulas have done more real service of a rough sort in psychology than the Spencerian one that the essence of mental life and bodily life are one, namely, "the adjustment of inner to outer relations." Such a formula is vagueness incarnate; but because it takes into account the fact that minds inhabit environments which act on them and on which they in turn react; because, in short, it takes mind in the midst of all its concrete relations, it is immensely more fertile than the old-fashioned "rational psychology," which treated the soul as a detached existent, sufficient unto itself and assumed to consider only its nature and properties.[129]

According to Herbert Spencer, this adjustment of inner to outer, organism to medium, leads to "progressive adaptation."[130] When this adaptation is translated into psychological terms, Spencer arrives at his theory of mental inheritance, the cornerstone of *The Principles of Psychology*.

The Principles of Psychology is divided into four parts: the general analysis, special analysis, general synthesis, and special synthesis. In his preface Spencer explains that "the four parts of which this work consists, though intimately related to each other as different views of the same great aggregate of phenomena, are yet, in the main, severally independent and complete in themselves." The analysis deals with the study of human intelligence subjectively; the synthesis, objectively.[131] To translate this Spencerese: in his analysis, Spencer views the human mind philosophically, from the subjective, internal perspective, the single center of consciousness; in the synthesis, he views the same phenomena biologically, or objectively: each mind as a single part of a greater synthetic whole, the larger pattern of evolutionary development. The essence of *The Principles of Psychology* is to be found in the ingenious method by which Spencer mediates between analysis and synthesis, the claims of philosophy and biology, introspection and observation, intuition and experience; and asserts the harmonious coexistence and dynamic interpenetration of both.

Although Spencer claimed to ground his psychology on biology rather than metaphysical speculation, he did not believe that dissecting the brain like a turnip was any more efficacious, taken alone, than introspective cogitation. In claiming the unity of composition, that life and mind are one substance, Spencer did not intend simple materialism; like Spinoza, it is inaccurate to classify him as either materialist or idealist. In fact, what Spencer sought was a science of mind that would transcend biology; to unify the polarities of introspective idealists and their innate ideas (such as the "moral sense") with the empirical men of science, who grounded their utilitarian beliefs on sense experience. The hereditary transmission of innate mental characteristics was Herbert Spencer's key to all mythologies, his intended reconciliation of the Shaftesbury and the Benthamite schools; his chief claim to a science of mind that would combine the truths of the metaphysicians with the discoveries of the biologists.

In my discussion of Charles Bray and Harriet Martineau, I suggested that the bridge between Carlyle and Bentham for Bray, mystical experience and materialism for Martineau, was to be found in a blend of nineteenth-century romanticism with eighteenth-century rationalism, phrenology, and association psychology. In its original, "static," inception, Gall's phrenology argued for the unity of composition, mind as matter, innate mental characteristics determined in each individual at birth. But beginning with George Combe and Robert Chambers, these optimistic Victorian necessitarians added a "dynamic" belief in progress, adaptive change in accordance with circumstance. The law of universal causation remained invariable, as Mill and Comte had asserted; but the individual could also form new associative mental patterns, altering his innate constitution. And most significantly this new constitution could be passed on to the next generation.

George Henry Lewes's final words on the much-maligned science of phrenology were ones of praise: "Gall taught men the futility of looking inwards, and neglecting the vast mass of external observation which animals and societies afforded; he taught them *where* to seek the primary organic conditions—in inherited structures and inherited aptitudes. The effect of this teaching is conspicuous in modern works."[132] One of these modern works was *The Principles of Psychology*. The reader will recall that Spencer's introduction to psychology was phrenology during the decade of Charles Bray's *Philosophy of Necessity* and Robert Chambers's *Vestiges of Creation*, George Combe's proselytizing and Harriet Martineau's conversion. Robert M. Young argues persuasively that phrenology was also a seminal influence behind Spencer's psychological theories.[133] My discussion above of Combe and Chambers, Bray and Martineau, has suggested some of the ways in which Spencer's wedding of psychology to evolutionary biology was anticipated by other members of this Victorian circle, all of whom can be linked with phrenology.[134]

Hints of the evolutionary possibilities of phrenology can be found in the *Vestiges of Creation*. Chambers believes mental characteristics are innate: "The mental characters of individuals are inherently various . . . education and circumstance . . . are incapable of entirely altering these characters." And yet, he continues provocatively, "there is, nevertheless, a general adaptation of the mental constitution of man to the circumstances in which he lives." Might not environment alter heredity? And might not the development of the individual be parallel to that of the race?[135] Not surprisingly, young Charles Darwin took a strong interest in the evolutionary possibilities of phrenology: "One is tempted to believe phrenologists are right about habitual exercise of the mind, altering the head, & thus these qualities become hereditary," he writes in his notebooks in 1838. "To avoid stating how far I believe, in Materialism, say only that emotions, instincts, degrees of talent, which are hereditary are so because brain of child resembles parent stock.—(& phrenologists state that brain alters)."[136]

The phrenological cosmologies of Robert Chambers and George Combe, Charles Bray and Harriet Martineau, are intended to be equally biological and metaphysical; but prior to Herbert Spencer, the metaphysics clearly outweighed the biology. In 1855 Spencer not only had the phrenological background upon which to draw, but also the broader range of scientific sources he had explored with Lewes, from "transcendental anatomy" to the adaptation of the organism to the medium.

As early as 1841, in the *Philosophy of Necessity*, Charles Bray had anticipated Herbert Spencer's *Principles of Psychology*: "All moral rules are derived originally from Utility, but the pleasures and pains . . . on which they are based are transmitted to offspring and thus become intuitions."[137] But it is left to the reader of the *Philosophy of Necessity* to move inferentially from this statement to a reconciliation of Bray's transcendental with his empirical tendencies; Bray himself makes no overt connection. By contrast, in *The Principles of Psychology*, Spencer's synthesis is systematic and explicit, as he claims to "furnish a solution to the controversy between the disciples of Locke and those of Kant," combining "the experience-hypothesis and the hypothesis of the transcendentalists: neither of which is tenable by itself."[138]

"Before our generation," wrote William James in 1890, when empirical psychologists contended that sense experience was the basis of mental development, "it was the experience of the individual only that was meant." In his "brilliant and seductive" *Principles of Psychology*, Herbert Spencer wrought a seminal change: "When one nowadays says that the human mind owes its present shape to experience, he means the experience of ancestors as well. Mr. Spencer's statement of this is the earliest emphatic one."[139] In *Problems of Life and Mind*, George Henry Lewes rewrites Locke's famous metaphor in Spencerian terms: "The sensitive subject is no *tabula rasa*; it is not a blank sheet of paper, but a palimpsest."[140]

The heart of Spencer's argument for this new definition of an "experiential" school of psychology is to be found in chapter 3 of part 4 of The Principles of Psychology, the "Special Synthesis," "The Growth of Intelligence." There Spencer argues that all knowledge does come from experience, but expands the definition of experience to include "the experience of the *race* organisms forming its ancestry." Like the phrenologists Spencer believes in innate mental faculties; but he incorporates phrenology with association psychology, to arrive at the notion of mental development: "The familiar doctrine of association here undergoes a great extension. . . . The effects of associations are . . . transmitted as modifications of the nervous system."[141] Hereditary transmission is the key to this process by which each new mind is born, as a palimpsest, already imprinted with a rich mental heritage of so-called "innate" ideas: "Instinct may be regarded as a kind of organized memory."[142]

Spencer saves his biggest gun for the end: "As most who have read thus far have perceived," this notion of mental heredity implies "a tacit adhesion to the development hypothesis."[143] The racial mind of man develops over time, as its ancestral heritage grows ever more complex. What began as animal instincts evolve into higher mental processes: "That progressive complication of the instincts, which . . . involves a progressive dimunition of their purely automatic character, likewise involves a simultaneous commencement of Memory and Reason."[144] Spencer's definition of life as "the continuous adjustment of internal relations to external relations" is thus central to the *Principles*. In her notebooks in the early 1870s, George Eliot demonstrated her familiarity with the vocabulary of the *Principles of Psychology*: "We have, as well as we can, to arrive at the classification which is called the distinction between the Static & Dynamic—between what is an inherent quality or characteristic or need of the human being . . . & what is modifiable or doomed to disappear under successive changes."[145]

The year after Spencer's *Principles of Psychology* was published, Lewes wrote his essay on "Hereditary Influence, Animal and Human," which abounds with echoes of Spencer. Just as they had shared the unity of composition, the organism and the medium, and the development from homogeneity to heterogeneity between 1851–54, this intellectual friendship continued to be the source of rich reciprocation for both men. "We inherit the acquired experience of our forefathers—their tendencies, their aptitudes, their habits, their improvements," writes Lewes, commending to his readers the "original and remarkable 'Principles of Psychology' ": "In this work Heritage, for the first time, is made the basis of a psychological system; and we especially recommend any reader interested in the present article, to make himself acquainted with a treatise in every way so remarkable."[146] Twenty years later, in the five-volume *Problems of Life and Mind*, the influence of Spencer's evolutionary psychology continues to be strong and unmistakable: "Thought is an embodied process, which has its conditions in the history of the race no less than in that of the individual," writes Lewes. "We learn by individual experiences, registrations of feeling, rendered possible by ancestral experience."[147]

The Principles of Psychology completes the scientific argument of this study, closing a circle of thinkers that found its methodology in the universal causation of John Stuart Mill and the positivism of Auguste Comte, and its first practical application in the phrenologists' claim that the brain is the organ of the mind. Herbert Spencer's original contribution to the history of psychology grows directly out of the matrix of ideas shared by this Victorian circle: the *Principles* fuses holistic metaphysics with evolutionary biology in an exemplary incarnation of a distinctively Victorian frame of mind. But the final note of my history is to be sounded in a theological key: because for all these thinkers, science was ultimately the servant of a higher faith. Thus I conclude with what Spencer called the "ontological bearings" of the case.[148]

V. THE KNOWABLE AND THE UNKNOWABLE—HERBERT SPENCER: "PROGRESS: ITS LAW AND CAUSE" (1857)

How strange it would be if Physical Science should first reduce the explanation of all phenomena to a single force, and then Philosophy step in to reduce the logic of all explanation to a single formula. What a sword wherewith to open the world, our oyster!—Robert Lytton to George Henry Lewes, 1872

Herbert Spencer's 1857 essay, "Progress: Its Law and Cause" was incorporated three years later into part 1 of *First Principles*, as "The Unknowable."[149] As we have seen, it was in "Progress" that Spencer made the conceptual leap from von Baer's embryology to his grand Victorian cosmology on a biological model. Von Baer's development from homogeneity to heterogeneity had provided Spencer with a key to all mythologies, a formula that would unlock the mysteries of the universe by a plan according to which all the parts would be clearly connected within one stupendous whole. This evolutionary process constitutes the first half of the essay, the scientific "law" of Progress. In the second half, Spencer turns to its "cause": "The Unknowable."

George Eliot's interest in the Unknowable antedated Spencer's; she had quoted R. W. McKay in her first essay for the *Westminster* in 1851: "The known and the unknown are intimately connected and correlative."[150] "Progress: Its Law and Cause," in its original essay form and its later version in *First Principles*, was singled out by Eliot for more praise than any of Spencer's other work. In a letter to Sara Sophia Hennell on

5 June 1857, Eliot leaves no doubt that it is Herbert Spencer as the poet of the Unknowable with whom she resonates:

> I feel every day a greater disinclination for theories and arguments about the origin of things in the presence of all this mystery and beauty and pain and ugliness, that floods one with conflicting emotions.

> Didn't you like the conclusion of Herbert Spencer's article in the W[estminster] R[eview]? There was more feeling in it than we generally get in his writing.

Her response to *First Principles* is similar: "I think the first part ["The Unknowable"] superior to anything he has done before, and he says he feels the same himself: it is less barely intellectual—the considerations are larger." Reading proof of the second part, George Eliot continues to find herself "supremely gratified": "It is, as he says, a result of his riper thought." "It is the best thing he has done," she writes in December 1860; and later: "It is touching to see how his whole life and soul are being poured into this book."[151] Eliot's first scene of clerical life, "Amos Barton," was published in January 1857; that October she would begin her first full-length novel, *Adam Bede*. The germinating artist found in Spencer's "Progress" considerations larger than the merely intellectual, a response to the same "mystery and beauty and pain and ugliness" that she would envision in the poetic eye of her fictions. And yet, like her friend Herbert Spencer, George Eliot the novelist can hardly be said to embody a "disinclination for theories." For Eliot as for Spencer, poetry and science are inseparable.

Significantly, Herbert Spencer's first mention of the Unknowable comes in his most confident and visionary essay. The more Spencer knows, the more clearly he can define the boundaries of what *cannot* be known; or, to put this another way, Spencer came to know, with confident certainty, exactly what he could never hope to understand. The known and the unknown are the ultimate Victorian polarity, as Spencer himself realized: "A known cannot be thought of apart from an

unknown. . . . To carry further the metaphor before used,—
they are the positive and negative poles of thought; of which
neither can gain in intensity without increasing the intensity
of the other."[152]

The pivotal transition from the known to the unknowable
takes place at the halfway point in "Progress: Its Law and
Cause": "Does not the universality of *law* imply a universal
cause? . . . To do this [fathom cause] would be to solve that
ultimate mystery which must ever transcend human intelligence." Although the optimistic Victorian believes that he can
fully come to understand the "how?" of the physical world, its
universal causation and evolutionary processes, this finally
does not answer its "why?": "We are still in the dark respecting
those mysterious properties in virtue of which the germ, when
subjected to the fit influences, undergoes the special changes
that begin the series of transformations."[153] When George Eliot
read Darwin's *Origin of Species* in 1859, she was already an
enthusiastic adherent of the development hypothesis; but Darwin's definitive intellectual breakthrough prompted her to respond with a polar antithesis: "To me the Development Theory and all other explanations of processes by which things
come to be, produce a feeble impression compared with the
mystery that lies under the processes."[154]

"Progress," Spencer concludes, "is not an accident, not a
thing within human control, but a beneficent necessity."[155] In
his *Autobiography* Spencer writes that the essay on "Progress"
was intended as a "repudiation of materialism."[156] Like Bray
and Martineau, Spencer did not believe that matter was all.
Nor did he believe in an orthodox Christian God as first mover.
But Spencer's beneficent necessity emanates from what can
surely be called a religious sense of the universe.

Twentieth-century critics have tended to be unsympathetic
to Spencer's Unknowable, regarding it as at best an amusing
and at worst a pathetic Victorian attempt at spiritual survival
in a world without God. "His philosophy of religion is an illogical blend of reason and faith," writes Alfred Benn, "which,
as such, finds its proper place among the various schemes of

compromise and conciliation characteristically put forward by English thought when the religious revolution had entered on its acute phase."[157] In *The Great Chain of Being*, A. O. Lovejoy is even less respectful: "There is a purely metaphysical other-worldliness which is sometimes to be found completely disso-ciated from any corresponding theory of the nature of the good, and therefore from any otherworldly moral and reli-gious temper. Perhaps the oddest example of this is to be seen in those half-dozen irrelevant chapters about the Unknowable which Herbert Spencer . . . prefixed to the Synthetic Philos-ophy."[158]

But the response of Spencer's contemporaries was quite dif-ferent: James Hinton rejoiced that Spencer had "shown so many evidences of a truly religious nature."[159] For these Victo-rians the Unknowable was a happy and a necessary counterpart to their boundless optimism about the knowable; an intensely emotional counterbalance to their equally intense rationality. Harriet Martineau wrote in her *Autobiography* in 1855: "Wondrous beyond the comprehension of any one mind is the mass of glorious facts, and the series of mighty conceptions laid open; but the shadow of the surrounding darkness rests upon it all. The unknown always engrosses the greater part of the field of vision; and the awe of infinity sanctifies both the study and the dream."[160] In his autobiography Bray quotes George Combe and Herbert Spencer in tandem:

> As George Combe says, "We cannot tell what matter is, and we are travelling through a world in which all that we can comprehend is truly relationship and nothing more. We know that the relation-ship established between things, and between our mind and them, gives rise to certain impressions in us, but we can penetrate no deeper into the mysteries of nature." "No relation in conscious-ness," says Herbert Spencer, "can resemble or be in any way akin to its source beyond consciousness."[161]

These mysteries of nature were not daunting; they were a source of joy and inspiration. George Henry Lewes first found the Unknowable in *Faust*'s "streben nach dem unendlichen": "If we at the outset content ourselves with the Knowable and attainable, and give up the wild impatience of desire for the Unknowable and unattainable . . . knowledge can only be relative, never absolute."[162] "*What* life is we know not—cannot know. The mystery is impenetrable. No positive philosophy attempts to penetrate it," he writes in *Comte*.[163] Twenty years later he opened volume 2 of the First Series of *Problems of Life and Mind* (suggestively titled *The Foundations of a Creed*) in a similar vein: "The Universe is mystic to man, and must ever remain so."[164] Clearly, Herbert Spencer did not originate the concept of the Unknowable. He is giving voice to a sensibility central to this Victorian frame of mind.

When Spencer transmuted "Progress: Its Law and Cause" into part 1 of *First Principles* as "The Unknowable," he made explicit the implications of the earlier essay, by entitling chapter 1 "Religion and Science," to replace "cause" and "law." Science and religion are, for Spencer, simply empiricism and intuitionism writ large: "This conclusion which . . . expresses the doctrine of the English school of philosophy, recognizes also a soul of truth in the doctrine of the antagonist German school—this conclusion . . . brings the results of speculation into harmony with those of common sense; is also the conclusion which reconciles Religion with Science." We have traversed the full circumference of this Victorian circle, back to the Coleridgean polarity that found expression in Mill's essays on Bentham and Coleridge, when Spencer writes:

> Each side, therefore, has to recognize the claims of the other as standing for truths that are not to be ignored. He who contemplates the Universe from the religious point of view, must learn to see that this which we call Science is one constituent of the great whole. . . . While he who contemplates the Universe from the scientific point of view, must learn to see that this which we call Religion is similarly a constituent of the great whole. . . . It behooves each party to strive to understand each other, with the conviction that the other has something worthy to be understood; and with the conviction that when mutually recognized this something will be the basis of a complete reconciliation.[165]

What is that "something worthy to be understood" that will effect the "complete reconciliation" of religion and science?

According to Spencer it is the "largest fact to be found within our mental range," an "ultimate fact," that will "[unite] these positive and negative poles of human thought." And what is this "deepest, widest, and most certain of all facts," the fact that is common to both religion and science?: "that the Power which the Universe manifests to us is utterly inscrutable."[166] Paradoxically the knowledge of the Unknowable is "the most certain of all facts." The ultimate mysteries of the universe are shared by both science and religion.

Previous critics of George Eliot have made much of the influence of Feuerbach's Religion of Humanity on her intellectual development. Feuerbach would reduce all religion to psychology, viewing God simply as a projection of all that is noblest in man's own nature: "Religion is human nature reflected, mirrored in itself."[167] Although Feuerbach did indeed have a great deal to teach George Eliot about the anthropological aspects of religion, I believe it is incorrect to assume that her translation in 1854 of Feuerbach's *Essence of Christianity* resulted in a demystification of the Unknowable for her. In that same letter to Charles Bray of 15 November 1857—six months after the publication of "Progress"—in which she defends the innate moral sense of the individual against the implications of Bray's utilitarianism, George Eliot speaks of "the many proofs that urge upon us our own total inability to find in our own natures a key to the Divine Mystery. I could more readily turn Christian and worship Jesus again than embrace a Theism which professes to explain the proceedings of God."[168]

But George Eliot wrote of Spencer in 1875 that "every main bias of [her] mind had been taken before [she] knew him."[169] Long before Spencer articulated it in *First Principles*, these Victorians sought in a wide variety of ways to reconcile religion and science, the emotions and the intellect, the unknowable and the knowable. In her first review essay for the *Westminster* on R. W. McKay, published six months prior to her first meeting with Spencer, George Eliot "[could not] resist giving a long extract" from McKay's "admirable" section on faith: "Religion and science are inseparable. No object in nature, no subject of contemplation, is destitute of religious tendency and meaning." Let me urge my readers to this essay itself, to the fascinating and lengthy passage from McKay that George Eliot quotes in full. "Faith is, to a great extent, involuntary; it is a law or faculty of our nature, operating silently and intuitively to supply the imperfections of our knowledge"; conversely, "the capacity of belief must be taught how to build securely, yet not arrogantly, on the data of experience." Ideally "faith and knowledge tend mutually to the confirmation and enlargement of each other."[170]

Knowing and feeling are literally, not just metaphorically, linked for these Victorians. Subjective and objective truths, intuitive expressions and sensory impressions, are two refractions of the same reality; transcendental visions are both a mystical impulse and a localized biological phenomenon. The Unknowable is also a scientific fact. "We find no room for matter at all. . . . We find only force or power, and that not separate from its source, or from God.[171] Bray, the reader will remember, draws upon Eastern mysticism, German idealism, and Spinoza for his concept of force: "There is but one infinite substance, and that is God"; but also, equally, on contemporary scientific theories of electricity and magnetism: "Science, then, proves the unity of Force."[172] Force bridges the physical and the metaphysical, operating in accordance with laws common to both matter and spirit.

Herbert Spencer's *Unknowable* has a great deal in common with Charles Bray's *force*:

> Though he may succeed in resolving all properties of objects into manifestations of force, he is not thereby enabled to conceive what force is; but finds, on the contrary, that the more he thinks about it, the more he is baffled. Similarly, though analysis of mental actions may finally bring him down to sensations as the original materials out of which all thought is woven, he is none the forwarder; for he cannot in the least comprehend sensation. Inward and outward things he thus discovers to be alike inscrutable in their ultimate genesis and nature. He sees that the Materialist and Spiritualist controversy is a mere war of words; the disputants being equally absurd—each believing he understands that which it is impossible for any man to understand.[173]

Spencer once again rejects any simple dichotomy of materialism and spiritualism; any view that sees the world purely as a
product of material forces, or conversely, entirely reducible to
subjective sensations. According to Spencer both physical
forces and mental sensations are manifestations of the same,
"primordial," force: "Those modes of the Unknowable which
we call motion, heat, light, chemical affinity, etc., are alike
transformable into each other, and into those modes of the
Unknowable which we distinguish as sensation, emotion,
thought,"[174] Not surprisingly, Charles Bray quotes this passage approvingly in his autobiography, also printing there a
letter he received from Spencer in 1881 in which the synthetic
philosopher asserts the same belief: "There is not only a correlation between physical force and that which we know as
feeling, but the one is, under the conditions specified, transformed into the other. In fact, I can perceive no other possible
interpretation of the phenomena."[175]

Another of the many interests George Henry Lewes shared
with Herbert Spencer was the concept of force. Although he
rejected Charles Bray's mesmeric force as a simplistic and unscientific notion in 1866, Lewes had discussed force as early as
1853, in an essay on "English Philosophy" in the *Leader*:
"The Organic is *reproductive*. . . . It thus becomes a *centre
of Force* . . . that which is true of the organical . . . is
equally true of the Mind; it is also a centre of Force."[176] In the
1870s Lewes turned to an extended discussion of force and
cause as "Problem V" of *The Foundations of a Creed* in *Problems of Life and Mind*. In chapter 1, "The Conception of
Force," Lewes, always the intellectual historian, summed up
previous definitions of *Force*—including Herbert Spencer's
Unknowable and Charles Bray's *imaginary entity*—before offering his own definition of the term:

> The word Force is a symbol which has many meanings. It varies
> in different works, and often in different passages of the same
> work. Sometimes it stands for the Unknowable, whose manifesta-
> tions are the objective universe; sometimes it is the common mea-
> sure by which all phenomena are rendered intelligible; sometimes
> it is an imaginary entity supposed to take up its habitation in sub-

> stances, passing freely from one to the other . . . sometimes it is
> the simple synonyme of cause, sometimes of strength, sometimes
> of motion; now confounded with, and now distinguished from,
> Energy. . . . But the physicist has his cohesive, diffusive, elastic
> forces, the chemist has his affinity, the biologist his vital forces,
> and the psychologist his moral forces,—which are not so readily
> reducible to the mathematical formula.

> If we consider what all these different meanings have in common,
> it will be found that the definition I have proposed—the Activity
> of Matter, or the Changes in the Felt—comprises them all.[177]

Characteristically, Lewes the positivist would unify physics,
chemistry, biology, and psychology under the common law of
force. "The activity of Matter, or the changes in the Felt," are
one and the same—simply viewed from the objective and subjective sides of the circle.

"Our world arises in Consciousness," Lewes writes in *Problems of Life and Mind*;[178] and much of Lewes's later thought
has a real kinship with Charles Bray's philosophy. Bray asserted that "the material order may exist only as mental."[179]
"Matter, the real, with which we have to deal, is saturated with
Mind, since it is the Felt," writes Lewes in the important essay
"Spiritualism and Materialism" (1876) that summarizes much
of *Problems*.[180] Charles Bray also quotes Lewes approvingly in
his autobiography: "All our knowledge *springs from*, and is
limited by, Feeling. The universe represented in that knowledge can only be a picture of a system of things as those exist
in relation to our sensibility."[181] Bray then goes on to argue
that this limitation—"We know only our own feelings"—has
its virtues: "We may be thankful . . . for if, as George Eliot
says, we had a keen vision and feeling for all ordinary life, it
would be like hearing the grass grow and the squirrel's heart
beat; and we should die of that roar which lies on the other side
of silence."[182] This famous passage is, of course, taken from
Middlemarch. I will turn to that novel in the chapter that
follows; but let me emphasize here that this picture of limited
human perceptions—the Unknowable—must be viewed in
conjunction with the microscopic eye of the novelist's power-

ful narrator, focusing its intense illumination on the "particular web" of Middlemarch.[183] These Victorian visionaries never falter in their optimistic exploration of the knowable, despite their acute awareness of its limitations. For they all believe in what Lewes called "the invisible continuous Cosmos, which is conceived as an uniform Existence, all the modes of which are interdependent."[184] Because the cosmos is continuous, the web of the created world, however apparently tangled, must finally have a coherent pattern, a meaningful order.

A healthy respect for the limitations of human understanding must not stand in the way of legitimate distinctions between that which is truly unknowable and that which is merely as yet unknown. "All our knowledge *springs from*, and is *limited by*, feeling"; but Lewes—and all his Victorian compatriots—do not stop with the felt; but rather, seek, to translate it into the known: "The facts of Feeling which sensation differentiates; Theory integrates. What we experience as Feeling, we systematize as Science. Hence the speculative effort, thoroughly justifiable, to reduce all phenomena to one Cause, all laws to one law, to see the Many in the One, and the One in the Many, as Plato divined."[185] If I had to select a single statement, from the many quoted in this study, to epitomize the frame of mind shared by these Victorians, it would be this one. John Stuart Mill's universal causation, Auguste Comte's positivism, George Combe's phrenological philosophy, Robert Chambers's evolutionary cosmology, Charles Bray's and Harriet Martineau's mesmeric force, Lewes's search through the annals of philosophy and science, Herbert Spencer's Law of Progress: each can be seen as an effort, grounded upon a belief in the continuous Cosmos, to "reduce all phenomena to one Cause, all laws to one law." "Without general conceptions," Lewes writes in *Problems of Life and Mind*, "particular experiences would be like the scattered leaves of the Sibyl; unless each leaf be read in connection with the others, its significance is concealed, for in itself it has no significance."[186]

But just as the known and the unknown are intimately connected, so the polarities of analysis and synthesis go hand-in-hand, as the diastole and systole of human reason. Intuitive faith leads back to scientific fact. These Victorians were more often armchair scientists than practicing technicians, and subsequent advances have relegated many of their most-cherished scientific beliefs to the dusty attic of historical oddities; yet each, in his own fashion, embraced with scientific energy and enthusiasm the individuality and the multiplicity of the continuous cosmos—its "heterogeneity"—as a necessary complement to the poetics of its fundamental unity. Once again, it is George Henry Lewes who sums this up best, in the concluding paragraph of *The Foundations of a Creed*:

> This unification of all the modes of Existence by no means obliterates the distinction of modes, nor the necessity of understanding the special characters of each. Mind remains Mind, and is essentially opposed to Matter, in spite of their identity in the Absolute; just as Pain is not Pleasure, nor Color either Heat or Taste, in spite of their identity in Feeling. The logical distinctions represent real differentiations, but not distinct existents. If we recognize the One in the Many, we do not thereby refuse to admit the Many in the One.[187]

There has been a great deal of emphasis in this study on the dynamic interpenetration of polar opposites. But it should be stressed here that, as Samuel Taylor Coleridge and Herbert Spencer insisted, the highest unity—the one in the many—also implies the most intense individuality—the many in the one.

Whether these Victorian cosmologies are persuasive may be debatable; whether the cosmos is, in fact, "continuous," is certainly still as much a question of faith as of proof for the twentieth century as it was for the nineteenth. And these Victorians themselves, despite the radiant illumination of their apparently boundless optimism, were forced to expand the boundaries of the dark Unknowable on every side, even as they claimed new territories for the known.

In the context of all the forward-looking energy of this Victorian vision, we should not forget that many of these ideas depend upon intellectual foundations laid long before the nineteenth century. None more so than "the Many in the One, the One in the Many," which, George Henry Lewes reminds us, was expounded by Plato in the fourth century B.C. Plato, for all his search after absolutes and unswerving belief in their existence, knew how small man stood in the midst of the continuous cosmos: "The soul is confronted with the Many by means of Sense, and by means of Reason it detects the One in the Many; i.e. the particular things perceived by Sense awaken the recollections of Universals or ideas. But this recollection of Truth is always more or less imperfect. Absolute Truth is for the Gods alone."[188] Looking back upon these Victorians as they attempt to scale Mount Olympus, they must at times appear, if not foolish, at least foredoomed to failure. But surely their *hubris* is worthy not only of our sympathy, but of our admiration—and perhaps, of our envy.

1. Hock Guan Tjoa, *George Henry Lewes: A Victorian Mind* (Cambridge, Mass., 1977), p. 135.

2. Lewes here playfully echoes the fictional Casaubon's "Key to All Mythologies" in *Middlemarch*, which Eliot was writing simultaneously with *Problems*. See George Henry Lewes, *George Eliot Letters*, 5:291, 350, 364, 370.

3. George Henry Lewes, *Problems of Life and Mind. Third Series. Problem the First. The Study of Psychology: Its Object, Scope and Method* (Boston, 1879), p. 54. In the preface to the first volume, Lewes says that "its origin may be said to go so far back as 1836" (*Problems. First Series. The Foundations of A Creed* [Boston, 1874-75], 1:v).

4. Johann Wolfgang von Goethe, quoted in "Goethe as a Man of Science," p. 261. Another German, Ludwig Feuerbach, uses the same metaphor in *The Essence of Christianity* (which Eliot was translating while Lewes researched his biography of Goethe). In Eliot's translation: "As the action of the arteries drives the blood into the extremeties, and the action of the veins brings it back again, as life in general consists in perpetual systole and diastole; so it is with religion. In the religious systole, man propels his own nature from himself, he throws himself outward; in the religious diastole, he receives the rejected nature into his heart again" (Feuerbach, *Essence*, trans. George Eliot [1854; rpt. New York, 1957], p. 468). Eliot herself uses the metaphor in *Middlemarch* (see "Finale," p. 249).

5. George Henry Lewes, "Spiritualism and Materialism," *Fortnightly Review* 25 (1876):713.

6. Rosemary Ashton, *The German Idea* (Cambridge, England, 1980), p. 121. In this study of Coleridge, Carlyle, Lewes, and Eliot, Ashton assumes Lewes's "permanent change of opinion away from the *a priori* philosophical approach" (p. 114).

7. Young, *Mind, Brain, and Adaptation*, p. 163.

8. Jack Kaminsky, "The Empirical Metaphysics of George Henry Lewes," *Journal of the History of Ideas* 13 (1952):314, 322. Similarly Tjoa accurately states that Lewes "earnestly tried to meet the two divergent intellectual demands of his age: the one a seasoned empiricism imposing procrustean measures upon all intellectual activity, and the other a swelling need for a kind of 'religious rationalism,' a meaningful vision of man and things (*Lewes*, pp. 117-18). But he is skeptical of Lewes's optimism; his "positivistic enthusiasm" is "too extravagant" (p. 136). Tjoa incorrectly interprets this extravagant optimism as "the strained effort to put up a brave front" (p. 137).

9. George Henry Lewes, review of *Letters on the Laws*, *Leader*, 22 February 1851, p. 178; 8 March 1851, p. 227; 1 March 1851, pp. 201, 203, 202. Gordon Haight claims that Lewes's "devastating reviews" of the book were the cause of hostility between Lewes and Martineau (see Haight, *George Eliot Letters*, 2:123n), fuel to the fire of her moral indignation in 1854.

10. Lewes, review of *Letters on the Laws*, *Leader*, 1 March 1851, p. 202. Compare this "transcendental faculty" with the "intuitive faculty" in the *Letters* (p. 76).

11. Lewes, "Spiritualism and Materialism," p. 483. Lewes does not date this experience. George Levine writes perceptively of Lewes: he "is in the paradoxical position of any empiricist who seeks systemic wholeness. Committed to common sense, he finds himself in a reality that runs counter to what common sense reveals. . . . His language must move from appearances to realities in a rhythm that is so directly reminiscent of religious language that it is difficult to avoid the connection" ("George Eliot's Hypothesis of Reality," *Nineteenth Century Fiction* 35 [1980]:9).

12. George Henry Lewes, "The Heart and the Brain," *Fortnightly Review* 1 (1865):66. My attention was drawn to this essay by Bray's approving quotation of it (*On Force*, p. 20).

13. Lewes, "Heart and the Brain," p. 74.

14. George Henry Lewes, "Subject, Subjective," *Penny Cyclopaedia* (London, 1842), 23:185.

15. George Henry Lewes, "Substance," *Penny Cyclopaedia*, 22:198.

16. George Henry Lewes, "Spinoza, Spinozism," *Penny Cyclopaedia*, 22:351-52.

17. George Henry Lewes, marginalia on Hallam's *Introduction to the Literature of Europe*, quoted in *The George Eliot-George Henry Lewes Library*, ed. William Baker (New York, 1977), p. 85.

18. George Henry Lewes, "Spinoza," *Fortnightly Review* 4 (1866):386-87.

19. See Francis Espinasse, *Literary Recollections* (New York, 1938), p. 276n.

20. George Henry Lewes, "Spinoza's Life and Works," *Westminster Review* 39 (1843):397-98.

21. Lewes, *Biographical History*, p. 493.

22. Lewes, "Spinoza's Life and Works," pp. 385, 404, 406.

23. Brabant's friendship with Coleridge was documented by his son-in-law, W. M. W. Call, in "Unpublished Letters, Written by Samuel Taylor Coleridge in 1815-16," *Westminster Review* 93, n.s. 37 (1870):341-64; 94, n.s. 38 (1870):1-24.

24. Haight, *George Eliot Letters*, 1:158n. Haight suggests that the work in question was the *Tractatus*, given Brabant's and Eliot's interest in the "higher criticism." He

cites Mathilde Blind, *George Eliot* (London, 1883) as the source of the information that Eliot was translating "De Deo," chiding Blind for her ignorance that this is the opening chapter of the *Ethics*; and then implies that Blind's mistake undermines her credibility. But the source of Blind's information was probably W. M. W. Call's "George Eliot, Her Life and Writings," *Westminster Review* 116 (1881):154-98. Call writes: "Miss Evans had translated about ten years previously, the first part ('De Deo') of Spinoza's great treatise, for the edification of a philosophical friend" (161). As Brabant's son-in-law and a personal friend of Eliot, Call was in a good position to have accurate information. Given the "friend" Charles Bray's necessitarian interests, the *Ethics* was a likely subject. Regardless, it seems that Eliot would have known both *Ethics* and *Tractatus* in the early 1840s.

25. George Eliot to Sara Sophia Hennell, *George Eliot Letters*, 1:231.

26. Mrs. Charles Bray to George Eliot, *George Eliot Letters*, 1:280n.

27. George Eliot to Mr. and Mrs. Charles Bray, *George Eliot Letters*, 1:321. See Hilda Hulme, "Language of the Novel: Imagery," in *Middlemarch: Critical Approaches*, ed. Barbara Hardy (London, 1967), pp. 118-24 on Eliot and the *Ethics*; see also Dorothy Atkins, *George Eliot and Spinoza* (Salzburg, 1980).

28. The scandal raging over her liaison with Lewes may have been the source of Eliot's request to Bray in March 1856: "By the way, when Spinoza comes out, be so good as not to mention *my* name in connection with it. I particularly wish not to be known as the translator of the Ethics, for reasons 'too tedious to mention' " (Eliot to Bray, *George Eliot Letters*, 2:233; see also 2:197).

29. Haight, *George Eliot Letters*, 2:189n; see 8:156-60 for Lewes's correspondence with Bohn.

30. David Friedrich Strauss, quoted in Robert Willis, *Benedict de Spinoza: His Life, Correspondence, and Ethics* (London, 1870), 3:4n.

31. I am indebted for the following summary to Alasdair MacIntyre, "Spinoza," *Encyclopedia of Philosophy* (New York, 1967), 7:530-41.

32. Benedict Spinoza, *Ethics*, trans. R. H. M. Elwes (1883; rpt. New York, 1955), part 2, prop. 7, note, p. 86.

33. Spinoza, *Ethics*, part 1, prop. 29, p. 68; prop. 33, note 2, p. 74; appendix, p. 77.

34. Spinoza, *Ethics*, part 4, prop. 57, note, p. 225.

35. Spinoza, *Ethics*, part 3, prop. 58, note, p. 172; part 4, prop. 47, note, p. 221; part 5, prop. 24, p. 260; part 5, prop. 36, note, p. 265.

36. Thomas McFarland, *Coleridge and the Pantheist Tradition* (Oxford, 1969), p. 169.

37. In this small Victorian world, Willis was also Eliot's and Lewes's physician: "Dr. Willis, by the way, is a phrenologist, and was a most intimate friend of Spurzheim for whom he had great respect and affection," Eliot writes Bray in 1855 (*George Eliot Letters*, 2:210). Willis translated Spurzheim's *Anatomy of the Brain* in 1826; his translation and commentary, *Benedict de Spinoza: His Life, Correspondence, and Ethics* (1870) is listed in the Lewes-Eliot library (William Baker, *The Libraries of George Eliot and George Henry Lewes* [Victoria, Canada, 1981], p. 119).

38. Leslie Stephen, "Spinoza," *Fortnightly Review* 34 (1880):755. Similarly, Frederic Copleston writes: "The system of Spinoza is . . . two-faced. . . . If one stresses

the metaphysical aspect, one will tend to think of Spinoza primarily as a 'pantheist'. . . . If one stresses . . . the 'naturalistic' aspect, one will tend . . . to see in the philosophical system the sketch of a programme for scientific research" (*A History of Philosophy, Descartes to Leibniz* [New York, 1963], 4:234-35).

39. George Henry Lewes Journal, quoted in Haight, *George Eliot: A Biography*, pp. 271-72.

40. Eliot found little to recommend in Lewes's fiction. She writes Spencer from Broadstairs in July 1852: "I have read Deerbrook [by Harriet Martineau] and am surprised at the depths of feeling it reveals. Rose, Blanche, and Violet, too—at least the first two volumes—the third I have left behind and (damaging fact, either for me or the novel!)—I don't care to have it" (*George Eliot Letters*, 8:51).

41. Spencer, *Autobiography*, 1:410, 399, 400, 435.

42. George Henry Lewes, review of *Social Statics, Leader*, 12 April 1851, p. 348; 22 February 1851, p. 178. Lewes's review articles appeared on March 15, March 22, and April 12, 1851.

43. George Eliot to Charles Bray, *George Eliot Letters*, 1:364. In the same letter, Eliot recommends Atkinson's and Martineau's *Letters* for review in the *Coventry Herald*. On 16 February 1852, Eliot writes Bray that she is a "hideous hag" with a headache, and thus unable to show visitor Sara Sophia Hennell about town. Fortunately, the "dear creature" accommodates herself by "sitting quietly by my fire and reading Social Statics with many interjections" (*George Eliot Letters*, 2:11).

44. Herbert Spencer to Edward Lott, 25 April 1852, quoted in Haight, *George Eliot: A Biography*, p. 112.

45. George Eliot to Charles Bray, *George Eliot Letters*, 2:22, 29.

46. See these letters in full, George Eliot to Herbert Spencer, *George Eliot Letters*, 8:50-52, 56-57, 61.

47. Spencer, *Autobiography*, 1:458, 460.

48. Haight says that Eliot was introduced to Lewes on 6 October 1851 (*George Eliot: A Biography*, p. 127); but I note she was at least acquainted with his opinions on *Social Statics* when she met Spencer at the Chapman's the previous week (see [ms. p. 246]).

49. See Haight, *George Eliot: A Biography*, pp. 127, 128, 135, 173, 135-36.

50. Spencer, *Autobiography*, 2:236-37. Compare Eliot's version of the friendship in her *Letters*, 6:426.

51. George Eliot to Sara Sophia Hennell, *George Eliot Letters*, 2:40. In a similar vein, see 2:128; 6:426; 7:344. In his *Autobiography* Spencer quotes Eliot saying of him, "You have such a passion for generalizing, you even fish with a generalization" (2:237). At least Spencer had a sense of humor on the subject.

52. George Eliot to Sara Sophia Hennell, *George Eliot Letters*, 7:344.

53. Peel, *Herbert Spencer*, p. 1. In his anthology *English Literature and British Philosophy* (1971), S. P. Rosenbaum feels little need to apologize for Spencer's absence: "Herbert Spencer is missing . . . although with Spencer it is also questionable how important his ideas were for any really enduring works of English literature" ("Introduction," p. 4). Spencer's friendship with George Eliot should cast doubt on that assertion.

54. Peel, *Herbert Spencer*, p. 26. Similarly, Alfred Benn: "Spencer had an inherited English fondness for the conciliation of divergent principles which fell in admirably with his own extraordinary powers of synthesis and generalization" (2:223).

55. Spencer, *Autobiography*, 1:260.

56. Spencer, *Social Statics*, p. 27. See pp. 11-27 for Spencer's discussion of the "Doctrine of Expediency."

57. Spencer, *Social Statics*, pp. 13, 24. There are many similarities between Spencer's assessment of the limitations of Utilitarianism and John Stuart Mill's reaction to the philosophy of his father and Jeremy Bentham in his *Autobiography*.

58. Spencer, 1850 "Preface" to *Social Statics*, p. xv; *Social Statics*, p. 18.

59. George Eliot to Charles Bray, *George Eliot Letters*, 2:14.

60. George Eliot to Charles Bray, *George Eliot Letters*, 2:403. Eliot spoke publicly along the same lines the year before in her essay, "The Natural History of German Life," when she bemoaned "the tendency created by the splendid conquests of modern generalization, to believe that all social questions are merged into economical science, and that the relations of men to their neighbours may be settled by algebraic equations" (in Pinney, p. 272).

61. George Henry Lewes, "Hereditary Influence," *Westminster Review* 66 (July-Oct. 1856):161.

62. Robert M. Young writes: Spencer believes in "the faculty of the 'Moral Sense.' In his argument for such a faculty, Spencer reveals the detailed influence of phrenology on his psychological thinking" (*Mind, Brain, and Adaptation*, pp. 155-56, 154).

63. George Eliot to Charles Bray, *George Eliot Letters*, 2:403.

64. Spencer, *Social Statics*, pp. 54, 55. See Peel, *Herbert Spencer*, pp. 102-11 for a discussion of Spencer's philosophy as "a transformation of Calvinist themes" (p. 103), along lines very similar to my discussion of Bray in chapter 3.

65. Spencer, *Social Statics*, p. 4.

66. Spencer, *Social Statics*, p. 44; my emphasis.

67. Spencer, *Social Statics*, p. 80.

68. See Spencer, *Social Statics*, p. 447: "Social philosophy may be aptly divided . . . into statics and dynamics; the first treating of the equilibrium of a perfect society, the second of forces by which society is advanced towards perfection."

69. Spencer, *Social Statics*, pp. 73, 454.

70. Spencer, *Social Statics*, pp. 482-83, 490, 499.

71. Spencer, *Autobiography*, 2:8.

72. Spencer, *Autobiography*, 1:490.

73. Spencer, *Social Statics*, quoted in Lewes's review, *Leader*, 15 March 1851, p. 249.

74. Spencer, *Autobiography*, 2:101.

75. Spencer, *Autobiography*, 1:399.

76. Spencer, *Autobiography*, 1:436.

77. Herbert Spencer, "The Laws of Organic Form," *British and Foreign Medico-Chirurgical Review* 23 (1859):191, 198, 201.

78. George Henry Lewes, "Lyell and Owen on Development," *Leader*, 18 October 1851, p. 997.

79. Herbert Spencer, "The Development Hypothesis," *Leader*, 20 March 1852; rpt. in *Essays Scientific, Political, and Speculative* (New York, 1904), 1:5.

80. As J. D. Y. Peel writes: "Spencer's approach was unlike that of his biological contemporaries . . . in that he did not start off from a phenomenon to be explained, but from ethical and metaphysical positions to be established. Consequently, he was an evolutionist long before Lyell, Huxley, and Darwin" (*Herbert Spencer*, p. 132).

81. George Henry Lewes, "Mr. Darwin's Hypothesis," *Fortnightly Review* 4 (1868):497.

82. Johann Wolfgang von Goethe, quoted in George Henry Lewes, *The Life of Goethe*, 2d ed. (London, 1864), p. 170.

83. Lewes, *Life of Gothe*, p. 35. Similarly, in his novel *Ranthorpe*, Lewes's fictional hero Thornton muses: "Goethe, my young friend, was the last man in the world to deserve the epithet cold. What makes boobies call him so, is the magnificent supremacy which his reason always exercised over his passions" (*Ranthorpe* [1847; rpt. Athens, Ohio, 1974], p. 171).

84. Lewes, *Life of Goethe*, p. 520.

85. Spencer, *Autobiography*, 1:485. Though Lewes's claim is, characteristically, a more modest one: "The antithesis to Poetry, as Wordsworth felicitously said, is not Prose, but Science. Therefore have Poets and Men of Science, in all times, formed two distinct classes, and never, save in one illustrious example, exhibited the twofold manifestation of Poetry and Science working in harmonious unity: that single exception is Goethe" ("Goethe as a Man of Science," p. 258).

86. Lewes, *Life of Goethe*, p. 342.

87. Lewes, "Goethe as a Man of Science," p. 260.

88. Lewes, "Goethe as a Man of Science," p. 267.

89. George Henry Lewes, "Life and Doctrine of Geoffroy St. Hilaire," *Westminster Review* 61 (1854):178, 180.

90. Herbert Spencer, "Transcendental Physiology," *National Review*, October 1857, rpt. in *Essays*, 1:63. Similarly, in *The Principles of Psychology*: "There exists a *unity of composition* throughout all the phenomena of intelligence" (p. 329).

91. Lewes, "Goethe as a Man of Science," p. 261. Another interesting link between Goethe and this Victorian circle: Lewes writes that when phrenologist Gall visited Jena in 1805, Goethe attended his lectures: "Instead of meeting this theory with ridicule, contempt, and the opposition of ancient prejudices . . . Goethe saw at once the importance of Gall's mode of dissection . . . and of his leading views. . . . Gall's doctrine pleased him because it determined the true position of Psychology in the study of man . . . showing the identity of all mental manifestation in the animal kingdom" (*Life of Goethe*, p. 486).

92. Lewes, "Goethe as a Man of Science," p. 272.

93. Goethe, quoted in Lewes, "Goethe as a Man of Science," p. 268. In reworking this essay into "The Poet as a Man of Science" for the *Life*, Lewes gives a slightly different version of this passage, and also its source: *Zur Morphologie* (*Life of Goethe*, p. 355).

94. Lewes, "St. Hilaire," p. 189.

95. Eliot, "The Natural History of German Life," in Pinney, p. 287.

96. George Henry Lewes, "Mr. Darwin's Hypothesis," *Fortnightly Review* 3 (1868):356.

97. French historian Georges Banguilhem writes: "There was no biologist or physician in France between 1840 and 1860 who . . . did not have to deal either directly with the themes of Comte's biological philosophy [the dualism of life and matter, the correlation of organism and environment] or indirectly with that philosophy through the themes developed from it" ("La philosophie biologique d'Auguste Comte et son influence en France au xixe siècle," quoted in Simon, *European Positivism*, p. 114).

98. Comte, *Cours*, in Lenzer, p. 164.

99. Lewes, *Comte's Philosophy*, p. 167.

100. Spencer, *Principles of Psychology*, p. 374.

101. Lewes, *Problems of Life and Mind, The Foundations of a Creed*, 1:112; 2:21.

102. Spencer, *Autobiography*, 2:9, 14.

103. W. B. Carpenter, *Principles of Comparative Physiology*, new American edition, from 4th revised English edition (Philadelphia, 1854), p. 48. See Young, *Mind, Brain, and Adaptation*, p. 168n for a long and informative note on von Baer. In fact both Darwin and Spencer twisted von Baer to their own purposes: the German himself was opposed to the development hypothesis (Lewes does note this in his essay on von Baer).

104. T. H. Huxley, review of W. B. Carpenter's *Principles of Physiology*, "Science," *Westminster Review* 63 (1855):242.

105. Herbert Spencer, "Progress: Its Law and Cause," *Westminster Review* 67 (1857), rpt. in *Essays*, 1:10.

106. See Millhauser, *Just Before Darwin*, pp. 86–87, for a comparison of Chambers and Spencer.

107. George Henry Lewes, "Von Baer on the Development Hypothesis," *Leader*, 25 June 1853, p. 617.

108. Lewes, *Life of Goethe*, p. 354.

109. George Eliot to Sara Sophia Hennell, *George Eliot Letters*, 2:220.

110. George Eliot to Herbert Spencer, *George Eliot Letters*, 8:51.

111. See Spencer, *Autobiography*, 2:10 for Spencer's explanation of his earliest published use of the word "homogeneity."

112. Eliot, "The Progress of the Intellect," in Pinney, p. 29. In his essay on "Idea and Image in the Novels of George Eliot," W. J. Harvey writes: "All external evidence . . . points to Spencer rather than Darwin as the prime intellectual influence concerning [Eliot's] ideas on Evolution" (though he goes on, somewhat inaccurately, to add: "Spencer's claims to scientific seriousness are now completely exploded"). He also notes Eliot's close friendship with Robert Chambers and her familiarity with the *Vestiges* (in *Critical Essays on George Eliot*, ed. Barbara Hardy [London, 1970], p. 157). Since "The Progress of the Intellect" was written before she knew Spencer's work, Chambers must be considered a key source of Eliot's belief in development.

113. Charles Darwin to George Henry Lewes, *George Eliot Letters*, 8:425.

114. Lewes, "Mr. Darwin's Hypothesis," *Fortnightly Review* 3:355; 4:66; 3:356. Lewes's essays on Darwin appear in vols. 3 (1868):353-73, 611-29 and 4:61-80, 492-501. In "George Eliot's Hypothesis of Reality," George Levine states that "for Lewes and George Eliot, following Darwin, the highest organism is both the most complexly differentiated from its rudimentary origins and the most integrated in other organisms" (8). Levine is correct, but Spencer, not Darwin, is the source of this idea.

115. Peel sums up the distinction between Spencer and Darwin: "Darwin's theory accounted for the secular transformation of each species by the mechanism of natural selection, while Spencer's attempted to explain the total configuration of nature, physical, organic, and social, as well as its necessary process" (*Herbert Spencer*, p. 142). Young argues that Spencer was "more seminal than directly contributory," since he was not a practicing scientist; he notes Darwin's influential later work in evolutionary psychology. He draws a parallel between Gall and Spencer: "Both advocated studies which they did not successfully conduct themselves" (p. 190). Although Darwin had worked in the application of evolutionary theory of psychology in his early notebooks, he did not publish on the subject until 1871, in *The Descent of Man*.

116. Spencer, *Autobiography*, 1:453.

117. George Eliot to Sara Sophia Hennell, *George Eliot Letters*, 2:165.

118. George Eliot to Mrs. Wathen Mark Wilks Call, *George Eliot Letters*, 2:476; George Eliot to Sara Sophia Hennell, *George Eliot Letters*, 2:213. We catch a glimpse of Lewes's characteristic sense of humor in his letter to Spencer on the *Principles*: "I hope the book sells. If it can get a decent *nucleus* of a public it is sure to make its way; all that surrounds the nucleus being as you know a *sell*" (George Henry Lewes to Herbert Spencer, *George Eliot Letters*, 8:151).

119. George Eliot to Sara Sophia Hennell, *George Eliot Letters*, 2:228.

120. George Henry Lewes, "Life and Mind," *Leader*, 3 November 1855, p. 1,062. This is the third part of Lewes's review of Spencer's *Principles of Psychology*, preceded by "Herbert Spencer's Psychology" (*Leader*, 20 October 1855, pp. 1,012-13) and "History of Psychological Method" (*Leader*, 27 October 1855, pp. 1,036-37).

121. George Henry Lewes, "Herbert Spencer's *Principles of Psychology*," *Saturday Review*, 1 March 1856, pp. 353, 352.

122. Review of Herbert Spencer's *Principles of Psychology*, *British Quarterly Review* 22 (1855):598.

123. R. H. Hutton, "Atheism," *National Review* 2 (1856):122. See also the "Theology and Philosophy" section of the *Westminster Review* 65 (January, 1856):234-40 for a similar discussion.

124. Lewes, "Herbert Spencer's Psychology," p. 1,013.

125. Lewes, "Herbert Spencer's Psychology," p. 1.013.

126. See Lewes, *Biographical History*, pp. 602, 646, 744.

127. Lewes, *Problems of Life and Mind, Foundations of a Creed*, 1:77.

128. Spencer, *Principles of Psychology*, p. 374. The review of the *Principles* in the *British Quarterly Review* drew an explicit parallel between Spencer and Comte on this subject: the relation of life and "outward environments" in the *Principles* is "precisely that put forth by the author of the Positive Philosophy" (p. 597).

129. William James, *The Principles of Psychology* (1890; rpt. New York, 1950), 1:6. The second edition of Spencer's *Principles* was James's textbook for his first class

of undergraduates in psychology (see James Kennedy, *Herbert Spencer* [Boston, 1978], p. 47). Lewes praises Spencer's definition of life in the 1870s in *Problems of Life and Mind. Second Series. The Physical Basis of Mind* (London, 1877), p. 33. Bray quotes Spencer's definition several times in his autobiography, without citing Spencer as its author (was it so well-known that he need not do so?) (see *Phases of Opinion*, pp. 203, 207–9).

130. Spencer, *Autobiography*, 2:12.

131. Spencer, *Principles of Psychology*, "Preface," pp. iii–iv.

132. Lewes, *Problems of Life and Mind. Third Series. Problem the First. The Study of Psychology* (Boston, 1879), p. 77.

133. "Adaptation was a major issue in *Social Statics*, and Spencer's conception of it was derived directly from phrenology"; before Spencer, "no psychologists except Gall and his followers had so emphatically made the connection of mind with life, and the adaptation of the mental functions to the environment, central to their views" (Young, *Mind, Brain, and Adaptation*, p. 169).

134. In "a few remarks on the tenets of the phrenologists," Spencer attacks them as "wrong in assuming there is something specific and unalterable in the natures of the various faculties" (*Principles*, p. 610). Although this static view of the mind was true of Gall, modifiability of faculties became a central tenet from Combe onwards, as evidence in my discussion of Chambers, Bray, and Martineau.

135. Chambers, *Vestiges of Creation*, pp. 180, 181, 183.

136. Darwin, "M and N Notebooks," in *Darwin on Man*, pp. 271, 276.

137. Bray, *Philosophy of Necessity*, 2d ed., p. 87.

138. Spencer, *Principles of Psychology*, pp. 578, 581. Benn summarizes the obvious philosophical limitations of Spencer's grandiose claim: "Spencer believed that by his theory of inherited ancestral experience he had reconciled the opposing views of Kant and Mill. In reality he had done nothing of the kind. He had considerably extended the ground occupied by the empirical school, and furnished them with a plausible reply to one of the objections previously urged against their explanation of necessary truths; but he had done no more. The main contention of Kant and his followers, which is that no amount of experience can give universality and necessity to a proposition, still remained unanswered" (*History of Rationalism*, 2:173).

139. James, *Principles of Psychology*, 2:625.

140. Lewes, *Problems of Life and Mind, Foundations of a Creed*, 1:149.

141. Spencer, *Principles of Psychology*, p. 526; summary of *Principles* in *Autobiography*, 1:548–49.

142. Spencer, *Principles of Psychology*, pp. 555–56.

143. Spencer, *First Principles*, quoted in Bray, *Phases of Opinion*, pp. 98–99.

144. Spencer, *Principles of Psychology*, p. 556.

145. Eliot, "More Leaves," p. 373.

146. Lewes, "Hereditary Influence," 161n. Similarly, see Eliot in a letter to Bray on historian Henry Buckle: "He holds that there is no such thing as *race* or hereditary transmission of qualities!" (*George Eliot Letters*, 2:415).

147. Lewes, *Problems of Life and Mind, Foundations of a Creed*, 1:202, 220.

148. Spencer, "Progress," p. 60.

149. See Herbert Spencer, *First Principles* (1862; rpt. New York, 1879), p. xvii, for the publishing history of the book, which appeared between October 1860 (part 1) and June 1862 (part 6).

150. R. W. McKay, quoted in Eliot, "The Progress of the Intellect," in Pinney, p. 33.

151. George Eliot to Sara Sophia Hennell, *George Eliot Letters*, 2:341; George Eliot to Sara Sophia Hennell, *George Eliot Letters*, 3:358; George Eliot to Sara Sophia Hennell, *George Eliot Letters*, 3:364; George Eliot to Mme Eugène Bodichon, *George Eliot Letters*, 3:367; George Eliot to Sara Sophia Hennell, *George Eliot Letters*, 4:9.

152. Spencer, *First Principles*, pp. 107-8.

153. Spencer, "Progress: Its Law and Cause," pp. 30, 45, 58.

154. George Eliot to Mme Eugène Bodichon, *George Eliot Letters*, 3:227.

155. Spencer, "Progress," p. 58.

156. Spencer, *Autobiography*, 1:86.

157. Benn, *History of Rationalism*, 2:204.

158. Lovejoy, *Great Chain of Being*, p. 28.

159. James Hinton, "Herbert Spencer's *Principles of Biology*," in *Chapters on the Art of Thinking* (London, 1879), p. 368. Much of the original *Principles of Psychology* was incorporated into the *Principles of Biology* in the 1860s.

160. Martineau, *Autobiography*, 2:417.

161. Bray, *Phases of Opinion*, p. 252.

162. Lewes, *Life of Goethe*, p. 479. Lewes cites this as the "moral" of *Faust*. Eliot uses an epigraph from *Faust* in *Middlemarch*: "Zum höchsten Dasein immerfort zu streben" (p. 579).

163. Lewes, *Comte*, p. 215.

164. Lewes, *Problems of Life and Mind, Foundations of a Creed*, 2:3.

165. Spencer, *First Principles*, pp. 98-99, 21.

166. Spencer, *First Principles*, pp. 24, 46.

167. Feuerbach, *Essence of Christianity*, p. 63.

168. George Eliot to Charles Bray, *George Eliot Letters*, 2:403.

169. George Eliot to Elizabeth Stewart Phelps, *George Eliot Letters*, 6:163-64.

170. R. W. McKay, quoted in Eliot, "Progress of the Intellect," in Pinney, pp. 33, 33-34.

171. Bray, *Philosophy of Necessity*, 2d ed., p. 443.

172. Bray, *On Force*, pp. 49, 51.

173. Spencer, "Progress," p. 61.

174. Spencer, *Principles of Psychology*, quoted by Bray in *Phases*, pp. 98-99.

175. See Bray, *On Force*, p. 14; Herbert Spencer to Charles Bray, 7 March 1881, quoted in *Phases of Opinion*, p. 100. See also *On Force*, pp. 35, 78 for quotations from *First Principles* which document the compatibility between Bray and Spencer. Thirty-three years after Lewes's review of *Social Statics*, Spencer is still spoken of in the same breath as Spinoza: "There is but one Reality in the universe, which Physical Philoso-

phers call 'Force;' and Metaphysicians 'Noumenon.' It is the 'Substance' of Spinoza, and the 'Being' of Hegel" (*Phases of Opinion*, p. 101).

176. George Henry Lewes, "English Philosophy," *Leader*, 16 July 1853, p. 693.

177. Lewes, *Problems of Life and Mind, The Foundations of a Creed*, 2:307.

178. Lewes, *Problems of Life and Mind, The Foundations of a Creed*, 2:11.

179. Bray, *Phases of Opinion*, p. 254.

180. Lewes, "Materialism and Spiritualism," p. 488.

181. Lewes, quoted in Bray, *Phases of Opinion*, p. 261.

182. George Eliot, *Middlemarch*, quoted in Bray, *Phases of Opinion*, p. 261.

183. Eliot, *Middlemarch*, p. 105.

184. Lewes, *Problems of Life and Mind, The Foundations of a Creed*, 2:25. I am indebted to George Levine, "George Eliot's Hypothesis of Reality," for drawing my attention to this passage.

185. Lewes, *Problems of Life and Mind, The Foundations of a Creed*, 2:25.

186. Lewes, *Problems of Life and Mind, The Foundations of a Creed*, 2:228-29.

187. Lewes, *Problems of Life and Mind, The Foundations of a Creed*, 2:451.

188. Plato, paraphrased in Lewes, *Biographical History*, p. 223. The *Biographical History* contains a discussion of Plato on pp. 209-29. See the "Philebus" dialogue for Plato's discussion of the many in the one, the one in the many.

"The Many in The One, The One in The Many":
George Eliot's *Middlemarch* (1871–1872) as
Victorian Cosmology

*This long and anxious dwelling with experience and matter
and the fluctuations of individual things, drags down the
mind to earth, . . . removing and withdrawing it from the
serene tranqulity of abstract wisdom, a condition far more
heavenly. Now to this I readily assent; and indeed this which
they point at as so much to be preferred, is the very thing of
all others which I am about. For I am building in the human
understanding a true model of the world, such as it is in fact,
not such as man's own reason would have it to be; a thing
which cannot be done without a very diligent dissection and
anatomy of the world.—Bacon,* Novum Organum

Although it has looked before and after, the focus of this history has been two decades, from the late 1830s to the late 1850s. George Eliot figures prominently in this Victorian circle as editor, essayist, and friend. Her most original genius was to be reserved for fiction; but she did not begin to write novels until 1856, at age 36. It has often been remarked that Eliot is unique among Victorian novelists, in the extent to which her artistic career was preceded by an apprenticeship to the seminal intellectual movements of her age. This study provides ample evidence for that assertion. It also adds an important dimension to George Eliot's intellectual biography, filling in the formative associations with Charles Bray's Coventry circle and the London era of the *Westminster Review* editorship.

Among previous biographical studies of Eliot, Gordon Haight's *George Eliot* (1968) contains a meticulous account of the facts of her life, but shies away from exploring the ideological contexts of those early years. More recent biographers have ventured into the interpretive realm, most notably, Ruby Redinger in *George Eliot: The Emergent Self* (1975); but their bias has been toward the emotive side of George Eliot's development. Much recent criticism, psychological or feminist in bias, is similarly slanted towards Eliot's heart rather than her head.[1] But the image of the painfully homely provincial spinster, the "Strauss-sick" renegade from Evangelical piety, the young woman editor in a man's world, the sexual heretic cast out from Victorian drawing rooms, must be counterbalanced by a clearer vision of George Eliot as a solidly established member of a Victorian circle of brilliant theoreticians, ambitious synthesizers, and progressive optimists. Much has been made of George Eliot's migraine headaches and her emotional dependence on George Henry Lewes; not enough has been said of her confident and aggressive intellectuality. A clearer understanding of the formative years of Eliot's intellectual development can provide new ways of reading her novels. This finale, a reading of *Middlemarch*, is intended as a suggestive illustration of that claim rather than an exhaustive exploration of its possibilities.

In a novel whose characters are so often seeking a vocation, trapped in the wrong vocation, or striving anxiously to fulfill the obligations and potential of the vocation they have chosen, Middlemarch's auctioneer Borthrop Trumbull is uniquely self-satisfied: "Surely among all men whose vocation requires them to exhibit their powers of speech, the happiest is a prosperous provincial auctioneer keenly alive to his own jokes and sensible of his encyclopaedic knowledge."[2] Language is Borthrop Trumbull's medium, and he wields it powerfully. "Being an auctioneer," George Eliot wryly tells her reader, Trumbull "was bound to know the nature of everything" (229); he "would have liked to have the universe under his hammer, feeling that it would go at a higher figure for his recommendation" (442). George Eliot enjoys her own gentle jokes in depicting the Middlemarch auction in chapter 60. Trumbull's remarkable success lies in his endless ability imaginatively to alter his point of view—and thus, that of his customer: "'I have in my hand . . . an ingenious contrivance—a sort of practical rebus, I may call it; here, you see, it looks like an elegant heart-shaped box, portable—for the pocket; there, again, it becomes like a splendid double flower—an ornament for the table; and now'—Mr. Trumbull allowed the flower to fall alarmingly into strings of heart-shaped leaves—'a book of riddles; No less than five hundred printed in a beautiful red'" (443).

The sibylline and sympathetic narrator of Middlemarch poses the "riddles" of human nature in the "heart-shaped leaves" of her novel, mirroring "this mighty volume of events / The world, the universal map of deeds."[3] On one hand the Victorian map of Middlemarch bears resemblance to Trumbull's grandly visionary description of that most Victorian of portrait heroes, the Duke of Wellington: "a [fine] subject—of the modern order, belonging to our own time and epoch." Trumbull, who "knows the nature of everything," knows also the limits of that knowledge; his picture is a subject "the understanding of man could hardly conceive; angels might, perhaps, but not men, sirs, not men" (443). Yet although the universe may pass under Borthrop Trumbull's hammer, it does so one particular piece at a time: "Now ladies," he tells his audience, "this tray contains a very recherchy lot—a collection of trifles for the drawing room table—and trifles make the sum of human things—nothing more important than trifles" (442–43). Under the measuring observation and shaping imagination of its author, George Eliot's vision of *Middlemarch*, like Borthrop Trumbull's of Middlemarch, strives toward angelic understandings with an emphatic insistence on the trifles of which any synthetic "sum" must be made.

Like the auctioneer George Eliot approached this subject "of the modern order" with "encyclopaedic knowledge." In the *Leader* in 1850, George Henry Lewes presaged his love for the woman he was to meet a year later when, under his gadfly persona "Vivian," he excoriated merely "clever women" at the expense of truly wise ones: "The women whose minds are stored with the writings of poets, moralists, and historians, who have thought upon the questions which affect the inner life of man, who have observed and analyzed the passions, watched society, traced the operation of moral laws . . . those women I find to be . . . adored by their humble servant."[4] George Eliot was worthy of Lewes's adoration. In 1949 historian of ideas Basil Willey made the often-quoted observation that "probably no English writer of the time, and certainly no novelist, more fully epitomizes the century; her development is a paradigm, her intellectual biography a graph, of its most decided trend."[5] George Eliot's contemporaries were immediately responsive to the distinctively Victorian qualities of *Middlemarch*: "What she writes is so full of her time," claimed reviewer Sidney Colvin in the *Fortnightly*,

> saturated with modern ideas, and poured into a language of which every word bites home with peculiar sharpness to the contemporary consciousness. . . . We are afraid of exaggerating the meaning such work will have for those who come after us, for the very reason that we feel its meaning so pregnant for ourselves. If, in-

deed, the ideas of to-day are certain to be the ideas of to-morrow
and the day after, if scientific thought and the positive synthesis
are indubitably to rule the world, than any one, it should seem,
might speak boldly enough to George Eliot's place.[6]

Of course, so much of the Victorian "to-day," its scientific
thought and its positive synthesis, *has* been buried with the
cast-off intellectual oddities of another age. *Middlemarch* has
endured because of its timeless human truths rather than its
dated ideological underpinnings. But I believe that an appreciation of some of the ways in which it manifests a distinctively
contemporary consciousness can both add significantly to our
understanding of this literary masterpiece and provide a final
epitome of the frame of mind shared by this circle of Victorian
intellectuals.

Scores of critical treasure-hunters have excavated the encyclopaedic "stratum of conglomerated fragments" this Victorian genius left behind her in the form of letters, essays, and
novels.[7] Anna Kitchel's publication of Eliot's "Quarry for
Middlemarch" in 1950 and Jerome Beaty's *"Middlemarch"
From Notebook to Novel* a decade later have more recently
been followed by publication of the complete *Middlemarch*
notebooks, transcribed and edited, providing ample evidence
for the breadth of George Eliot's learning and the minute research at the foundations of this remarkable novel.[8] The previous chapters of my study document many important intellectual sources upon which George Eliot could draw for the
topography of her Victorian world. For example, the reader
who knows something of magnetism and mesmerism will read
passages like the following in a new way: "When Mrs. Casaubon was announced he started up as from an electric shock,
and felt a tingling at his finger-ends. . . . every molecule in
his body has passed the message of a magic touch. . . . For
effective magic is transcendent nature; and who shall measure
the subtlety of those touches which convey the quality of soul
as well as body?" (285). The relation between innate disposition and external objects, the dilemmas of determinism shared
by these Victorians, can illuminate the dialogue between those

two gentlemen of chapter 4's epigraph:

> *1st Gent.* Our deeds are fetters that we forge ourselves.
> *2nd Gent.* Ay, truly: but I think it is the world
> That brings the iron. (25)

Dr. Tertius Lydgate, searching for "certain primary webs or tissues, out of which the various organs—brain, heart, lungs, and so on—are compacted" (110) is, of course, a Spencerian transcendental anatomist. And so forth; such a list could be continued at length. Scholarly essays have been written, and remain to be written, on the resonant interweavings of contemporary ideas about determinism, or positivism, or biology, or evolutionary theory, in George Eliot's fiction.[9] Much that I have said in chapters 1 through 4 should stimulate the reader familiar with Eliot's novels.

But source-hunting is not my primary intention here. For surely the whole of this great novel is more than the sum of such particular parts. For each of these thinkers, the details of positivist logic or phrenological dissection or evolutionary embryology were merely the means to a much larger end: the foundations for a Victorian cosmology. Rather than syllogisms or skulls, character and plot were to be George Eliot's data, the particulars in which she would embody her generalizations. "Ideas are often poor ghosts; our sun-filled eyes cannot discern them. . . . But sometimes they are made flesh; . . . they are clothed in a living human soul, with all its conflicts, its faith, and its love. Then their presence is a power," she writes in her first fiction, *Scenes of Clerical Life.*[10] The incarnation is to be a literal one, as a Victorian sensibility defines its shape in the complex yet coherent human web of Middlemarch society.

II. A VICTORIAN SENSIBILITY: THE POETRY OF THE REAL

The aesthetic faculties are . . . intermediate between the purely moral and the purely intellectual faculties.—Lewes, Comte's Philosophy of the Sciences, *1853.*

"Every limit is a beginning as well as an ending," George
Eliot opens her "Finale" (607). After eighty-six chapters she
ends her narrative with the "great beginning" of marriage; but
remember that she also began *Middlemarch* with the marriages
of her heroine Dorothea and hero Lydgate, exploding at the
outset any conclusive linear myth of happily ever after. On the
circumference of the Victorian circle traced by my book, endings similarly return us to beginnings. At the opposite pole of
the nineteenth century from Coleridge's *Theory of Life*,
George Eliot's *Middlemarch* can be read as a finale that interacts dynamically with Coleridge's prelude to the Victorian age.
"Who that cares much to know the history of man, and how
the *mysterious* mixture behaves under the varying *experiments*
of Time, has not dwelt, as least briefly, on the life of Saint
Theresa," the novel's "Prelude" begins (3; my emphasis).
Thus *Middlemarch* opens: with mystery and experiment, the
unknowable and the knowable, inextricably intertwined. In
this first paragraph, the narrator's synthesizing sensibility is
mirrored in her heroine, Saint Theresa.[11] The glory of Theresa's "epos," her "epic life," is exemplified by her ability to
translate passionate emotion—"the rapturous consciousness
of life beyond self"—into constructive action—"the reform of
a religious order" (3).

By contrast the second and third paragraphs of the three-par-
agraph "Prelude" present a world without order. In the second
Eliot depicts a life spiritually inadequate, one in which modern-day Theresas lack "coherent social faith" (3). She then goes
on, in the third, to mock the equal inadequacy of a simplisti-
cally empirical cosmos, those who believe that "the social lot
of women might be treated with scientific certitude" (4). The
twentieth-century reader might be tempted simply to conclude
that Eliot's contemporary men and women, without the centering force of Saint Theresa's Catholic church, are doomed to
disorder, "dim lights and tangled circumstances" (3); and that
scientific certitude offers little that is really certain to replace
the fallen idols of orthodox faith.

But the confident tone of the narrator's opening words, the

ease with which she moves from the mystical to the empirical, cannot be overlooked. The fallible and confused modern-day Theresas must be juxtaposed with Eliot's omniscient narrator, with her much broader view of "the history of man": "With dim lights and tangled circumstance they tried to shape their thought and deed in noble agreement; but after all *to common eyes* their struggles *seemed* mere inconsistency and formlessness" (3; my emphasis). These struggles only seem formless. Is not a finer and fuller vision possible to the uncommon eye— the all-seeing "I" of the novelist? This uncommon eye is both intuitive and empirical; it can give clearer shape to spiritual inconsistency and refine simple scientific certitudes into less rigid forms: "Meanwhile the indefiniteness remains, and the limits of variation are really much wider than anyone would imagine" (4). The uncommon eye can contain the polarities of mystery and experiment; it can mediate between the chaos of formlessness and the reductiveness of unrefined structures.

The final words of the "Prelude" describe the failed Saint Theresa of the modern age, "foundress of nothing, whose loving heart-beats and sobs after an unattained goodness . . . are dispersed among hindrances, instead of centering in some long-recognisable deed" (4). As so many critics of *Middlemarch* have observed, the novel overflows with failed monistic cosmologists, seeking the wrong Key to All Mythologies or the nonexistent Universal Tissue—systems no more valid than phrenology or mesmerism. "I have made up my mind not to run that risk of never attaining a failure," Will Ladislaw tells Dorothea Brooke (165). The unknowable lies at the boundary of the known; but the search for a center must continue. "Difficulties of thought and acceptance of what is without comprehension belong to every system of thinking. The question is to find the least incomplete," George Eliot writes in 1874.[12] Both the novelist and her characters search for what Dorothea Brooke calls "the fullest truth, the least partial good" (151). The uncommon eye persists in seeking the order of the continuous cosmos.[13]

Source-hunting for *Middlemarch*'s models has inspired

small scholarly conflagrations for a century. Where did Eliot get the name Casaubon? Was he a portrait of Mark Pattison? Dr. Brabant? George Henry Lewes? But George Eliot herself answered the question: "When a young friend put the question direct: 'But from whom, then, did you draw Casaubon?' George Eliot, with a humorous solemnity, which was quite in earnest, nevertheless, pointed to her own heart."[14] No novel in the English language can boast a more fully-articulated cast of characters than *Middlemarch*. But the one of George Eliot's creative identity is refracted in the many of a diverse group of fictional individuals.[15]

The first two chapters of the novel introduce two most dissimilar reflections of that narrator who coupled mystery so easily with experiment. In chapter 1 Dorothea Brooke: Dorothea, we quickly learn, is both a religious mystic and a would-be social reformer: "'How very beautiful these gems are!' said Dorothea, under a new current of feeling, as sudden as the gleam. 'It is strange how colours seem to penetrate one, like scent. . . . They look like fragments of heaven'" (10). But a page later, Dorothea switches from "fragments of heaven" to bricks and mortar: "Here, Kitty, come and look at my plan; I shall think I am a great architect, if I have not got incompatible stairs and fireplaces" (11).

This same theme is orchestrated in quite another way in the paragraph that immediately follows Dorothea's architectural outburst, as chapter 2 opens with an abrupt introduction to that "pulpy" (52) proponent of many-sidedness, Dorothea's uncle:

> "Sir Humphry Davy?" said Mr. Brooke, over the soup, in his easy smiling way, taking up Sir James Chettam's remark that he was studying Davy's Agricultural Chemistry. "Well, now, Sir Humphry Davy: I dined with him years ago at Cartwright's, and Wordsworth was there too—the poet Wordsworth, you know. Now there was something singular. I was at Cambridge when Wordsworth was there, and I never met him—and I dined with him twenty years afterwards at Cartwright's. There's an oddity in things, now. But Davy was there: and he was a poet too. Or, as I may say, Wordsworth was poet one, and Davy was poet two. That was true in every sense, you know. [11–12]

It is easy to identify George Eliot with her "ardent, theoretic, and intellectually consequent" heroine (21); but she also shares much with her wise fool Brooke, who "goes into" science, theology, history, and political economy with equal fervor: "Pigeon-holes will not do" (14). "I should learn everything then," says Dorothea (21); Brooke is George Eliot's affectionate parody of the same encyclopaedic impulse, and his amusing ramblings always contain a germ of truth: "I have always been in favor of a little theory: we must have Thought" (13). It is significant that Brooke's first words in the novel are of Sir Humphry Davy and William Wordsworth, "poet one" and "poet two," "in every sense."[16] Art and science, intuitive imagination and empirical observation, are not mutually exclusive. Brooke is a far cry from Goethe or Spinoza!—but he nonetheless speaks to the ideal of the poet-scientist.

Of course Middlemarch has both its own poet-scientist and scientific poet, in Tertius Lydgate and Will Ladislaw. For Lydgate, as for George Henry Lewes, heart and brain are the dual lords of life, both literally and metaphorically. Lydgate's search for a vocation is fulfilled by the "intellectual passion" of his scientific research (107). In a brilliant stroke of imagination on Eliot's part, her scientific hero "kindles" that passion by discovering a passage "on the valves of the heart" in a book on anatomy. It is through the medium of language, a metaphoric leap of the poetic imagination, that Lydgate first becomes a scientist: "He knew that *valvae* were folding doors, and through this crevice came a sudden light startling him with his first vivid notion of finely-adjusted mechanism in the human frame" (106-7). In *The Principles of Success in Literature* (1865), George Henry Lewes drew the distinction between the appeal of science to the intellect, and art to the emotions. As might be expected, Lewes quickly goes on to deny any necessary separation of the two processes: "But having recognized the broadly-marked differences, we are called upon to ascertain the underlying resemblances. Logic and Imagination belong equally to both."[17] Likewise, Lydgate's research is "the most perfect interchange between science and art" (108). Like the nonfictional Victorian cosmologist, his methodology emphasizes the mutual interaction of general and particular, theory and practice: "The two purposes would illuminate each other: the careful observation and inference which was his daily work . . . would further his thought as an instrument of larger inquiry." The "great idea" and the "arduous practice of his profession" are "twin object[s]" (109). Like Dorothea Brooke, Tertius Lydgate is a would-be architect, who seeks to realize his theory in the concrete world of physical objects: "Living bodies . . . must be regarded as consisting of certain primary webs or tissues, out of which the various organs—brain, heart, lungs, and so on, are compacted, *as the various accommodations of a house are built up* in various proportions of wood, iron, stone, brick, zinc and the rest" (110; my emphasis). Following Bichat, Lydgate performs minute dissections in his serach for "ultimate facts."[18]

At first glance Will Ladislaw scarcely seems to be a scientist, though he is unmistakably a poet. Will tells Dorothea: "To be a poet is to have a soul so quick to discern that no shade of quality escapes it, and so quick to feel, that discernment is but a hand playing with finely-ordered variety on the chords of emotion—a soul in which knowledge passes instantaneously into feeling, and feeling flashes back as a new organ of knowledge."[19] Although Will does recognize that feeling and knowing work in tandem, something is missing from this scheme, as Dorothea quickly points out: "But you leave out the poems. . . . I think they are wanted to complete the poet" (166). "The true seeing is within," Ladislaw idealistically argues with his painter friend Naumann (142). But Naumann disagrees: he wants "the idealistic in the real" (159). Abstract imagination without concrete realization—the poet without his poems—is only half of the equation.

Will never shows any interest in science, but he does find his ultimate vocation as a politician, becoming "an ardent public man" in later years (610): "He studied the political situation with as ardent an interest as he had ever given to poetic metres" (337). He is "a sort of Burke with a leaven of Shelley," thinks Mr. Brooke in his wonderfully muddled way (366)—but as always, there is a leaven of truth in Brooke's inspired foolishness. For politics is both Ladislaw's science and his poetry; his way of translating the ideal into the real. Romantic visions are transformed into concrete political proposals (just as Saint Theresa's mysticism led to the reform of a religious order).[20] However skeptical she may be about the details of the political process, George Eliot, setting her novel on the eve of the first reform bill and writing from the vantage-point of the second, knows how profoundly the particular lives of her provincial characters will ultimately be altered by the large evolutionary forces of political and social change in the Victorian era that is immediately to follow *Middlemarch*. Eliot takes Shelley's "Defense of Poetry" quite literally: her poet is the *acknowledged* "legislator of mankind."[21] For this Victorian sensibility, the ideal politician would also be the ideal poet, the man of particular legislation and sweeping imaginative vision: a fusion of polar opposites.[22] In this light Mr. Brooke's unlikely marriage of Burke and Shelley takes on more serious meaning as the political defender of tradition and order is counterbalanced by the poetical proponent of revolutionary change.

As critics of *Middlemarch* have often noted, one of the chief unifying principles of the novel is the way in which characters not directly linked by plot provide thematic contrasts with one another. One such example is illustrated above: Lydgate the scientist—the empiricist who is also a transcendental anatomist; and Ladislaw the poet—the intuitive visionary who deals in practical legislation. Before turning to the ways in which George Eliot embodies a Victorian sensibility in the plot and structure of her novel, let me extend my discussion of character by noting that Ladislaw and Lydgate are only one of the many such polar pairs that interact dynamically upon the mind of the reader: the unassuming brown sparrow Mary Garth and the preening white dove Rosamond Vincy; the open-minded Reverend Camden Farebrother and the zealous Evangelical bigot Bulstrode; the emotionally ossified religious scholar Casaubon with his dusty fragments, and the virile scientific researcher Lydgate with his vital connections; generous-spirited

Dorothea and egotistical Rosamond; male Lydgate who chan-
nels his aggressive ambition into an ardent career, female Dorothea who seeks intellectual fulfillment through the submis-
sive hero-worship of marriage; "uncle" Brooke who takes
young Ladislaw under his nebulous political patronage,
"uncle" Garth who tutors young Fred Vincy in concrete agricultural management; the list could be continued at length. It
could be said that George Eliot's characterizations in *Middlemarch* are a Spencerian combination of individuation and interdependence. Concerned with the "minutiae of mental
make" (111) in every character, George Eliot paints a brilliantly individualized portrait of each, yet draws them together
in the mind of her reader through the mediums of Middlemarch, a common humanity, and the novelist's philosophy of
the one in the many, incarnate in the narrator's vision of a
larger whole.

I conclude my discussion of character in *Middlemarch* with
the polar antithesis to Mr. Brooke, Caleb Garth. The contrasts
are obvious: Brooke the wealthy landowner and Garth the es-
tate agent stand at opposite poles of Middlemarch's social spectrum; "the Garths were poor," but "did not mind it" (186).
Brooke is the most foolish character in the novel, a childish
figure benevolently tolerated by his friends and actively mocked
by the larger community, but Caleb Garth's wisdom is questioned by none, including his author. Garth's refusal to act as
Bulstrode's agent is the *coup de grâce* to the banker's ruination
in Middlemarch. The narrator clearly feels a special affection
for Caleb: "(Pardon the details for once—you would have learned
to love them if you had known Caleb Garth)," she apologizes
to her reader (171). Brooke is lost in airy fancies and half-baked
theories; Garth is the consummately practical man: "He was
ready to accept any number of systems, like any number of
firmaments, if they did not obviously interfere with the best
land-drainage, solid building, correct measuring, and judicious
boring (for coal)" (185).

Like Dorothea Brooke and Tertius Lydgate, Caleb Garth is
a would-be architect. And like them he too meets with setbacks.

The first thing we learn about him is that he "had failed in the building business" (170); yet we catch our first glimpse of Garth, when Fred Vincy comes to confess his financial pecadillos, "absorbed in a plan for Sir James Chettam's new farm-building" (171). Caleb Garth is the most unqualifiedly heroic of *Middlemarch*'s characters—not because of his success (which is minimal) but because of his sensibility, that undaunted striving for "the fullest truth" that incarnates the ideal in the everyday. Caleb's work is also his religion, in the truest sense of that word: "Getting a bit of good contriving and solid building done," he tells his wife, is "a great gift from God" (295). Caleb Garth is a practical empiricist: "A good deal of what I know can only come from experience," he advises Fred Vincy; "you are young enough to lay a foundation yet" (409). But the foundation of Garth's creed is as intuitive as it is rational; he speaks to Fred "with the air of a man who felt himself to be saying something deeply religious" (409). And here, the pragmatic Caleb Garth interacts dynamically with his polar opposite, Mr. Brooke. For Caleb Garth too articulates a vision of the whole; he too is a poet-scientist.

It is not surprising that Dorothea Brooke—who at the outset of *Middlemarch* stated her desire to "learn everything," so that "there would be nothing trivial about our lives. Everyday-things with us would mean the greatest things" (21)—should four hundred pages later meet up with Garth and experience growing "confidence" in his "knowledge." The beautiful young heiress and the old workman find they have similar goals: " 'Most uncommon!' repeated Caleb. 'She said a thing I often used to think myself when I was a lad:—"Mr. Garth, I should like to feel, if I lived to be old, that I had improved a great piece of land and built a great many cottages, because the work is of a healthy kind while it is being done, and after it is done, men are the better for it." Those were the very words: she sees things in that way' " (402). Yet just as Dorothea's architectural blueprints were juxtaposed to the "fragments of heaven" in her jewelry (10-11), so Garth follows his account of the pragmatic work of building with an imaginative vision: "You would like to hear her speak, Susan. She speaks in such plain words, and a voice like music. Bless me! it reminds me of bits in the 'Messiah'—'and straightway there appeared a multitude of the heavenly host, praising God and saying;' it has a tone with it that satisfies your ear." Laborers' cottages are not the only structures in which Caleb Garth glories: "Caleb was very fond of music, and when he could afford it went to hear an oratorio that came within his reach, returning from it with a profound reverence for this mighty structure of tones" (402).

And so, Caleb Garth hears the angels sing. At the conclusion of *Middlemarch*, Dorothea Brooke is granted a redemptive vision of the larger whole, as she looks out her window to "the largeness of the world and the manifold wakings of men to labour and endurance" (578). But it is Caleb Garth who experiences the most comprehensive vision, a panorama closest to the omniscient narrator's own bird's-eye view of "that myriad-headed, myriad-handed . . . social body." Like his creator Garth recognizes the poetry of the real, the sublime in the mundane:

> It laid hold of his imagination in boyhood. The echoes of the great hammer where roof or keel were a-making, the signal-shots of the workmen, the roar of the furnace, the thunder and plash of the engine, and the huge trunk vibrating star-like in the distance along the highway, the crane at work on the wharf, the piled-up produce in warehouses, the precision and variety of muscular effort wherever exact work had to be turned out,—all these sights of his youth had acted on him as poetry without the aid of the poets, had made a philosophy for him without the aid of philosophers, a religion without the aid of theology. [185]

III. BUILDING A NOVEL: THE PART AND THE WHOLE

We need not shrink from this comparison of small things with great; for does not science tell us that its highest striving is after the ascertainment of a unity which shall bind the smallest things with the greatest? In natural science, I have understood, there is nothing petty to the mind that has a large vision of relations, and to which every single object suggests a vast sum of conditions. It is surely the same with the observation of human life.—George Eliot, The Mill on the Floss, *1860*

Critics of *Middlemarch* have often pointed out that George Eliot's description of Lydgate's microscopic visions sounds as much like the enterprise of a psychological novelist as it does the work of a research scientist:[23] "He wanted to pierce the obscurity of those minute processes which prepare human misery and joy, those invisible thoroughfares which are the first lurking-places of anguish, mania, and crime, that delicate poise and transition which determine the growth of happy or unhappy consciousness" (122). When Lydgate quotes his "favourite bit from an old poet" to his wife Rosamund, he is surely voicing an ambition shared by his creator:

> What good is like to this,
> To do worth the writing, and to write
> Worthy the reading and the world's delight?
> [320]

In fact, Lydgate's poetry sits more comfortably upon a Victorian novel than it does a treatise on anatomy.

It is a familiar observation that still bears repeating that virtually every major character in *Middlemarch* is in search of a key to all mythologies, on an evolutionary scale from Dorothea's spiritual yearning "after some lofty conception of the world" (6) and Lydgate's intellectual search for the primary tissue (111), down to the "central poising force" (359) of Celia Brooke Chettam's maternal instinct and, at the lowest level, the froglike Rigg-Featherstone's avaricious aspiration for a money-changer's shop in which he might "have locks all round him of which he held the keys" (381). This desire for a vision of the whole does not originate with *Middlemarch*, however; it is a theme that can be traced throughout George Eliot's fiction. We find it in her heroines: in *The Mill on the Floss*'s Maggie Tulliver, "thirsty for all knowledge . . . yearning for something that would link together the powerful impressions of this mysterious life";[24] and *Felix Holt*'s Esther Lyon: "Her life was a heap of fragments, and so were her thoughts: some great energy was needed to bind them together."[25] The blind scholar Bardo of *Romola* foreshadows Casaubon's arachnae ambitions: "That great work in which I had desired to gather, as into a firm web, all the threads that my research had laboriously disentangled . . . was cut off by the failure of my sight."[26] No character is more consumed by this ambition than the eponymous hero of Eliot's final, and most visionary, novel, *Daniel Deronda*: "He felt the inward bent towards comprehension and thoroughness . . . he felt a heightening discontent with the wearing futility and enfeebling strain of a demand for excessive retention and dexterity without any insight into the principles which form the vital connections of knowledge."[27]

In my opening discussion of Coleridge's *Theory of Life*, I observed how closely Eliot's "Notes on Form in Art" translated Coleridge's "individuation" into formal aesthetic principles.[28] But long before these notes of 1868, Herbert Spencer had made an aesthetic application of that scientific model. Spencer mentions in his *Autobiography* that the famous Spencerian password, "heterogeneity," first appeared not in a scientific but in a literary context, in an essay on the "Philosophy of Style" published in the *Westminster* under George Eliot's editorship in 1852. In that same essay, Spencer argues that a perfect literary composition will "answer to the description of all highly-organized products of both men and nature. It will be, not a series of like parts simply placed in juxtaposition, but one whole made up of unlike parts that are mutually dependent."[29] As early as her first published writing, "Poetry and Prose, From the Notebook of an Eccentric" (in Charles Bray's *Coventry Herald* in 1846) George Eliot had herself applied the same sensibility that animated the positivist, the phrenologist, and the transcendental anatomist, to the writer's craft: "I love to think how the perfect whole exists in the imagination of the artist. . . . I love to watch the artist's eye . . . scrupulously attentive to the details of his actual labour, yet keeping ever in view the idea which that labour is to fulfill. I say to myself—this is an image of what our life should be,—a series of efforts directed to the production of a contemplated whole."[30]

In the preceding chapters of this study, I have attempted to delineate the ways in which each of these Victorian thinkers sought to make it whole. All of their systems share a temperamental tendency to mediate between head and heart, that sensibility which Eliot personifies in the poet-scientists, the passionate intellectuals, the realistic idealists of her novel. The second common denominator found in this Victorian frame of mind is what Atkinson and Martineau called "the true cosmical view of Nature: the sense of variety in unity, and unity in variety: the whole in the parts and the parts in the whole."[31] The part/whole antithesis is, of course, closely linked to the head/heart dichotomy: the rational empiricist dissects the parts; the passionate idealist intuits the whole. *Middlemarch* is George Eliot's own aspiration toward a key to all mythologies, her effort to incarnate a monistic conception of the world. It is to the larger organism of *Middlemarch* as a whole, the structure of the novel and the strategies of its narrator, to which I now turn in order to view this novel as Eliot's own distinctive embodiment of a Victorian cosmology.

The reader will remember that in 1851, Atkinson and Martineau had proclaimed, "While we dilate the sight in the sense of the Unity of Nature, . . . we must not forget to contract the sight to every particular and circumstance."[32] In 1876 Lewes would write, echoing his hero Goethe, "Analysis and synthesis are the systole and diastole of science."[33] Similarly, when George Eliot builds her fictional structure, she makes an aesthetic application of *her* hero Lydgate's scientific dictum: "There must be a systole and diastole in all inquiry"; "A man's mind must be continually expanding and shrinking between the whole human horizon and the horizon of an object-glass" (468). The uncommon eye of *Middlemarch*'s narrator focuses with alternating but equal intensity on the whole and the part. Within a single paragraph, Eliot can shift from "a careful telescopic watch [of] . . . the parishes of Tipton and Freshitt" to "a microscope directed on a water-drop" (44); from the telescopic horizon of human society to the microscopic object-glass of the individual psyche.[34]

On one hand, *Middlemarch: A Study of Provincial Life* takes as its building-blocks the entirety of the social organism. In the *Cours de philosophie positive,* Auguste Comte had observed this social organism from afar:

> Can we conceive of a more marvelous spectacle, in the whole range of natural phenomena, than the regular and constant convergence of an innumerable multitude of human beings, each possessing a distinct and, in a certain degree, independent existence, and yet incessantly disposed, amidst all their discordance of talent and character, to concur in many ways in the same general development, without concert, and even consciousness on the part of most of them, who believe that they are merely following their personal impulses?[35]

Similarly, in Social Statics Herbert Spencer argued that

> This union of many men into one community—this increasing mutual dependence of units which were originally independent— this gradual segregation of citizens into separate bodies, with reciprocally subservient functions—this formation of a whole, consisting of numerous essential parts—this growth of an organism, of which one portion cannot be injured without the rest feeling it—may all be generalized under the law of individualization.[36]

Both visions are mirrored in Eliot's sweepingly telescopic vantage-point. "Watching keenly the stealthy convergence of human lots," the novelist "sees a slow preparation of effects from one life on another":

> Old provincial society had its share of this subtle movement: had not only its striking downfalls, its brilliant young professional dandies who ended by living up an entry with a drab and six children for their establishment, but also those less marked vicissitudes which are constantly shifting the boundaries of social intercourse, and begetting new consciousness of interdependence. Some slipped a little downward, some got higher footing: people denied aspirates, gained wealth, and fastidious gentlemen stood for boroughs; some were caught in political currents, some in ecclesiastical, and perhaps found themselves surprisingly grouped in consequence; while a few personages or families that stood with rocky firmness amid all this fluctuation, were slowly presenting new aspects in spite of solidity, and altering with the double change of self and beholder. Municipal town and rural parish gradually made fresh threads of connection. [70-71]

This synthetic incarnation of a dynamic social organism is temporal as well as spatial. In 1871 George Eliot is writing a historical novel set forty years earlier; and her telescopic vision traces fundamental unities of human nature across the space of all recorded history: "In fact, much the same sort of movement and mixture went on in old England as we find in older Herodotus" (71).

But Eliot's microscopic vision places an equal emphasis on the "play of minute causes" (44) within each unique and individuated part of this human whole. She is equally concerned with "heterogeneity," the "endless minutiae by which [each character's] view . . . was gradually changing with the secret motion of a watch-hand." (144). It is impossible to do justice by summary example to the brilliant particularity with which the novelist "pierce[s] the obscurity of those minute processes" (122) within each of her characters. Casaubon's realization of his own mortality, "a man . . . now for the first time looking into the eyes of death," with its mingling of the trivial and the sublime—"the pathos of a lot where everything is below the level of tragedy except the passionate egoism of the sufferer" (310-11) or Bulstrode's soliloquy of self-justification leading to his murder of Raffles—"the rigid outline with which acts present themselves to onlookers . . . was broken into little sequences, each justified as it came by reasonings which seemed to prove it righteous" (452)—these can only be randomly offered as a suggestion of the incredibly rich microscopic particularity of the novel's psychological analysis.

But we must keep in mind that this is a world of dynamic polarities in which opposites interpenetrate. Reread George Eliot's description of old provincial society on the preceding page and note the underlying biological metaphor of "subtle movement" and "fresh threads of connection." Eliot's telescopic vision, sweeping over time and space, is equally microscopic: she focuses on the "particular web" of *Middlemarch* (105), intricately and uniquely woven in a highly specified historical moment and well-mapped place. Conversely, the microscopic "minutiae of mental make" (111) of each character

must be subsumed into fundamental unity: "A human being
. . . is a very wonderful whole" (300). And transcending the
individuated whole of Dorothea Brooke or Tertius Lydgate or
Fred Vincy is the larger whole of human nature. Casaubon's
small shivering self in the face of death or Bulstrode's calculat-
ing rationalizations resonate with universal insight into human nature, as *Middlemarch*'s omniscient and moralizing narrator so constantly reminds her reader: "We are all of us born
in moral stupidity, taking the world as an udder to feed our
supreme selves" (156). In reading *Middlemarch* we are each
drawn into a greater human whole by virtue of the novelist's
insistence that her particular psychological insights must be
constantly enlarged into universal moral truths.

But even the most optimistic of organicists must come to
terms with the fact that the Victorian cosmologies of *Middlemarch*'s characters, one after another, seem to fail; their visions
proving, if not incorrect, at least inadequate. Saint Theresa
may have been "centered," but Dorothea Brooke is "incal-
culably diffusive" (613). If George Eliot attempts her own key
to all mythologies in *Middlemarch*, she does so with a keen sense
of the very real hazards of such an enterprise. But there has
been a consensus among George Eliot's critics that because
Middlemarch contains so many doomed searchers for that elu-
sive key, therefore Eliot must believe that the enterprise is inherently futile, that the monist entertains a false view of reality.[37] But once we have placed George Eliot within this
Victorian circle, such an interpretation becomes difficult to
sustain. Again and again Eliot's closest intellectual associations and deepest friendships are with men and women not unlike Tertius Lydgate and Dorothea Brooke, searchers for universal tissues and binding theories. I believe that George Eliot
shares their aspirations.

That "eminent philosopher" among George Eliot's friends
who can "dignify" the mundane by the "serene light of science" has been (arguably) identified as Herbert Spencer.[38] But
the actual historical source of Eliot's famous parable of the
pier glass is not particularly important; any eminent philosopher searching for a centering system runs this risk:

Your pier-glass or extensive surface of polished steel made to be rubbed by a housemaid, will be minutely and multitudinously scratched in all directions; but place now against it a lighted candle as a centre of illumination, and lo! the scratches will seem to arrange themselves in a fine series of concentric circles round that little sun. It is demonstrable that the scratches are going everywhere impartially, and it is only your candle which produces the flattering illusion of a concentric arrangement, its light falling with an exclusive optical selection. [194-95]

In a provocative essay on "Narrative and History" in *Middlemarch*, critic J. Hillis Miller has argued that "in each case the character is shown to be mystified by a belief that all the details he confronts make a whole governed by a single center, origin, or end. In each case the narrator demystifies the illusion." Miller asserts that *Middlemarch* is George Eliot's "subversion" of the "metaphysics" of wholeness, her deconstruction of the universe.[39] But is Miller's "illusion" George Eliot's? Miller's reading would stress the "minute and multitudinous" disorder of those scratches; I would emphasize the "centre of illumination." "The phenomena constituting the external reality to us are presented discontinuously," writes George Henry Lewes in *Problems of Life and Mind*; "and it is the office of Philosophy so to connect them that their actual continuity be discovered."[40] The continuous cosmos is no illusion for these Victorians, even though their systems may prove inadequate to embody it.

The illusion of the pier glass-gazer—and the potential pitfall of the eminent philosopher—lies in mistaking the part for the whole, not in believing that there *is* such a thing as wholeness. Any reading of the pier glass parable must begin by stressing that each "little sun" *is* in itself "a wonderful whole." George Eliot insists throughout *Middlemarch* on the integrity of each unifying consciousness: "Mr. Casaubon, too, was the centre of his own world; if he was liable to think that others were providentially made for him, and especially to consider them in light of their fitness for the author of a 'Key to All Mythologies,' this trait is not quite alien to us, and, like the other mendicant hopes of mortals, claims some of our pity"

(62). Eliot validates every such center, demanding her readers' sympathetic response and educating her characters to similar insight: "He had an equivalent centre of self," Dorothea realizes (157).

"Things must be *recognized as separate wholes* before they can be recognized as wholes composed of parts, or before those wholes again can be regarded as relatively *parts of a larger whole*," Eliot writes in "Notes on Form."[41] But if we are to escape the illusion of the pier glass, the separate whole, each center of consciousness, must finally be seen in the context of the larger whole. This broader vision is the province of the uncommon eye of the omniscient narrator, the synthetic philosopher who can see the order inherent in the dim lights and tangled circumstance that is hidden to the common eyes of the novel's characters—and its readers. If George Eliot is to succeed in making it whole with *Middlemarch*, she must demonstrate this interconnectedness. Like Caleb Garth, Dorothea Brooke, and Tertius Lydgate, George Eliot is an architect, building her novel on the philosophical foundations of a Victorian frame of mind. The structure of *Middlemarch* is Eliot's own blueprint for wholeness. Where our common eye is limited to the small candle of self, the omniscient narrator's is not.

Multiplicity is concomitant to unity; "trifles make the sum of human things," as Borthrop Trumbull says. The rich, abundant, and carefully detailed subject matter of *Middlemarch* underscores this point most obviously. But Eliot also emphasizes multiplicity in more subtle structural ways. "In watching effects, if only of an electric battery, it is often necessary to change our place and examine a particular mixture or group at some distance from the point where the movement we are interested in was set up," she writes (292; and note the electrical metaphor). Eliot self-consciously shifts her novelistic viewpoint throughout, to emphasize that every circle contains innumerable circles, each with its center and circumference. Take the famous opening of chapter 29: "One morning, some weeks after her arrival at Lowick, Dorothea—but why always Dorothea? Was her point of view the only possible one with regard to this marriage? . . . Mr. Casaubon had an intense consciousness within him" (205); or similarly, chapter 53:

> Joshua himself was thinking that the new moment now was not
> far off when he should settle on the North Quay with the best ap-
> pointments in Safes and Locks.
>   Enough. We are concerned with looking at Joshua Rigg's sale
> of his land from Mr. Bulstrode's point of view. [382]

The deliberate awkwardness with which Eliot makes her tran-
sitions from one center of consciousness to another serves to
emphasize her point: this multiplicity is an important aspect
of the novel's fundamental wholeness. Like her auctioneer
Trumbull, Eliot insists that the events of *Middlemarch* be
"viewed in many different lights" (323).

The phrase "point of view" becomes a *leitmotif* in *Middlemarch*: "Sir James Chettam, for example, whom she constantly considered from Celia's point of view, inwardly debat-
ing whether it would be good for Celia to accept him" (7); "Mr.
Brooke, seeing Mrs. Cadwallader's merits from a different
point of view, winced a little when her name was announced
in the library" (39); " 'He is no better than a mummy!' (The
point of view has to be allowed for, as that of a blooming and
disappointed rival)" (43); "It is a narrow mind which cannot
look at a subject from various points of view" (49); " 'She is not
in the least Evangelical,' said Rosamund, reflectively, as if that
religious point of view would have fully accounted for perpetual crepe" (77). Such a list could be continued at length: the
above examples are taken only from book 1.[12] Paradoxically,
the author's self-consciously shifting focus serves to draw attention to the continuity and cohesiveness of the omniscient
narrator's larger vision.

Juxtaposing its myriad parts, the multilayered plot of *Middlemarch* is structured in such a way as to draw further attention to the larger whole. In the midst of her own marital crises,
Dorothea Brooke's attention is drawn randomly out her window to Peter Featherstone's funeral, to a scene which

> aloof as it seemed to be from the tenor of her life, always afterwards
> came back to her at the touch of certain sensitive points in mem-
> ory, just as the vision of St. Peter's at Rome was inwoven with

moods of despondency. Scenes which make vital changes in our
neighbours' lot are but the background of our own, yet, like a particular aspect of the fields and trees, they become associated for us
with the epochs of our own history, and make a part of that unity
which lies in the selection of our keenest consciousness. [238]

"Scenes which make vital changes in our neighbours' lot are
but the background of our own": each character in the novel is
a "little sun," a circle with a center whose circumference is
coincident with the center of another. Each character's consciousness is "inwoven" with the external medium of Middlemarch in an apparently random manner—one center may
touch another circumference at any given point—but the final
result is a unity that balances part and whole, overlapping circles that ideally coalesce to form one great sphere.

The plot of the novel underscores this belief. George Eliot's
narrative deliberately displaces central moments in the lives of
her characters to the periphery of other lives. Eliot opens the
"Finale" of her novel on the note of "Marriage, which has been
the bourne of so many narratives" (607); *Middlemarch* is no
exception: the marriages of Dorothea and Casaubon, Rosamond and Lydgate, provide the novel with its predominant
subject matter. But Eliot's focus is a curious one: we never see
the central event of marriage itself take place in the novel. After
a long depiction of her courtship, Dorothea's wedding is an
offstage event, mentioned in passing at a windy dinner party
gossip session on the feminine virtues among a number of minor characters: "Miss Brooke, however, was not again seen by
either of these gentlemen under her maiden name. Not long
after that dinner party she had become Mrs. Casaubon, and
was on her way to Rome" (69). Celia, Dorothea's sister, ob-
trudes upon a moment of marital crisis between Mr. and Mrs.
Casaubon "on a second visit to Lowick, probably the last before her marriage" (207). Lydgate's marriage is dated by Mary
Garth, busy sewing the trousseau: "Rosamond Vincy . . . is
to be married next week, and she can't be married without this
handkerchief" (292). That the marriage has taken place is revealed in a chapter which centers on Casaubon's discovery of

his fatal illness: "One of the professional calls made by Lydgate soon after his return from his wedding journey was to Lowick Manor" (305). The doctor's marriage is of peripheral concern to Dorothea, facing her husband's fatal heart condition: "'Is Mrs. Lydgate at home,' said Dorothea, who had never, that she knew of, seen Rosamond, but now remembered the fact of the marriage" (315). The reader's only clue to the moment of these great centering events of a life is through their casual impingement on the lives of other characters, themselves absorbed in their own crises.

Marriage is the best, but not the only, example of this deliberate displacement of centers. The reader discovers that Fred Vincy has undergone a serious illness, but the fact is noted in an analysis of Lydgate's conflicts with Middlemarch's other physicians: "This had happened before the affair of Fred Vincy's illness had given to Mr. Wrench's enmity towards Lydgate more definite personal ground" (331). Mrs. Vincy's dismay over Fred's social descent to become Caleb Garth's assistant prompts her husband to remind her of their daughter Rosamond's miscarriage, another offstage event: "I'm sure I felt for her being disappointed of her baby; but she got over it nicely," Mrs. Vincy replies (416). The reader is not present at the event, nor does he even experience either Rosamond's or Lydgate's reactions to it. We are reminded in chapter 52 that Fred Vincy has reformed, "now returned from Omnibus College with his bachelor's degree" (375); but the narrative picks up Fred only in Middlemarch, where the events of his life overlap with those of the other characters in the novel. Dorothea paces the "virtual tomb" of Lowick in despair: "It was Sunday, and she could not have the carriage to go to Celia's, who had lately had a baby" (348); this is the only description of that event, which for Celia herself is a "central poising force" (359). The decentralized web of Eliot's plot underscores her belief that one decisively central psychic event is inseparable from a multitude of everyday external occurrences; each part, every individuated, heterogeneous drama, is subsumed into a larger whole, Middlemarch—and *Middlemarch*.

Has George Eliot, finally, made it whole? She begins the "Finale" of her novel with the admission that she has not: "Every limit is a beginning as well as an ending. Who can quit young lives after being long in company with them, and not desire to know what befell them in their after-years? For the fragment of a life, however typical, is not the sample of an even web" (607). Just as George Eliot plays with polarities by opening her novel with happy endings and closing it with new beginnings, so the form of *Middlemarch* oscillates between wholeness and open-endedness: the exhaustively-documented known of the novel's narrative and the amorphous unknown beyond the space of its pages; that which can be predicted and analyzed in human nature and that which remains mysteriously unknowable. Yet even as George Eliot admits to the limitations of her fictional vision; which must, after all, restrict itself to a particular time and place, a suitable number of pages, etc.—"Every limit is a beginning as well as an ending"—does she perhaps intend subliminally to remind the reader that omniscience is associated with divinity as well as with Victorian narrators? "I am Alpha and Omega, the beginning and the ending, saith the Lord, which is, and which was, and which is to come" (Revelation 1:8); in my beginning is my ending. The novelist's sphere may only be a faint type of God's vision of the great world itself; but the eye of the fictional creator is as close as mere mortals can come to Bacon's "true model of the world" as seen by the eye of the Creator.

Let me return one final time to "Notes on Form in Art" and George Eliot's definition of "the highest example of Form": "The relation of multiplex interdependent parts to a whole which is in itself in the most varied & therefore the fullest relation to other wholes." What I would emphasize here is that apparently even the "highest Form" or wholeness is nonetheless "[related] to other wholes"; each perfect whole is "relatively [part] of a larger whole."[43] Any aspiration in *Middlemarch* toward an all-encompassing and self-contained wholeness is finally as much an illusion as that of the individual little suns in the pier glass.

But such illusions are the inescapable lot of mortal vision. And however inadequate they are to be cherished and commended, for they represent man's aspiration toward the transcendent, his momentary glimpses of the Unknowable. This passage from *Felix Holt* illuminates *Middlemarch* as well:

> For what we call illusions are often, in truth, a wider vision of past and present realities—a willing movement of a man's soul with the larger sweep of the world's forces—a movement towards a more assured end than the chances of a single life. We see human heroism broken into units and say, this unit did little—might as well not have been. But in this way we might break up a great army into units; in this way we might break the sunlight into fragments.[11]

The narrator of *Middlemarch* takes the "little suns" of her characters' small visions and weaves these "fragments of a life" into the larger fictional web of *Middlemarch*. But the whole of *Middlemarch* is itself only a small part of a larger whole. George Eliot's own key to all mythologies can unlock only partial truths. The centre of illumination provided by the uncommon eye of the novelist is only the faint type of a perfect vision of the ultimate whole:

> Who shall tell what may be the effect of writing? . . . As the stone which has been kicked by generations of clowns may come by curious little links of effect under the eyes of a scholar, through whose labours it may at last fix the date of invasions and unlock religions, so a bit of ink and paper which has long been an innocent wrapping or stop-gap may at last be laid upon under the one pair of eyes which have knowledge enough to turn it into the opening of a catastrophe. To Uriel watching the progress of planetary history from the Sun, the one result would be just as much of a coincidence as the other. [302]

Uriel, you will remember, is Milton's "Regent of the Sun," "The sharpest-sighted Spirit of all in Heaven" (*Paradise Lost*, 3:690–91). He is, quite literally, the eye of God:

> . . . one of the sev'n
> Who in God's presence, nearest to his Throne
> Stand ready at command, and are his Eyes

That run through all the Heav'ns, or down to th' Earth
Bear his swift errands over moist and dry,
O'er Sea and Land.

Paradise Lost, 3:648-53

Uriel is a wonderful figure for the Victorian monist; he knows
the unknowable, those things that, as Borthrop Trumbull
said, "the understanding of man could hardly conceive; angels
might, perhaps, but not men, sirs, not men" (443).[45] In comparison to Uriel's vision, even the knowing eyes that can unlock the mystery of the written word (the Victorian novelist's?)
are blind.

But remember that one character in *Middlemarch* does, in
fact, hear the angels sing: "Bless me! it reminds me of bits in
the 'Messiah'—'and straightway there appeared a multitude of
the heavenly host, praising God and saying;' it has a tone with
it that satisfies your ear," Caleb Garth tells his wife. And appropriately Caleb hears the angels' music in the "plain words"
of Dorothea Brooke (402). It is the most misguided and unre-
liable characters in *Middlemarch*, the likes of Fred Vincy, who
see the world from "an immeasurable depth of aërial perspective" (172). Farmer Garth is, quite literally, the closest to the
earth of any character in *Middlemarch*. And so it should be.
For in George Eliot's world, we catch glimpses of the transcendent ideal through the mundane real. The final emphasis in
any discussion of *Middlemarch*'s narrator should rest not on
her omniscience but on her common humanity; or rather, that
common humanity as the *source* of any omniscience she might
have. Eliot's narrator, like her characters, is ultimately more
clown than angel. But in *Middlemarch* Uriel is of little interest—it is Bulstrode or Rosamond or Casaubon who are to be
the subject of this particular vision.

Like all of her Victorian compatriots, George Eliot is a visionary who insists on remaining an empiricist. I conclude my
discussion of *Middlemarch* with the opening paragraph of
book 4, chapter 34. It is a perfect example, I think, of the whole
in the part, *Middlemarch* in microcosm:

It was on a morning of May that Peter Featherstone was buried. In the prosaic neighbourhood of Middlemarch, May was not always warm and sunny, and on this particular morning a chill wind was blowing blossoms from the surrounding gardens on to the green mounds of Lowick churchyard. Swiftly-moving clouds only now and then allowed a gleam to light up any object, whether ugly or beautiful, that happened to be within its golden shower. In the churchyard the objects were remarkably various, for there was a little country crowd waiting to see the funeral. [236]

Eliot's realism is resolutely "prosaic." This is the world of real weather, not vernal literary convention. It is a "particular morning," particularly described. Yet a "gleam" of visionary sunlight pierces the low-hanging clouds of this everyday view. It lights up "any object, whether ugly or beautiful." Eliot's creative vision penetrates to the poetry of the real. It illuminates things as they are; but it does so by the light of the imagination. And they are, always, "remarkably various." Although that visionary ray may suffuse everything in its path alike in a "golden shower," the "little country crowd" remains on *terra firma*, each unmistakably his quotidian self.

1. Sandra M. Gilbert and Susan Gubar suggest that Eliot's intellectuality typifies her "need to evade identification with her own sex" (*The Madwoman in the Attic* [New Haven, 1979], p. 466). They dismiss Eliot's intellectual backgrounds: "As the token female in an intellectual circle that included such eminent thinkers as Spencer, Jowett, Froude, and Mazzini, Eliot might have suspected that . . . 'She was that most disagreeable of all monsters, a blue-stocking—a monster that can only exist in a miserably false state of society, in which a woman with but a smattering of learning of philosophy is classed along with singing mice and card playing pigs' (George Eliot to John Sibree Jr., *George Eliot Letters*, 1:245). Eliot, of course, had far more than a smattering of learning or philosophy. . . . But this could only serve to make her more freakish in her society" (p. 467).

2. Eliot, *Middlemarch*, p. 441. Further references will be cited in parentheses in the text.

3. Eliot, *Middlemarch*, p. 502; epigraph to chapter 68, from Daniel's *Musophilus*.

4. George Henry Lewes, "Clever Women," *Leader*, 1 June 1850, p. 237.

5. Willey, *Nineteenth Century Studies*, p. 260.

6. Sidney Colvin, review of *Middlemarch*, *Fortnightly Review* 19 (1873), rpt. in *George Eliot: The Critical Heritage*, ed. David Carroll (New York, 1971), pp. 331-32.

7. George Eliot to Maria Lewes, *George Eliot Letters*, 1:29.

8. For the contents of their libraries, see *The George Eliot-George Henry Lewes Library: An Annotated Catalogue of Their Books at Dr. Williams' Library, London* (New York, 1977); and *The Libraries of George Eliot and George Henry Lewes*, ed. William Baker (Victoria, B. C., Canada, 1981). In addition to *Gerorge Eliot's "Middlemarch" Notebooks*, ed. John Clark Pratt and Victor A. Neufeldt (Berkeley, 1979), Joseph Wiesenfarth has edited *A Writer's Notebook: 1854-1879* (Charlottesville, Va., 1981) that contains previously unpublished notes and never-reprinted essays, completing Pinney's earlier edition of the *Essays*. The gold-mine for the scholar remains Gordon Haight's meticulously-edited nine volumes of *The George Eliot Letters*.

9. The earliest and still among the best work on Eliot's intellectual backgrounds is Basil Willey's chapter in *Nineteenth Century Studies*, emphasizing Eliot and the Biblical critics. Bernard Paris continues Willey's emphasis in *Experiments in Life: George Eliot's Quest for Values* (Detroit, 1965), which centers on Feuerbach and the "religion of humanity." U. C. Knoepflmacher's *Religious Humanism and the Victorian Novel* (Princeton, 1965) places Eliot within a larger Victorian context, again in the same vein as Willey and Paris.

Less has been done on Eliot's scientific backgrounds. W. J. Harvey's classic essay on "Idea and Image in the Novels of George Eliot" (in *Critical Essays on George Eliot*, ed. Barbara Hardy [London, 1970]) provides a deft exploration of the Victorian notion that "we are the sum of our origins and development" (p. 153) as embodied in Eliot's fiction and within a contemporary context that includes Spencer, Chambers, Lewes, and Darwin. Studies like Robert Greenberg's "Plexuses and Ganglia: Scientific Allusion in *Middlemarch*," *Nineteenth Century Fiction* 30 (1975), or Michael York Mason's "*Middlemarch* and Science: Problems of Life and Mind," *Review of English Studies* 22 (1971):151–72 have traced specific scientific allusions in the novel to some of their sources. George Levine is the best writer on the philosophical world-view behind Eliot's interest in contemporary science; his "Determinism and Responsibility" compares Eliot and Mill (*PMLA* 77 (1962), rpt. in *A Century of George Eliot Criticism*, ed. Gordon S. Haight [Boston, 1965]). Elizabeth Ermarth's "Incarnations: George Eliot's Conception of 'Undeviating Law'" (*Nineteenth Century Fiction* 29 (1974-75):273–86) is a worthy successor to Levine on the same subject. Levine's superb recent essay, "George Eliot's Hypothesis of Reality," *Nineteenth Century Fiction* 35 (1980):1–28, compares Eliot's and Lewes's later thought.

For essays on George Eliot and positivism, see chapter 1, note 63.

10. George Eliot, "Janet's Repentance," *Scenes of Clerical Life* (1858: rpt. Harmondsworth, England, 1973), p. 364.

11. See N. N. Feltes, "George Eliot and the Unified Sensibility," *PMLA* 79 (1964):130–36: "*Middlemarch* and George Eliot's other works and letters, express a view of the human personality in which wholeness is all, a view remarkably close to that expressed by G. H. Lewes in *Problems of Life and Mind*" (136). In *Religious Humanism* Knoepflmacher makes the point that "a majority of Victorians were to regard George Eliot as one who combined at least the 'essence' of the Church with the predominant 'spirit of science'" (p. 28). *Middlemarch*, says Knoepflmacher, "thrives on paradox. It is a mystic's rejection of religion and a rationalist's plea for irrationality" (p. 114).

12. George Eliot to the Hon. Mr. Henry Frederick Ponsonby, *George Eliot Letters*, 6:100.

13. George Levine writes: "Although *Middlemarch* is concerned with the obstacles to the ideal and the limits of knowledge, its narrator is the altruistic scientist who perceives 'unapparent relations' and the continuities behind the discontinuities. Through all its questioning of history, narrative, and language, the book implies the continuous cosmos it is too wise to impose upon the common life of Middlemarch" ("George Eliot's Hypothesis of Reality," p. 16).

14. F. W. H. Meyers, "George Eliot," *Century Magazine* 23 (1881), quoted in Haight, *George Eliot: A Biography*, p. 450.

15. For the purposes of this discussion, I shall treat "George Eliot" and the narrator of *Middlemarch* as one and the same; I also assume some contiguity between the views of the real Marian Evans and her fictional persona.

16. Sir Humphry Davy (1778-1829) was a chemist who produced new theories of light and heat. His *Elements of Agricultural Chemistry*, which Sir James reads, was published in 1810. He gave a course of lectures on galvanism at the Royal Institution in 1801, and retained "electro-chemistry" as a lifelong interest. It is literally true that Davy was a poet-scientist, writing youthful poems such as "The Sons of Genius" before turning to the laboratory (see *Dictionary of National Biography*, 5:637). Coleridge said of him: "If he had not been the first chemist, he would have been the first poet of his age"; he attended Davy's scientific lectures "to increase his stock of metaphors." But Southey considered Davy a better scientist than poet: "He had all the elements of the poet; he only wanted the art" ("Sir Humphry Davy," *Encyclopaedia Brittanica*, 11th ed. (New York, 1910), 7:871-73).

17. George Henry Lewes, *The Principles of Success in Literature* (1865; rpt. Berkeley, Calif., 1901), p. 64.

18. Note that Lydgate performs "galvanic experiments" (p. 112) in his search for "ultimate facts"; he is an "electro-biologist." As David Carroll writes: "Lydgate is pursuing the interaction of mind and matter to the apotheosis—the discovery of mind in matter—where their separateness will be resolved and paradise will eventually be regained" ("*Middlemarch* and the Externality of Fact," in Ian Adam, ed., *This Particular Web: Essays on "Middlemarch"* [Toronto, 1975], p. 77).

19. Ladislaw's poetic principles closely parallel Eliot's notion of "Romanticism, which has helped to fill some dull blanks with *love* and *knowledge*" (p. 140; my emphasis). Note also Eliot's use of the phrenological term *organ*.

20. This theme can be found throughout Eliot's fiction; for example, in *Adam Bede* (1859): "All passion becomes strength when it has an outlet from the narrow limits of our personal lot in the labour of our right arm, the cunning of our right hand, or the still, creative activity of our thought" ([Boston, 1968], p. 180); and *Daniel Deronda* (1876): "For, look at it one way, all actions men put a bit of thought into are ideas— say, sowing seed, or making a canoe, or baking clay; and such ideas as these work themselves into life and go on growing with it, but they can't go apart from the material that set them to work and makes a medium for them" ([Harmondsworth, England, 1967], p. 583).

21. Percy Shelley, *Defense of Poetry*, rpt. in *English Romantic Writers*, ed. David Perkins (New York, 1967), p. 1,087. Like Coleridge's *Theory of Life*, Shelley's *Defense*

was written in the romantic period (1821) and published in the Victorian age (1840). Much that Shelley says about poetry resonates with Ladislaw's character as poet-politician: "The most unfailing herald, companion, and follower of the awakening of a great people to work a beneficial change in opinion of institution, is poetry" (p. 1,086).

22. Barbara Hardy writes of Will, "He writes no more poems, and perhaps the reader knows why"; "Will's lyric is not only unaware of social links between its passionate moment and lower forms of variants, it is also unaware of the thickly peopled world. In this invariably social novel, we are perpetually reminded of the community" (*"Middlemarch* and the Passions," in Adam, *This Particular Web*, pp. 19, 20). I would suggest that Will's "politics" *become* his "poetry," his incarnation of the idealistic in the real.

23. David Carroll writes that Eliot "acts out the dialectic of Lydgate's research where the energy of the mind bathes the unintelligible evidence in its own ideally illuminated space" (*"Middlemarch* and the Externality of Fact," p. 86). George Levine compares Lydgate's research to the scientific work of Lewes and W. K. Clifford ("George Eliot's Hypothesis of Reality," pp. 12-14).

24. Eliot, *The Mill on the Floss*, p. 320.

25. George Eliot, *Felix Holt* (1866; rpt. Harmondsworth, England, 1979), p. 320.

26. George Eliot, *Romola* (1863; rpt. Harmondsworth, England, 1980), p. 97.

27. Eliot, *Daniel Deronda*, p. 220.

28. A number of critics have applied "Notes on Form in Art" to *Middlemarch*, but to disparate ends. Darrell Mansell reads the essay as evidence that Eliot "is more anxious . . . than most Victorian novelists that her novels be considered as organic wholes" ("George Eliot's Conception of 'Form,'" *Studies in English Literature* 5 [1965]:655); conversely, J. H. Miller finds that "against the notion of a work of art which is an organic unity . . . George Eliot opposes the concepts of a text made of differences and of human lives which have no unitary meaning. . . . George Eliot presents a view of artistic form as inorganic, acentered, and discontinuous" ("Narrative and History," *English Literary History* 41 [1974]:468).

29. Herbert Spencer, "Philosophy of Style," *Westminster Review* 58 (1852):247. "Heterogeneity" appears on the same page: "increasing heterogeneity in our modes of expression." Lewes's essay on "Goethe as a Man of Science" was in the same issue.

30. George Eliot, "Poetry and Prose from the Notebook of an Eccentric," in Pinney, pp. 17-18.

31. Martineau and Atkinson, *Letters*, p. 256.

32. Martineau and Atkinson, *Letters*, p. 256.

33. Lewes, "Materialism and Spiritualism," p. 713.

34. Critics from Henry James onward have loved to talk about "parts" and "wholes" in Eliot's fiction. As James's Theodora says: "George Eliot's intentions are extremely complex. The mass is for each detail and each detail is for the mass" (*"Daniel Deronda*: A Conversation," *Atlantic Monthly* [1876], rpt. in Carroll, *Critical Heritage*, p. 431). Excellent essays have been written on both the whole and the parts. Isobel Armstrong takes the larger view: "These generalizations exert an extraordinary pressure on the particular facts of the narrative. They place them, with a sort of mild

and tactful deliberation, *sub specie aeternitatis*" (" 'Middlemarch': A Note on George
Eliot's 'Wisdom,' " in Hardy, *Critical Essays*, p. 129); conversely, Barbara Hardy provides a masterful dissection of the parts in "The Surface of the Novel: Chapter 30" (in
"Middlemarch": Critical Approaches to the Novel [London, 1967]): "Looking hard at
the part . . . brings out other aspects of organization—the local configurations of
scene and chapter. . . . I want to say that some parts are simple and not symbolic,
but that other, larger units are more intricately and systematically organized than I
had imagined" (p. 150).

Brian Swan singles out the part/whole relationship as central to Eliot's notion of
symbolic form: "one in which everything is related to everything without sacrificing
its own *quidditas*, the actuality of its present existence" (*"Middlemarch*: Realism and
Symbolic Form," *English Literary History* 39 [1972]:289). For Swan, Eliot is thus simultaneously "realistic" and "symbolic."

35. Comte, *Cours*, in Lenzer, pp. 270–71. In his study of Comte, Lewes paraphrases
this same passage almost verbatim (see *Comte*, p. 263).

36. Spencer, *Social Statics*, p. 497.

37. This notion is a staple of *Middlemarch* criticism. Gillian Beer writes: "The typical concern of the intellectual characters of the book is with visions of unity, but a
unity which seeks to resolve the extraordinary diversities of the world back into a single answer"; but they are wrong: "any single interpretation of experience will mis-
lead" ("Myth and the Single Consciousness: *Middlemarch* and 'The Lifted Veil,' " in
Adam, *This Particular Web*, pp. 102, 111). Similarly, W. J. Harvey: "We know that
George Eliot was generally suspicious of anything in the nature of *a* key to the meaning of life" ("The Intellectual Background of the Novel," in Hardy, *"Middlemarch"*:
Critical Approaches, p. 35). George Levine agrees: "George Eliot . . . had discarded
the many religious and epistemological assumptions of her inherited culture, including the convention that a single unitary theory of reality could certainly be established" ("George Eliot's Hypothesis," p. 7).

38. See N. N. Feltes, "George Eliot's 'Pier-Glass': The Development of a Metaphor," *Modern Philology* 67 (1969):69–71. It is now almost taken for granted that the
philosopher is Spencer, although Feltes's actual evidence for the identification is less
than decisive, consisting of a faint parallel between the pier glass and a metaphor
about the effect of moonlight on water that Spencer used in the *Study of Sociology*.
Hilda M. Hulme suggests that the philosopher may be Lewes himself, and quotes
Lewes's use of a mirror image from Bacon's *Novum Organum* in his 1843 essay on
Spinoza ("The Language of the Novel: Imagery," in Hardy, *"Middlemarch"*: *Critical
Approaches*, p. 123). Clearly, Eliot had many models from which to choose. The philosopher may well personify any Victorian synthesizer, rather than a particular indi-
vidual.

39. Miller, "Narrative and History," pp. 464, 470.

40. Lewes, *Problems of Life and Mind, Foundations of a Creed*, 1:163. Levine's
essay "George Eliot's Hypothesis of Reality" contains a timely defense against decon-
structionist readings: "Our subversive readings tend to neglect the primary object to
which these self-conscious deconstructions of our common-sense traditions of order
and narrative are preliminary: the reconstruction of meaning and order that is Lewes's
objective as well" (p. 6; see pp. 5–6).

41. Eliot, "Notes on Form," in Pinney, p. 432; my emphasis.

42. See also pp. 165, 205, 224, 250, 284, 301, 321, 375, 382, and 430. Hardy argues that *Middlemarch*'s "shifting point of view is the structural equivalent for its theme of illusion, and the insistent rotation . . . puts each illusion in its place amongst the rest and lets the contradictions stand" (*The Novels of George Eliot* [1959; rev. ed. London, 1963], p. 96).

43. Eliot, "Notes on Form," in Pinney, pp. 433, 432.

44. Eliot, *Felix Holt*, pp. 276–77.

45. George Levine also sees Uriel as the personification of transcendent vision: "The novel is not an intuition embracing the universe but an intuition that, to 'Uriel,' what we take as discontinuous will be in fact continuous, that the invisible continuous cosmos is there, waiting for an all-embracing Uriel-like intuition" ("George Eliot's Hypothesis of Reality," p. 17).

"A response to the mystery of things, together with the sense of awe and wonder that it produces, is one of the great human sanctities for George Eliot" (Harvey, "Idea and Image," in Hardy, *Critical Essays*, pp. 172-73): "She continued to feel a longing, if not for the transcendent, at least for the numinous, the incandescent, the mysterious" (Beer, "Myth and the Single Consciousness," in Adam, *This Particular Web*, p. 91).

BIBLIOGRAPHY

This bibliography lists only those works cited directly in the text; it is exclusive of footnote references.

Abrams, M. H. *The Mirror and the Lamp: Romantic Theory and the Critical Tradition.* Oxford, 1953. Reprint, 1971.

Adam, Ian, ed. *This Particular Web: Essays on "Middlemarch."* Toronto, 1975.

Ashton, Rosemary. *The German Idea: Four English Writers and the Reception of German Thought 1800–1860.* Cambridge, 1980.

Bacon, Francis. *Selected Writings.* Edited by Hugh G. Dick. New York, 1955.

Baker, William. *The George Eliot-George Henry Lewes Library: An Annotated Catalogue of Their Books at Dr. Williams' Library, London.* New York, 1977.

―――. "George Henry Lewes's Annotations to Coleridge's *The Friend* (1837)." *Library* 31 (March 1976):31–36.

―――. *The Libraries of George Eliot and George Henry Lewes.* Victoria, British Columbia, Canada, 1981.

Barfield, Owen. *What Coleridge Thought.* Middletown, Ct., 1971.

Bate, Walter Jackson. *From Classic to Romantic: Premises of Taste in Eighteenth Century England.* 1946. Reprint, New York, 1961.

Benn, Alfred William. *The History of English Rationalism in the Nineteenth Century.* 2 vols. London, 1906.

Brabant, R. H. and Thomas Moore. "The State of Protestantism in Germany," *Edinburgh Review* 54 (1831):238–55.

Bray, Charles. *The Education of the Feelings.* 2d ed. London, 1849.

―――. *On Force, Its Mental and Moral Correlates; and on That Which is Supposed to Underlie All Phenomena; with Speculations on Spiritualism, and Other Abnormal Conditions of Mind.* London, 1866.

―――. *Phrases of Opinion and Experience During a Long Life: An Autobiography.* London, n.d.

―――. *The Philosophy of Necessity; or, The Law of Consequences; As Applicable to Mental, Moral, and Social Science.* 2 vols. London, 1841.

―――. *The Philosophy of Necessity; or, The Law of Consequences; As Applicable to Mental, Moral, and Social Science.* 2d ed., rev. London, 1863.

Buckley, Jerome Hamilton. *The Victorian Temper: A Study in Literary Culture.* New York, 1951.

Carpenter, W. B. "Electro-Biology and Mesmerism." *Quarterly Review* 93 (1853): 501-57.

―――. *Principles of Comparative Physiology.* New American Edition, from 4th rev. English Edition. Philadelphia, 1854.

Carroll, David, ed. *George Eliot: The Critical Heritage.* New York, 1971.

Chambers, Robert. *Vestiges of the Natural History of Creation. With a Sequel.* New York, 1859.

Coleridge, Samuel Taylor. *Collected Letters.* Edited by Earl Leslie Griggs. Vol. 4 (1815-19). Oxford, 1959.

―――. *Formation of a More Comprehensive Theory of Life.* In *Selected Poetry and Prose of Samuel Taylor Coleridge.* Edited by Donald Stauffer. New York, 1951.

―――. *The Friend.* Edited by Barbara E. Rooke. 2 vols. Princeton, 1969.

―――. *Inquiring Spirit: a New Presentation of Coleridge from His Published and Unpublished Prose Writings.* Edited by Kathleen Coburn. London, 1951.

―――. *The Notebooks of Samuel Taylor Coleridge.* Edited by Kathleen Coburn. Vol. 3 (1808-19). Princeton, 1973.

―――. *Specimens of the Table Talk of Samuel Taylor Coleridge.* Edinburgh, 1905.

Combe, George. *The Constitution of Man Considered in Relation to External Objects.* Sixth American ed. from the 2d English ed. Corrected and Enlarged. Boston, 1838.

Comte, Auguste. *Cours de philosophie positive.* Translated by Harriet Martineau. In *Auguste Comte and Positivism, The Essential Writings.* Edited by Gertrud Lenzer. New York, 1975.

Cross, John Walter. *Life of George Eliot.* 2 vols. 1885. Reprint. London, 1908.

Davies, John D. *Phrenology: Fad and Science.* New Haven, 1955.

DeGiustino, David. *Conquest of Mind: Phrenology and Victorian Social Thought.* London, 1975.

DeLaura, David, ed. *Victorian Prose: A Guide to Research.* New York, 1973.

Dickens, Charles. *Hard Times.* Edited by George Ford and Sylvère Monod. New York, 1966.

Drummond, James. *The Life and Letters of James Martineau.* New York, 1902.

Dunn, Waldo Hilary. *James Anthony Froude: A Biography.* 2 vols. Oxford, 1961.

Eagles, John. "What Is Mesmerism?" *Blackwood's* 70 (1851):70–83.

Eiseley, Loren. *Darwin's Century.* 1958. Reprint, New York, 1961.

"Electro-Biology." *Westminister Review* 55 (1851):312–28.

Eliot, George. *Adam Bede.* Edited by John Paterson. Boston, 1968.

―――. *Daniel Deronda.* Edited by Barbara Hardy. Harmondsworth, Middlesex, Eng., 1967.

————. *Essays of George Eliot.* Edited by Thomas Pinney. New York, 1963.

————. *Felix Holt.* Edited by Peter Coveney. Harmondsworth, Middlesex, Eng., 1975.

————. *George Eliot's "Middlemarch" Notebooks.* Edited by John Clark Pratt and Victor A. Neufeldt. Berkeley, 1979.

————. "Literature." *The Leader*, 13 May, 1854, p. 447.

————. *Middlemarch: A Study of Provincial Life.* Edited by Gordon S. Haight. Boston, 1956.

————. *The Mill on the Floss.* Edited by A. S. Byatt. Harmondsworth, Middlesex, Eng., 1979.

————. "Miss Martineau's Translation of Comte." *Leader*, 3 December, 1853, pp. 1,171-72.

————. "More Leaves from George Eliot's Notebook." Edited by Thomas Pinney. *Huntington Library Quarterly* 29 (1966):353-76.

————. *Romola.* Edited by Andrew Sanders. Harmondsworth, Middlesex, Eng., 1980.

————. *Scenes of Clerical Life.* Edited by David Lodge. Harmondsworth, Middlesex, Eng., 1973.

Encyclopedia of Philosophy. 8 vols. New York, 1967.

Espinasse, Francis. *Literary Recollections.* New York, 1938.

Feuerbach, Ludwig. *The Essence of Christianity.* Translated by George Eliot. 1854. Reprint, New York, 1957.

Froude, James Anthony. "Materialism: Miss Martineau and Mr. Atkinson." *Fraser's* 43 (1851):418-34.

Froude, James Anthony. *The Nemesis of Faith.* 2d ed. London, 1849.

Gaskell, Elizabeth. *Life of Charlotte Bronte.* Edited by Alan Shelston. Harmondsworth, Middlesex, Eng., 1975.

Gibbon, Charles. *The Life of George Combe.* 2 vols. London, 1878.

Goodfield-Toulmin, June. "Some Aspects of English Physiology: 1780-1840." *Journal of the History of Biology* 2 (1969):283-320.

Grove, W. R. "Mesmerism." *Blackwood's* 57 (1845):219-41.

Gruber, Howard E. *Darwin on Man: A Psychological Study of Scientific Creativity. Together with Darwin's Early and Unpublished Notebooks.* Transcribed and annotated by Paul H. Barrett. New York, 1974.

Haight, Gordon S. *A Century of George Eliot Criticism.* Boston, 1965.

————. *George Eliot: A Biography.* New York, 1968.

————, ed. *The George Eliot Letters.* 9 vols. New Haven, 1954-55, 1978.

Halévy, Eli. *England in 1815.* Translated by E. I. Watkin and D. A. Barker. 1924. Reprint, London, 1960.

Hardy, Barbara, ed. *Critical Essays on George Eliot.* London, 1970.

————. *"Middlemarch": Critical Approaches to the Novel.* London, 1967.

Harris, Wendell V. *The Omnipresent Debate: Empiricism and Transcendentalism in Nineteenth-Century English Prose.* DeKalb, Ill., 1981.

Hearnshaw, Leslie S. *A Short History of British Psychology, 1840-1940.* London, 1964.

Herrnstein, Richard J. and Edwin G. Boring, eds. *A Source Book in the History of Psychology.* Cambridge, Mass., 1965.

Hickson, W. R. "Life and Immortality." *Westminster Review* 56 (1851):168-228.

Hinton, James. *Chapters on the Art of Thinking, and Other Essays.* Edited by C. H. Hinton. London, 1879.

―――. "Physiological Riddles." *Cornhill Magazine* 2 (1860):421-31.

Houghton, Walter E. *The Victorian Frame of Mind, 1830-1870.* New Haven, 1957.

Hutton, R. H. "Atheism." *National Review* 2 (1856):97-123.

Huxley, T. H. "Joseph Priestley." In *Society and Culture and Other Essays.* New York, 1890, pp. 102-34.

―――. "Mental Physiology and Pathology." In "Science," *Westminster Review* 61 (1854):266-70.

―――. Review of *Comparative Physiology,* by W. B. Carpenter. In "Science," *Westminster Review* 63 (1855):241-47.

―――. Review of *Vestiges of the Natural History of Creation,* by Robert Chambers. *British and Foreign Medico-Chirurgical Review* 13 (1854):425-39.

―――. "Science," *Westminster Review* 61 (1854):254-57.

James, William. *The Principles of Psychology.* 2 vols. 1890. Reprint, New York, 1950.

Kaminsky, Jack. "The Empirical Metaphysics of George Henry Lewes." *Journal of the History of Ideas* 13 (1952):314-32.

Kaplan, Fred. *Dickens and Mesmerism: The Hidden Springs of Fiction.* Princeton, 1975.

―――. "'The Mesmeric Mania': The Early Victorians and Animal Magnetism." *Journal of the History of Ideas* 35 (1974):691-702.

Kitchel, Anna. *George Lewes and George Eliot.* New York, 1933.

Review of *Letters on the Laws of Man's Nature and Development* by Harriet Martineau and Henry George Atkinson. *Westminster Review* 55 (1851):83-92.

Levine, George. "George Eliot's Hypothesis of Reality." *Nineteenth Century Fiction* 35 (1980):1-28.

Lewes, George Henry. "Auguste Comte." *Fortnightly Review* 3 (1865-66):385-410.

―――. *The Biographical History of Philosophy.* Library Edition. New York, 1866.

―――. *Comte's Philosophy of the Sciences: Being an Exposition of the Principles of the "Cours de philosophie positive" of Auguste Comte.* London, 1853.

―――. "The Development Hypothesis of the 'Vestiges.'" *Leader,* 13 August 1853, pp. 784-85; 20 August 1853, pp. 812-14; 27 August 1853, pp. 832-34; 10 September 1853, p. 883.

―――. "English Philosophy." *Leader,* 16 July 1853, pp. 692-93; 23 July 1853, pp. 716-17.

―――. "Goethe as a Man of Science." *Westminster Review* 58 (1852):258-72.

―――. "The Grounds of Belief." *Leader,* 26 November 1853, pp. 1,147-48.

―――. "The Heart and the Brain." *Fortnightly Review* 1 (1865):66-74.

―――. "Herbert Spencer's *Principles of Psychology.*" *Saturday Review*, 1 March 1856, pp. 352-53.

―――. "Herbert Spencer's Psychology." *Leader*, 20 October 1855, pp. 1,012-13.

―――. "Hereditary Influence, Animal and Human." *Westminster Review* 66 (1856):135-62.

―――. "History of Psychology Method." *Leader*, 27 October 1855, pp. 1,036-37.

―――. Review of *Letters on the Laws of Man's Nature and Development*, by Harriet Martineau and Henry George Atkinson. *Leader*, 22 February 1851, p. 178; 1 March, 1851, pp. 201-3; 8 March 1851, pp. 227-28.

―――. "Life and Doctrine of Geoffroy St. Hilaire." *Westminster Review* 61 (1854): 160-90.

―――. "Life and Mind." *Leader*, 3 November 1855, pp. 1,062-63.

―――. *The Life of Goethe.* 2d ed. London, 1864.

―――. "Literature." *Leader*, 14 January 1854, p. 40.

―――. "Lyell and Owen on Development." *Leader*, 18 October 1851, pp. 996-97.

―――. "A Mesmeric Quack." *Saturday Review*, 2 February 1856, pp. 262-63.

―――. "Mr. Darwin's Hypothesis." *Fortnightly Review* 34 (1868):353-73, 611-29; 4 (1868):61-80, 492-501.

―――. "Modern Metaphysics and Moral Philosophy of France." *British and Foreign Review* 15 (1843):353-406.

―――. "Noble on Insanity." *Leader*, 24 December 1853, pp. 1,240-42.

―――. "Phrenology and Phrenologists." *Leader*, 10 December 1853, pp. 1,192-93.

―――. "Phrenology and Physiology." *Leader*, 7 January 1854, pp. 20-21.

―――. "Phrenology in France." *Blackwood's* 82 (1857):665-74.

―――. "A Precursor of the Vestiges." *Fraser's* 56 (1857):526-31.

―――. *The Principles of Success in Literature.* 1865. Reprint. Berkeley, Calif., 1901.

―――. *Problems of Life and Mind. First Series. The Foundations of a Creed.* 2 vols. Boston, 1874-75.

―――. *Problems of Life and Mind. Second Series. The Physical Basis of Mind.* London, 1877.

―――. *Problems of Life and Mind. Third Series. Problem the First. The Study of Psychology: Its Object, Scope and Method.* Boston, 1879.

―――. *Problems of Life and Mind. Third Series. Problems 2-4.* Boston, 1880.

―――. Review of *Social Statics*, by Herbert Spencer. *Leader*, 15 March 1851, pp. 248-50; 22 March 18, 1851, 274-75; 12 April 1851, 347-48.

―――. "Spinoza." *Fortnightly Review* 4 (1866):385-406.

―――. "Spinoza, Spinozism." *Penny Cyclopaedia.* Vol. 22. London, 1842.

―――. "Spinoza's Life and Works." *Westminster Review* 39 (1843):372-407.

―――. "Spiritualism and Materialism." *Fortnightly Review* 25 (1876):479-93, 707-19.

―――. "Subject, Subjective." *Penny Cyclopaedia.* Vol. 23. London, 1842.

―――. "Substance." *Penny Cyclopaedia.* Vol. 22. London, 1842.

————. Review of *Système de Politique Positive*, by Auguste Comte, in "Contemporary Literature of France." *Westminster Review* 57 (1852):346–50.

————. "Von Baer on the Development Hypothesis." *Leader*, 25 June 1853, pp. 617–18.

Locke, John. *An Essay Concerning Human Understanding.* Edited by Peter H. Nidditch. Oxford, 1975.

Lovejoy, Arthur O. "The Argument of Organic Evolution Before 'The Origin of Species,' 1830–1858." In *Forerunners of Darwin: 1745–1859.* Edited by Bentley Glass, Oswei Temkin, and William Strauss. Baltimore, 1959.

————. *The Great Chain of Being: A Study in the History of An Idea.* 1936. Reprint. New York, 1960.

McFarland, Thomas. *Coleridge and the Pantheist Tradition.* Oxford, 1969.

Martineau, Harriet. *Autobiography.* 3 vols. London, 1877.

————. *Biographical Sketches, 1852–1868.* 3d ed. London, 1870.

————. Letters on Mesmerism. *Athenaeum*, 23 November 1844, pp. 1,070–72; 30 November 1844, pp. 1,093–94; 7 December 1844, pp. 1,117–18; 14 December 1844, pp. 1,144–46; 21 December, 1844, pp. 1,173–74.

————, and Henry George Atkinson. *Letters on the Laws of Man's Nature and Development.* London, 1851.

————. *The Positive Philosophy of Auguste Comte, Freely Translated and Condensed.* 2d ed. 2 vols. London, 1875.

Martineau, James. "Mesmeric Atheism." *Prospective Review* 7 (1851):224–62.

Mill, John Stuart. *Auguste Comte and Positivism.* 4th ed. London, 1891.

————. *Autobiography.* Edited by Jack Stillinger. Boston, 1969.

————. *The Earlier Letters of John Stuart Mill, 1812–48.* Edited by Francis E. Mineka. Vol. 13 of *Collected Works.* Toronto, 1963.

————. *Mill on Bentham and Coleridge.* Edited by F. R. Leavis. London, 1950.

————. *A System of Logic, Ratiocinative and Inductive.* Edited by J. M. Robson. Vols. 7–8 of *Collected Works.* Toronto, 1973.

Miller, J. Hillis. "Narrative and History." *ELH* 41 (1974):455–73.

Millhauser, Milton. *Just Before Darwin: Robert Chambers and the "Vestiges of Creation."* Middletown, Conn., 1959.

Mineka, Francis Edward. *The Dissidence of Dissent: The Monthly Repository, 1806–1838.* Chapel Hill, 1944.

Newman, Francis. Review of *Vestiges of the Natural History of Creation*, by Robert Chambers. *Prospective Review* 1 (1845):49–82.

Newman, John Henry. *Apologia Pro Vita Sua.* 1864. Reprint, New York, 1956.

Parssinen, Terry M. "Mesmeric Performers." *Victorian Studies* 21 (1977–78):87–104.

Peel, J. D. Y. *Herbert Spencer, The Evolution of a Sociologist.* New York, 1971.

Priestley, Joseph. *Disquisitions Relating to Matter and Spirit.* 2d ed., Improved and Enlarged. 2 vols. London, 1792.

————. *The Doctrine of Philosophical Necessity Illustrated, Being an Appendix to the Disquisitions Relating to Matter and Spirit.* London, 1777.

Review of *Principles of Psychology*, by Herbert Spencer. *British Quarterly Review* 22 (1855):596–98.

Review of *Principles of Psychology*, by Herbert Spencer. In "Theology and Philosophy," *Westminster Review* 65 (1856):234–40.

Robertson, John M. *History of Freethought in the Nineteenth Century*. 2 vols. London, 1929.

Robinson, Henry Crabb. *Henry Crabb Robinson on Books and Their Writers*. Edited by Edith Morley. 3 vols. London, 1938.

Rosenbaum, S. P., ed. *English Literature and British Philosophy*. Chicago, 1971.

Sedgwick, Adam. Review of *Vestiges of the Natural History of Creation*, by Robert Chambers. *Edinburgh Review* 82 (1845):1–85.

Shelley, Percy. *A Defence of Poetry*. In *English Romantic Writers*. Edited by David Perkins. New York, 1967, pp. 1,072–87.

Simon, W. M. "Auguste Comte's English Disciples." *Victorian Studies* 8 (1964–65):162–172.

———. *European Positivism in the Nineteenth Century: An Essay in Intellectual History*. New York, 1963.

Smith, W. H. "Comte." *Blackwood's* 53 (1843):397–414.

Snyder, Alice D. *Coleridge on Logic and Learning*. New Haven, 1929.

Spencer, Herbert. *An Autobiography*. 2 vols. New York, 1904.

———. *Essays, Scientific, Political, and Speculative*. Vol. 1. New York, 1904.

———. *First Principles of a New System of Philosophy*. 3d ed. New York, 1879.

———. "The Laws of Organic Form." *British and Foreign Medico-Chirurgical Review* 23 (1859):189–202.

———. "The Philosophy of Style." *Westminster Review* 58 (1852):234–47.

———. *The Principles of Psychology*. London, 1855.

———. *Social Statics: or, The Conditions Essential to Human Happiness Specialized, and the First of Them Developed*. 1850. Reprint, New York, 1865.

———. "The Universal Postulate." *Westminster Review* 60 (1853):513–60.

Spinoza, Benedict. *Ethics*. Translated by R. H. Elwes. 1883. Reprint, New York, 1955.

Stephen, Leslie. *History of English Thought in the Eighteenth Century*. 2 vols. 1876. Reprint. New York, 1962.

———. "Spinoza." *Fortnightly Review* 34 (1880):752–72.

Tennyson, Alfred. *In Memoriam*. Edited by Robert H. Ross. New York, 1973.

Tjoa, Hock Guan. *George Henry Lewes: A Victorian Mind*. Cambridge, Mass., 1977.

Review of *Vestiges of the Natural History of Creation*, by Robert Chambers. *British Quarterly Review* 1 (1845):490–513.

Wallace, Alfred Russel. *My Life*. 2 vols. New York, 1905.

———. *The Wonderful Century: Its Successes and Its Failures*. New York, 1899.

Webb, R. K. *Harriet Martineau: A Radical Victorian*. New York, 1960.

Wheatley, Vera. *The Life and Work of Harriet Martineau*. London, 1957.

Willey, Basil. *Nineteenth Century Studies: Coleridge to Matthew Arnold*. 1949. Reprint, New York, 1966.

Wilson, H. B. Review of *The Constitution of Man*, by George Combe. In "Contemporary Literature," *Westminster Review* 68 (1857):237.

Youmans, Edward L., ed. *The Correlation and Conservation of Forces: A Series of Expositions*. New York, 1865.

Young, Robert M. *Mind, Brain, and Adaptation in the Nineteenth Century: Cerebral Localization and Its Biological Context From Gall to Ferrier*. Oxford, 1970.

SUBJECT INDEX

NAME INDEX